Understanding governance in contemporary Japan

Manchester University Press

Understanding governance in contemporary Japan

Transformation and the regulatory state

Masahiro Mogaki

Manchester University Press

Copyright © Masahiro Mogaki 2019

The right of Masahiro Mogaki to be identified as the author of this work has been asserted by him in accordance with the Copyright, Designs and Patents Act 1988.

Published by Manchester University Press
Oxford Road, Manchester M13 9PL
www.manchesteruniversitypress.co.uk

British Library Cataloguing-in-Publication Data
A catalogue record for this book is available from the British Library

ISBN 978 1 5261 1468 6 hardback
ISBN 978 1 5261 1471 6 paperback

First published 2019
Paperback published 2022

The publisher has no responsibility for the persistence or accuracy of URLs for any external or third-party internet websites referred to in this book, and does not guarantee that any content on such websites is, or will remain, accurate or appropriate.

Typeset by
Servis Filmsetting Ltd, Stockport, Cheshire

Contents

List of figures and tables	vii
Preface	ix
Acknowledgements	xi
Abbreviations	xii

Part I: Conceptualising the Japanese state and governance

1	Introduction: transformation, governance and the state in the Japanese context	3
2	The change of governance and regulation	19

Part II: Evolving regulation and governance

3	The evolving core executive in response to burgeoning ICT	35
4	Regulatory state transformation with an unusual approach	64
5	Piecemeal transformation: anti-monopoly regulation	86
6	Breaking the egg shell	118

Part III: The nature of Japanese governance with the transformation of the state

7	Regulatory transformation and the core executive	137
8	Governance in Japan: the implications of the research	147

Appendix 1   List of Ministers of Post and Telecommunications
             (before January 2001) and Ministers of Internal
             Affairs and Communications (after January 2001)   164
Appendix 2   The anti-monopoly case process   167
References   170
Index   182

List of figures and tables

Figures

3.1	Timeline of the development of Japan's ICT regulation since the 1980s	37
5.1	Timeline of the development of Japan's anti-monopoly regulation	87
5.2	The JFTC's staff numbers and budget	101
8.1	The mode of regulation in the Japanese regulatory state	156
8.2	The mode of regulation in the Japanese regulatory state compared with the UK and New Zealand	158

Tables

1.1	Summary of state and state-transformation literature	11
2.1	Membership of the core executive	24
3.1	Primary authority before and after the 1985 telecommunications regulatory reform	39
3.2	Problems resulting from NTT's dominance in local landline telecommunications networks	42
3.3	The major elements of Jun'ichirō Koizumi's approach to strengthening the Cabinet	47
3.4	Relative strength of the actors in the ICT sector	60
4.1	Risks associated with independent regulators	73
4.2	Changes in the core executive actors' power	82
5.1	The key points of the 1953 AMA amendment	89
5.2	The chronological sequence of the oil cartel case	91
5.3	The key points of the 1977 AMA amendment	94
5.4	The key points of the amendment to the AMA in 2005	99

viii   Figures and tables

5.5	The number of applications to the leniency programme	99
5.6	The JFTC's staff numbers and budget	100
5.7	Relative strength of the actors in anti-monopoly regulation	114
6.1	The merits and demerits of an independent regulator	124

Preface

Since the 1980s political scientists in the developed world have explored changes to the state in response to the challenge of governance. Yet the state and governance have not been key topics of debate within Japanese politics, despite significant changes being observed by commentators since the 1990s. The major focus has been on specific political and societal issues within the political arena, including the increasing power of politicians, changes to the electoral system and political parties, and the impact of private-sector actors, often mobilised by the body of pluralist and rational choice literature. As a collection of literature illuminating the key role of state actors, this does not employ an approach that pays attention to the state at a macro level in relation to governance. In particular, the state at a macro level has not been problematised despite being crucial to the debate regarding governance elsewhere.

To address this lacuna, this book explores the transformation of the Japanese state in response to a variety of challenges by focusing on two case studies: ICT (Information and Communications Technology) regulation and anti-monopoly regulation after the 1980s, which experienced disjunctures and significant transformation within the period, with particularistic approaches embracing competition. The case studies set up the state as the key locus of power in contrast to the pluralist and rational choice schools, and the analytical framework is drawn from key theories of governance and the state including the concepts of the core executive and the regulatory state. The book explores the extent to which there is asymmetric dominance on the part of Japan's core executive through an examination of developments in the Japanese regulatory tradition since the 1980s. With its particular approach that employs a government ministry as the regulator, the analysis of ICT regulation reveals how the Japanese state has been transformed in response to specific challenges under its political tradition. Anti-monopoly regulation offers another example of state transformation, with an independent administrative commission as regulator in contrast to the ministerial ICT regulator. Developments under the Democratic Party of Japan and the Liberal Democratic Party governments also confirm the findings of the case studies. This book concludes that the transformation of the Japanese state in the two case studies can be characterised as regulatory state development, with a view that the state at a macro level is the key locus of power. In so doing, it reveals the transformation of the state and governance in a Japanese context and offers an example of the new governance school addressing the state, its transformation and the governance of the political arena in Japanese politics and beyond, setting out a challenge to the established body of pluralist and rational choice literature in Japanese politics.

Acknowledgements

The assistance and understanding of the people around me were vital for completing this book. The kindness of those who accepted my interview requests in the Diet, government ministries, the Fair Trade Commission, the business community, consumer groups and professional communities was indispensable. Although I am unable to name each of the interviewees here in order to protect their confidentiality, I have no words to show my appreciation for their goodwill. The interviews also drew on the significant assistance of many people including Toshiyuki Minami, Akira Kaneko, Katsutoshi Ishioka and Jin Matsubara, who helped me to develop my strategy and secure appointments during my field work. At the University of Sheffield, Dave Richards, Martin J. Smith and Matt Flinders read the manuscript and offered comments and feedback, which formed the foundation of this book. Without their contribution this book would not have been published in its present form. The Department of Politics also offered crucial assistance financially and psychologically, including financial support for the field work. During the publication process, the anonymous reviewer offered comments that were useful in improving the manuscript. Throughout the process the staff of Manchester University Press, particularly Tony Mason, have offered useful and effective advice. I am indebted to Steve Hart for his tireless assistance. I would like to offer my gratitude to all for their generous support.

Abbreviations

AMA	Anti-monopoly Act, Japan (*Dokusen kinshi hō*)
BT	British Telecommunications plc (British Telecom)
CEFP	Council on Economic and Fiscal Policy, Japan
DPJ	Democratic Party of Japan
FCC	Federal Communications Commission, US
ICT	Information and Communication Technology
JFTC	Fair Trade Commission, Japan
Kantei	Prime Minister's Office [formally the Prime Minister's official residence]
Keidanren	Japan Business Federation (*Nippon Keizaidantai Rengōkai*)
LDP	Liberal Democratic Party, Japan
METI	Ministry of Economy, Trade and Industry, Japan (after 2001)
MIC	Ministry of Internal Affairs and Communications, Japan (after 2001)
MITI	Ministry of International Trade and Industry, Japan (before 2001)
MMC	Monopolies and Mergers Commission, UK
MMM	mixed-member majoritarian
MNO	mobile network operator
MOF	Ministry of Finance, Japan
MPT	Ministry of Post and Telecommunications, Japan (before 2001)
NCC	new common carrier
NHS	National Health Service, UK
NTT	Nippon Telegraph and Telephone Public Co. (before privatisation in 1985)/Nippon Telegraph and Telephone Co. (after privatisation in 1985)
OA	office automation facilities
OFT	Office of Fair Trading, UK

Oftel	Office of Telecommunications, UK (before 2003)
PARC	Policy Affairs Research Council, LDP, Japan (*Sēchō*)
Rinchō	Second Provisional Commission on Administrative Reform (*Rinji gyōsei chōsakai*), Japan
RPI	retail prices index
SCAP	Supreme Commander for the Allied Powers
SDPJ	Social Democratic Party of Japan
SII	Structural Impediments Initiative
SMD	single-member district
TDSC	Telecommunications Dispute Settlement Commission, MIC, Japan

Part I

Conceptualising the Japanese state and governance

1

Introduction: transformation, governance and the state in the Japanese context

The 2010s have seen a significant transformation in politics. The established governing regimes across the globe have been confronted by challenges that have undermined their traditional foundation of governing. The outcomes of the 2016 US presidential election and the 2016 referendum regarding the UK's EU membership can be interpreted as a wave of populist nationalism occurring on the home territory of classic, liberalist, Anglo-Saxon areas (Fukuyama 2017). This set of political upheavals accompanied the emergence of administrations concomitant with nationalist and populist discourses in a number of countries in Europe, Asia and Latin America, whose key characteristics include a challenge to established political norms within their respective political arenas. This set of events indicates that the established governing system is facing significant political challenges across the globe. Societal problems beyond the scope of the established governing mechanism have been highlighted as a key factor in mobilising the rise of populists and nationalists (Fukuyama 2016). A possible interpretation is that political regimes throughout the world are facing the 'challenge of governance', a term that expresses political developments since the 1970s. Indeed, developments characterised by the emergence of significant challenges to the established political system in the 2010s have a parallel in political developments after the 1970s. Therefore, exploring changes of governance is vital in addressing contemporary political challenges and the historical development of political arenas. This book will analyse the case of Japan as a specific example of changes of governance.

Given Japan's significant economic and industrial decline in the world's politico-economic arena and its slow response to globalisation and internationalisation in the 2010s, some readers may doubt the benefit of exploring the Japanese case. I offer the following reasons for examining the governance of Japan. First, its long history as a developed country outside Europe and America offers an example of the generalisable nature of political and economic issues beyond the specific context of western Europe and America. Second, although its relative decline in terms of economic size is inevitable, Japan retains its position as a large country significant enough to influence its region and beyond. The challenges to Japan are issues that others (e.g. Europe, China) are also facing, or will confront in the near future, such as regulatory transformation and governance. And lastly, the governance of Japan has been little explored. Indeed, in spite of works by scholars and journalists focusing on specific issues such as political groups, bureaucracy, societal issues, foreign policy and economic issues, few have explored changes of governance in Japan's political and economic arena as their core theme. The following section will consider the development of governance in Japan, heeding key political issues specifically affecting the course of the country's political development.

Governance, Japanese style

In the past forty years there has been a significant growth in the literature on governance within political science, in part as a response to the decline of the state's traditional role and capacity in developed countries. The governance literature seeks to offer new forms of analysis of governing systems in the transforming political arenas after the 1980s. This new set of approaches has prompted a renewed debate on the state. The debate on governance has helped bring the state back into political science literature partly because the period during which government was supposed to address many of the key political issues in society was replaced by a new era in which the term 'governance' was employed to address the set of governing processes. That is, examining 'government' no longer always responds to the issues of governing. Elsewhere, the concept of the state, not always heeded by political research despite its traditional significance, has re-emerged as a topic of debate in addressing political issues in transforming society. I define 'governance' here as the set of political systems that governs the state and society; the scope of the term covers the nexus of public administration actors and structures that are influential over policy-making and implementation, both those within the government and beyond.

The analysis of Japan's political arenas was dominated by approaches focusing on central government officials as key before the 1980s (Tsuji 1969; Johnson 1982). This reflects a period dominated by the stable administration of the Liberal Democratic Party (LDP), which had enjoyed continuous tenure since its establishment in 1955. In particular, the 1960s and early 1970s saw significant economic development called the 'High Growth Period' under the Hayato Ikeda (Prime Minister, 1960–64) and Eisaku Satō (Prime Minister, 1964–72) governments, in which the impact of government policy was regarded as a significant factor contributing to the rapid rise of living standards in the country. Although the nature of this rapid economic growth is a contentious topic, many recognise policy-making processes steered by government officials and overseen by LDP politicians as influential (Johnson 1982). This set of governing mechanisms had analogues to the Weberian state model. Unusual in Japan was the significant impact of ruling party politicians outside the Cabinet: they exerted influence over policy-making within the LDP's informal policy-making bodies including the Policy Affairs Research Council (PARC). They belonged to a community in which groups of politicians (*Zoku gi'in*) specialised in specific fields, many of whom were former Cabinet ministers responsible for particular policy areas (Inoguchi and Iwai 1987).

In the 1970s Japan encountered significant political and economic crises. The emergence of corruption scandals culminated in financial scandals involving Kakuei Tanaka (Prime Minister, 1972–74) and the Lockheed bribery scandals in 1976, part of which also directly involved Tanaka. These scandals resulted in public anger against the LDP and undermined its popular support. The 1973 oil crisis and the series of economic measures by then US President Nixon called the 'Nixon Shock' led to the end of the Bretton Woods system of monetary management. The concomitant economic turmoil prompted corporate scandals including price controls on everyday commodities by trading companies and cartels. The response to these political and economic crises was the gradual transformation of the LDP and political and economic structures. The financial scandals in the 1970s involving LDP politicians prompted strong antagonism against 'money politics' (*kinken seiji*), significantly exacerbating public distrust of the political system and politicians. The economic crisis led to a call for administrative reform, which was the prioritised project of the Yasuhiro Nakasone government (1982–87). Although the resulting privatisation of three public corporations (telecommunications and tobacco in 1985, railways in 1987) attracted significant attention, the impact of neoliberal policies was generally limited in the 1970s and 1980s because established and persistent political and economic structures resisted neoliberal reforms. Indeed, Japan has sometimes partially promoted policies based on a market-oriented philosophy, but it has been reluctant to thoroughly embrace them (Pierre and Peters 2000: 3) so as to protect its embedded structure. As such, governing in the 1980s retained the traditional approach mobilised by the government, although the influence of *Zoku gi'in* on policy-making processes increased (Inoguchi and Iwai 1987).

Transformation gradually emerged in the 1990s, prompted by a set of reforms including the 1994 political reform and the 1997 administrative reform, with concomitant societal changes. The 1994 political reform set out to address public anger against the LDP prompted by scandals involving several top LDP politicians in the late 1980s, such as the Recruit scandal in 1988 and Tokyo *Sagawa kyūbin* scandal in 1992. A key component of the reform was the replacement of the traditional single non-transferable voting (SNTV) system with the mixed-member majoritarian (MMM) system, together with the introduction of public funding for political parties. The impact of the electoral system changes reshaped the organisation of political parties. As members of the House of Representatives (*Shūgi'in*) are now selected from single-member districts (SMDs), where only a single candidate is elected as the representative, using the proportional representation (PR) system drawn from the party's PR candidate list, top party officials obtain significant leverage to administer their party by authorising candidates. The introduction of the government subsidy to political parties and concomitant restrictions on private entities' direct funding of each politician have set the framework that regulates Japan's political parties' finances. Under the new system, the party management receives government funds to allocate to local party branches headed by Diet members or their candidates. As Japan's Diet employs a bicameral system, with the power of the House of Representatives being superior to that of the House of Councillors in selecting a government, the impact of the reform was significant enough to reshape Japan's political landscape.

A key outcome of the 1994 political reform was the centralised power of party management within the respective parties, which has contributed to shaping a stronger Prime Minister and Cabinet since the 2000s. Another key contributory factor shaping a strong central government was the 1997 administrative reform adopted by the Ryūtarō Hashimoto administration in 1997, which strengthened the power of the Prime Minister and the Cabinet in relation to bureaucracy, together with the reorganisation of government organisations and the establishment of independent administrative agencies (*dokuritsu gyōsei hōjin*). After its implementation in 2001, the 1997 administrative reform transformed the civil service, which had been a key body of administrative power, into a set of organisations more systematically administered by the Prime Minister and the Cabinet. The explicit impact of this set of reforms was observed in the political project under the Jun'ichirō Koizumi administration (2001–06). The enactment of the 1998 Non-Profit Organisation Law also established the institutional foundation of non-government organisations in Japan, which have the potential to address activities traditionally overseen by the government. Although this has augmented the development of the sector, the organisations have not significantly affected the development of governance in Japan with either sizeable professional groups or clear strategies influential over the public sphere and policy-making (McCargo 2013: 179–80).

Although Japan's transformation of the state and governance attracted scholarly attention in the 1990s, its explicit impact was widely observed in the 2000s, including the tenure of the Koizumi administration. The LDP administration in this period saw the gradual and piecemeal development of elected officials, for example the Prime Minister and Cabinet ministers, who mobilised popular support through engaging in politicisation, and the contrasting decline of ruling party politicians outside the Cabinet – although some Cabinets had a comparatively short tenure. A key issue of the LDP administration in the 2000s was party governance. Indeed, a major challenge to the Koizumi government was its internal opponents within the LDP itself rather than opposition parties. The change of power relations within the LDP from politicians outside the Cabinet to Koizumi, the *Kantei* (Prime Minister's Office) and his ministers culminated in the 2005 postal reform and his victory over internal enemies within the LDP. After Koizumi's landslide victory in the 2005 general election, he dominated the country's political arena with unchallengeable power within the LDP in addition to the LDP's overwhelming majority in the National Diet. Koizumi's example exhibits the growing power of the Prime Minister and the Cabinet vis-à-vis politicians outside the Cabinet.

Elsewhere, the transformation of the relationship between the state and society after the 1990s through the reforms of regulation and public spending gradually changed the nature of government officials in policymaking. As typically observed in Information and Communications Technology (ICT) regulation, the bureaucratic approach gradually shifted its focus from discretionary measures including market entry permissions to those based on rules such as overseeing network interconnection disputes (Mogaki 2015). In particular, the policy projects explicitly mobilised by neoliberal rhetoric with the mantra of *Kan kara min e* [from the official to the private] under the Koizumi administration aimed to reform established economic structures, exemplifying reformist politics in the 2000s. The administration pursued spending cuts in public investment, privatisation (e.g. highways, postal services), deregulation and devolution through its prioritised structural reform projects. Together with the impact of the 1997 administrative reform, this set of measures reshaped the nature and power of civil servants in policy-making, who gradually refrained from acting as strategists. The government change from the Liberal Democratic Party to the Democratic Party of Japan (DPJ) that resulted from the landslide victory in the 2009 general election provided an explicit indicator of this trend.

Despite significant popular support in the 2009 general election, governance under the DPJ administration between 2009 and 2013 can be characterised by its unsystematic approach to governing and resulting turmoil, the insignificant impact of its domestic policies, and unpopular crisis management (RJIF 2013). The administration intended to replace the previous public policy-making processes under the LDP administration with its own, in which the Cabinet functioned as the sole body responsible for policy-making; for this purpose, it abolished its Policy Research Committee (PRC), the equivalent of the LDP's PARC. This measure did not work because of the DPJ's failure to incorporate bureaucracy smoothly into its policy-making machine. Rather, what the DPJ did was a gradual regression to the traditional approach established by the LDP through the revival of the PRC and its enhancement. In this way, the impact of the DPJ administration was not as striking as many observers initially expected. However, it marked a clear disjuncture between traditional governance under the LDP and a new period in which policy-making was steered by the Prime Minister and the Cabinet. The gradual decline in the power of LDP politicians outside the Cabinet in the 2000s was accelerated by the emergence of the DPJ administration. Their power has yet to recover within policy-making arenas as party politicians outside the Cabinet have failed to play a key role in policy-making since 2009 in either the DPJ or LDP administrations.

The power of the core, that is, the Prime Minister, the *Kantei*, the Cabinet and its ministers, grew in the 2000s including during the LDP Koizumi administration. The DPJ administration enhanced this trend but did not demonstrate a new mode of governance. What happened instead was the emergence of unstable conditions rather than a new equilibrium. Indeed, the DPJ administration has often been criticised for its lack of governing ability, for example its failure to form a consensus within the party and to mobilise bureaucracy to achieve its goals, which resulted in the failure of its governance reform initiatives, including its policy-making system led by elected officials (RJIF 2013; Zakowski 2015). Together with its status as a minority government within the House of Councillors resulting from the failed election in 2010, the administration exhibited insufficient ability to generate strong policy outcomes. Elsewhere, despite notable political disputes between the DPJ and opposition parties within the National Diet, under the DPJ-led Coalition government the state retained its significance in policy-making as it had in the LDP-led Coalition government of the 2000s, although its core experienced fluid changes of power between key actors.

The 2012 change of government from the DPJ to the LDP restored the LDP's previous policy-making framework, including the PARC's preliminary examination system. The ostensible outcome was the restoration of the previous regime and approach. However, a broader trend that reshaped the governance of Japan has significantly affected the LDP administration since 2012. As of 2018, the power of the Prime Minister has been regarded as key in Japan's policy-making process, together with his aides such as the *Kantei*, the chief Cabinet secretary and other Cabinet ministers. Although ruling party politicians outside the Cabinet have regained their previous position as actors in policy-making, few commentators have identified cases in which their impact has been comparable to that in the 1980s (Yomiuri online 2014). Likewise, few argue for government ministries as key strategists. Indeed, unlike Johnson's (1982) equivalent in the 1970s, the explicit impact of government ministries has been limited since 2012. This could reflect the fact that the institutional foundation of the Prime Minister's power was enhanced by the 1997 administrative reform and successive measures, including the establishment in 2014 of the Cabinet Bureau of Personnel Affairs which oversees the appointment of senior civil servants. The resulting performance of the LDP's Abe administration is, however, a topic for examination. The LDP administration since 2012 has experienced few internal conflicts because not only does the LDP President/Prime Minister authorise the registration of a candidate, but he has also not engaged in policy projects that would significantly undermine the interests and power of fellow LDP politicians (Pekkanen et al. 2016). The administration has enjoyed significant advantages from the weakness of opposition parties such as the DPJ/DP (the Democratic Party, the successor of the DPJ, established in 2016) (Noble 2016). Whether or not this dominance is sustainable in the absence of these factors remains to be seen.

The politics of Japan and its state

In the literature, three major schools address Japan and its politics regarding the state and power after the 1980s: the state-centric, the pluralist and rational choice. The state-centric school sets out the influential 'developmental state' thesis proposed by Johnson (1982). It regards the Japanese state as development-oriented or strategic under the domination of economic bureaucrats; this approach describes a state primarily concentrating on the economic development of the country.[1] The state retains a strong authority based on the Weberian model of bureaucracy, which is insulated from society and organised to maximise its efficiency. The developmental state thesis had a sustained and lasting impact, shaping the successive literature on Japan (Schaede 2000: 2). It was a watershed in the study of Japanese politics and had a significant impact on political science literature after the 1980s. As an example, Vogel (1996: 59) adapts Johnson to explore regulatory reforms in Japan and the UK, regarding the Japanese approach as the one pursuing better management of the sector; he employs an approach focusing on state actors and regulatory reforms, showing how the Japanese state asserted its will against the targeted industries such as telecommunications and financial services. The

2000s saw a successive body of literature drawing on the state-centric approach demonstrated by Vogel. For example, throughout his exploration of Japan's fiscal policy between the 1970s and 2000s, Wright (2002) illuminates the complicated decision-making mechanism, revealing the persistent dominance of the core executive within this sector exemplified by the Ministry of Finance (MOF). Elsewhere, George Mulgan (2005, 2006) in a similar vein identifies the Ministry of Agriculture, Forestry and Fisheries (MAFF) as a significant actor in shaping agricultural policies and reveals the MAFF's skilful approach to retaining its power and what she calls the 'interventionist state' (George Mulgan 2005: 9–44). One of the frequent criticisms (Calder 1993) of the statist approach involves its extensive emphasis on a particular state actor, for example the Ministry of International Trade and Industry (MITI) in Johnson (1982). As Johnson, along with others (e.g. Weiss 1998: 14–40), argues, the MITI has had significant capacity and performed well in the field of industrial policy. However, the MITI is not part of the central apparatus of the Japanese state because its responsibilities (industrial policy-making and implementation) do not include the core function of state steering. Structurally powerful government ministries such as the MOF are not sufficiently addressed.

The influential paradigm of the developmental state was challenged by the emergence of a pluralist literature such as Muramatsu and Krauss (1987) and Calder (1993), which highlights the importance of actors other than bureaucrats, such as party politicians and private-sector actors including long-term credit banks. Elsewhere, another school challenging the notion of the developmental state is that of rational choice. The rational choice literature understands Japan's politics to be the result of rational choices by actors, particularly party politicians facing elections. As an example of this school, Ramseyer and Rosenbluth (1993) conclude, through their analysis of Japanese politics with the principal–agent theory, that the ruling LDP at the time dominated Japan's policy-making by mobilising bureaucrats (Wright 1999: 949).

After the 1990s, these pluralist and rational choice schools started to report that significant changes were emerging in Japan (Yamamura 1997; Pempel 1998; Vogel 2006; Schaede 2008; Pempel 2010; Rosenbluth and Thies 2010). This literature focused on changes of actors and structures: bureaucracy was losing its traditional influence and private firms were taking more responsibility and risks (Vogel 2006; Schaede 2008). What is missing in these accounts is how the Japanese state at a macro level has evolved. Indeed, they focus on changes within the industrial and corporate sectors in reflecting on the recent changes that have taken place in Japan. The government and the public sector are not their major focus and state transformation is only partially described (see Table 1.1).

Table 1.1 Summary of state and state-transformation literature

Work	Approach	Description of the state	State transformation
Johnson 1982	state-centric	The state is led by the MITI with the 'safety valve' of politicians. Interest groups are insignificant.	Transformed to the MITI-led developmental state
Muramatsu and Krauss 1987	pluralist	The state is penetrated by interest groups.	Inside the state the LDP's power is growing. Bureaucrats are gradually losing influence.
Calder 1993	pluralist	The state is a pluralist theatre where actors struggle to formulate policies. Long-term credit banks are key for economic development.	
Ramseyer and Rosenbluth 1993	rational choice	The LDP as the principal utilises bureaucrats as the agent.	The electoral system has changed to cope with emerging urban voters. Traditional interest groups declined.
Pempel 1998	comparative politics/pluralist	A group of actors including the LDP and bureaucrats; it has a complicated relationship with societal actors such as interest groups.	Japan's regime has shifted from one based on agriculture and small businesses to one reliant on urban voters.
Vogel 1996	state-centric	Party politicians and bureaucrats collectively work to realise regulatory reforms.	The state has deployed its initiative through its regulatory policy instruments.
Schaede 2000	pluralist	The state has gradually lost its control over industries.	The state is losing its traditional grip. This void is exploited by self-regulation.
Wright 2002	historical institutionalism/ state-centric	The nexus of actors such as the MOF, Finance Ministry and the LDP shaped key fiscal policies through internal negotiations.	The state was inflexible in addressing emerging fiscal challenges such as spending and debt increase.

(*Continued*)

Table 1.1 Continued

Work	Approach	Description of the state	State transformation
George Mulgan 2005, 2006	state-centric	The MAFF is highlighted as the key state actor shaping the interventionist state in agriculture.	The state has been transformed in line with the MAFF's direction, which pursues a process of cumulative intervention
Vogel 2006	institutional economics (private firms-focused)	The state is described as an element of reform processes and is not addressed as a core theme.	The state is losing its authority in the economy. It has gradually abandoned industrial policy and embraced liberal reforms.
I'io 2007	leaning to pluralist	Politicians act as representatives of government ministries (bureaucrats)	The Prime Minister has strengthened their power and responsibility.
Schaede 2008	pluralist (not clearly mentioned, private firms-focused)	The state is described as an actor behind the transformation of private firms.	The state is losing its traditional authority over industry. Drastic regulatory reforms have been implemented.
Rosenbluth and Thies 2010	rational choice	The LDP controls the state machinery. The state acts so that the LDP election machine could generate the optimum electoral results.	The 1994 electoral reforms changed the Diet and the state. The LDP has been switching its support basis to more productive industries and urban voters from obsolete industries and interest groups.

Japanese politics research has hitherto tended to focus on individual issues such as particular actors in the political arena, eschewing accounts that seek to analyse the relationship between the state and society. In Johnson's (1982) developmental state model the key actor is economic bureaucrats, in particular the MITI. Although Muramatsu and Krauss (1987) recognise the increasing importance of party politicians

Introduction   13

(particularly the LDP's), bureaucracy continues to be identified as the dominant actor. They seek to highlight the transformation of the Japanese state in terms of a gradual shift in power from bureaucrats to party politicians; in so doing, they challenge the notion of bureaucratic domination (I'io 2007: 37). The pluralist literature illuminates the role of other state actors such as party politicians (Muramatsu and Krauss 1987) and societal actors such as major financial institutions (long-term credit banks, Calder 1993), interest groups (Pempel 1998) and trade associations (Schaede 2000). The pluralist literature has dominated accounts from within Japanese political science since the late 1970s as the major approach to explain Japan's democracy (I'io 2007: 37–8). Its approach to exploring Japan's political changes is not free from the criticism of pluralist literature in general (Smith 2005: 36–7); it fails to problematise and analyse the Japanese state at the macro level. Because the pluralist literature focuses on groups and implicitly assumes that 'the state is a neutral arena for groups', it struggles to address the state and state power at this level (Smith 2005: 37). Change is explained as the collection of the micro-level events of both state and societal actors and structures. Description and analyses of the state and societal actors are conflated, as Pempel's (1998) regime model shows. Change in the state is not deliberately drawn. In other words, the pluralist literature does not regard the transformation of the state as key because transformation takes place in what Calder (1993: 14) described as 'a pluralist theatre'.

The rational choice literature does not offer a remedy for this shortcoming in the pluralist literature, because its analytical focus is on actors (Elster 1989: 22, in Ward 2002: 65). The rational choice literature requires exogenous premises to illuminate changes of structure (Ward 2002: 88). Also, its methodological individualism and deductive explanations do not cope with accounts exploring state transformation at the macro level, because, like the pluralist literature, it does not explore macro-level subjects such as the transformation of the state. What it generates is aggregation drawn from micro-level enquiries. The dominance of these approaches leaves the exploration of the Japanese state at a macro level largely overlooked: this is the lacuna that this book intends to address. It sets out to challenge these dominant perspectives by offering an analysis of the Japanese state predominantly cast at the macro level. The next section elaborates my specific approach to achieving this goal.

About this book

I adopt an elitist account, locating power at the centre of the state, with a view that the central state is the key locus that is afforded particular and asymmetric resources that allow it to be the dominant actor influencing and steering society. To clearly set up the definition of this important concept with attention to the relevant debate, in this book we regard the state as an entity insulated from private interests, composed of established state organisations such as government ministries and other similar organisations, and monopolising coercive tools within its territorial boundaries (Weber 1978; Skocpol 1985; Mann 1993). Over time, the state's central organisation has been enhanced and its control on society has become more developed. The state has been reconstituted to respond to the recent challenges of an emergent era of governance, with a process of adaptation on the part of the core executive in relation to both resources and strategic-learning capabilities to reshape its existing capacities and develop new forms of intervention to sustain its position as the dominant actor in the policy-making arena. Such an approach illuminating the state at a macro level challenges the dominant views on Japan offered by pluralist and rational choice accounts. I set out to critique the existing dominance of pluralism by offering an elitist account of state power and power relations in Japan. Although the response of the state since the 1980s to its challenges has been a major topic of debate on governance in European political science, the Japanese state's response to challenges has remained unexplored. This is the core theme of this book: the transformation of the Japanese state after the 1980s.

The study of the core executive and the way it has adapted is at the heart of the analytical framework of this research. It draws on the principle of concept travelling (Sartori 1970), employing the core executive approach originating from British political science. It offers a framework depicting the specific resources, alongside the fluid and changeable nature of power within the core executive based on the interdependent relationships between key central actors, that allow the core executive collectively to establish an asymmetric position of dominance over other actors in the policy-making arena (Smith 1999). The concept of the core executive offers a framework to collectively analyse central government policy-making. Its key characteristics include its view that power is fluid and relational depending upon resource reliance and the resulting negotiations between actors to achieve their respective goals, and the scope with which institutions are considered through the analysis of structures and agency within the core executive and beyond (Smith 1999). The concept is also generalisable and polymorphous; the literature has demonstrated the benefit of the concept as an analytical framework in different cases (Itō 2006; Elgie 2011); elsewhere, exactly what comprises the core executive depends upon the nature of case studies. The concept of the core executive offers an ontological view of power that responds to the criticism of pluralist and rational choice literature, which regards power as observable: power depends on resources that are fluid within the core executive. The ontological view offers an approach that systematically and collectively analyses structure and agency.

To elaborate, the following functional definition by Rhodes (1995: 12) is beneficial for setting up the specific scope of the core executive in the case studies: 'all those organisations and procedures which coordinate central government policies, and act as final arbiters of conflict between different parts of the government machine'. The specific consideration regarding the case studies allows the concept of the core executive to shape the framework applicable to the case as a form of concept travelling. The resulting scope of the core executive is differentiated into a specific one for each case study, referring to its political conditions. This 'modification' enables the concept to analyse a variety of political cases. Specifically, referring to the previous examples of Japanese cases, this book embraces party politicians outside the Cabinet as key members of the core executive together with responsible government organisations. If one turns to the original definition set out by Rhodes, this modified scope offers a framework to analyse key actors with power together with structures. A model that eradicates non-Cabinet politicians will offer a view that misses a key part of the policy-making process.

Governance of key regulatory sectors has significantly transformed from a regime focusing on direct service provision by the state or public organisations (e.g. a public corporation) to one focusing on principal–agent regulation. Indeed, the state has increasingly used regulation as an administrative tool in addition to its traditional methods of authority, bureaucracy and force, because of perceived inadequacies within the existing bureaucratic tool kit (Smith 2009: 156).[2] The increasing use of regulation can exemplify the transformation of state power, prompting the emergence of a state focused more on rule-making, monitoring and enforcement either directly or indirectly (Smith 2009: 171; Levi-Faur 2012: 19–20). Highlighting this 'regulatory state' in the specific context of Japanese examples enables us to unfold how the state has been transformed in the selected case studies on regulation. In addition, I highlight the significance of regulation in the study of the state, society and power (Smith 2009). As Majone (1996: 54) contends, regulation is a core function of the state, together with the redistribution function and the stabilisation function. Although this book's exploration does not cover every part of the Japanese state, its focus on key examples of Japan's regulatory sectors presents useful insights for the study of the state and Japan. Indeed, the development of sectors of a key policy area can be understood as examples with strong explanatory power to reveal the transformation of the Japanese state in general, given their significance in Japan's political arena. This book will explore two case studies of regulation as key examples of state transformation. In so doing, it tries to offer a perspective applicable to cases beyond regulation.

16   Conceptualising the Japanese state and governance

If this book is predominantly concerned with analysing the extent to which the Japanese state, and in particular its core executive power, has been reconstituted after the 1980s, its core theme can be specified as follows: *During the era of the LDP government, the core executive pursued discretionary regulation within inner regulatory policy communities as a strategy to sustain its position of asymmetric dominance over actors within key policy sectors, with their actions shaped by a particular set of structures.* This proposition identifies a perpetuation of the asymmetric dominance of the central state through strategic adaptation on the part of the core executive. To explore this core theme, several overarching questions are posed:

- How has Japan's regulatory framework evolved over the last three decades?
- How has the core executive been successful in imposing its will on regulation?
- How have Japan's ministries shaped the organisational design of regulatory functions?
- How has the state's regulatory capacity changed?
- Why have the present power relations been constructed in the chosen regulatory fields?

Through an examination of this set of research questions, this book reveals the extent to which asymmetric dominance of the Japanese state in the transformative process has been sustained.

This book will set out the argument that the reconstituted state is a key characteristic of the Japanese state after the 1980s. The reconstitution of the Japanese state has come with a change of power within the core executive. Powerful party politicians outside the Cabinet acting as decision makers, and civil servants acting as strategists, administered the key sectors of ICT and anti-monopoly regulation in the 1980s and 1990s. In the 2000s the Cabinet emerged as a dominant actor but failed to take over the strategic role of civil servants. Mobilised by the change of power within the core executive – Cabinet ministers, party politicians outside the Cabinet and civil servants – the reconstitution of the state has transformed the Japanese state's developmentally oriented characteristics. The transformation, however, has not changed the essential nature of the state: the asymmetric dominance of the core executive. Rather, the core executive has mobilised the reconstitution. The Japanese state employed a developmentally oriented approach because the core executive of the time chose that option. If the core executive had chosen an alternative, the Japanese state would employ a different method. Therefore, the nature of the Japanese state is explained not by its specific approaches but by what makes it employ such approaches. The resulting Japanese regulatory state displays the equilibrium between accountability, independent implementation and frequent rule changes in response to circumstantial changes. Japan's ICT regulation does not prioritise independent implementation, but accountability and frequent rule changes. Elsewhere, anti-monopoly regulation has not had either frequent rule changes or the preparation to cope with them, but has managed its challenges so far by prioritising its independence; concern for accountability has been less pronounced than concern for independent implementation. This reflects the fact that Japan's anti-monopoly regulator does not have a robust link with politics, unlike other government ministries. The above set of claims challenges the traditional views of pluralist and rational choice literature by explicitly highlighting the significance of the state-level as key. It also evolves from the traditional statist view by embracing not a particular state actor, but a group of key state actors within a tangible political arena: the state at a macro level. The following chapters will set out to demonstrate these claims.

This book is composed of eight chapters examining two case studies of the Japanese state: ICT regulation and anti-monopoly regulation. Following this introductory chapter, Chapter 2 sets out the key analytical framework underpinning this study. It invokes the concept of the core executive developed within UK studies in the 1990s, in response to the change of governance in the political arena, and applies it to the Japanese case. It then sets out the context of the transformation of the Japanese state through governance literature. The changed context of governance can be aligned with the concomitant emergence of a regulatory response, a dynamic that has been commonly identified in several industrialised economies over the last three decades. Here, the concept of the regulatory state offers a framework within which this book analyses how the state steers society by regulation.

Part II is composed of the case study chapters. Chapters 3 and 4 explore the case of ICT regulation, starting from the 1985 regulatory reform. Chapter 3 analyses the power relations within the core executive. It reveals the ongoing dominance of the core executive in the sector, with changing power relations significantly prompting a shift in the dominant group among party politicians. Chapter 4 focuses on how the regulator has been located within the responsible ministry – the MPT/MIC – with an examination of state capacity within the sector. Then the chapter pulls together the analysis of the case study on ICT regulation. Chapters 5 and 6 explore the case of anti-monopoly regulation and the nature of the Fair Trade Commission (JFTC) as a rare independent regulator in Japan. Chapter 5 addresses the transformation of power relations in the sector; this is followed by an examination of the nature of the commission's independence and continuously growing state capacity in Chapter 6, which reveals a different story from its counterpart in ICT regulation.

Yet both case studies reveal the ongoing dominance of the core executive throughout the period studied. The analysis draws on elite interviews from current and former party politicians, civil servants, private firm officials, consumer group officials and professionals involved in the case studies: researchers and lawyers. All interviews were undertaken on an off-the-record-basis and no interviewee is named or specific role disclosed. This enabled interviewees to offer frank and unhindered views.

Part III draws together the insights from the case studies. Chapter 7 unites the findings of the case study chapters and sets out the argument for the emergence of the Japanese regulatory state based on changing power relations within the core executive, responding to the change of governance, highlighting two key characteristics: the asymmetric dominance of the core executive within the Japanese state and the emergence of a variation of the regulatory state in Japan. In so doing, it challenges the dominant positions within existing accounts of Japanese state–society relations: those of pluralism and rational choice. The final chapter reviews recent political developments, paying attention to the two regulatory sectors, and sets out the implications of this research and the subsequent political developments under the re-emergent LDP-led Coalition government.

Notes

1 Evans (1995: 12) also defines the developmental state, as the state not only has 'presided over industrial transformation but can be plausibly argued to have played a role in making it happen'.
2 To elaborate, decision makers have difficulty controlling implementers because of a substantial distance between the top and the bottom within bureaucracy and the considerable coordination needed to deliver the top's decisions through bureaucratic chains; decision makers also face the possibility that implementers might subvert decisions (Smith 2009: 156).

2
The change of governance and regulation

In the developed world, the dominance of the state before the 1970s brought government to the centre of the debate as a key concept; it was government that was supposed to govern and solve societal issues with its expanding projects and budgets, rather than the system of governance. The decline of government's traditional approach from the 1970s brought back 'governance', whose origin was a fourteenth-century French word *gouvernance*, as the focus of interest to explain the state's adaptation in response to the challenges outlined above (Pierre and Peters 2000: 1, 18). The concept of governance emerged as a new vehicle to address changing politics and society from the 1970s. In the past thirty years there has been a significant growth in the study of governance within political science. Governance literature seeks to offer new forms of analysis of the governing system under the emergent political conditions after the 1980s and 1990s. Interestingly, the debate on governance has helped bring the state back into political science literature, especially in Europe; for example, one school has proposed a hollowing out of the state (Rhodes 1997), while others have argued for the transformation or reconstitution of the state (Marsh et al. 2001; Sorensen 2004). Crucially though, the debate on the state and governance has not been significantly addressed in the analysis of Japan and its politics, where the tradition of pluralist and rational choice literature has continued to dominate. With the view that the state is the key locus of power in political arenas, my ontological perspective endorses the reconstituted-state thesis.[1] Placing the core theme – transformation of the Japanese state after the 1980s – in a broader context of the change of governance, I will demonstrate the utility of the reconstituted state thesis when applied to Japan, with the aim of exploring the extent to which the Japanese state has reconstituted itself rather than been hollowed out in response to transformational forces in the last three decades. This position draws from the view that state actors are in an asymmetrically advantageous position because the state makes its decisions within a close circle of core state actors: the core executive. State transformation is the set of processes reconstituting the state, in which the core executive exploits opportunities to reshape its existing capacities and develop new forms of intervention to sustain its position as the dominant policy-making actor (Richards 2008: 97–8). What is key here is the core executive's resources and strategic-learning capabilities, drawing on its asymmetric structural position within the government.

Within this broad analytical framework, I illuminate the concepts of the core executive and the regulatory state as key and elaborate my position with them; specifically, I set up an analytical framework on governance to explore the core theme by observing how the core executive has adapted to change and how the regulatory state has developed. The concept of the core executive, which emerged in the debate within the Anglo-Governance School,[2] aims at the core mechanism of the state based on its ontological view of power, which is fluid and relational within the core executive. The framework drawn from the concept analyses central government and its broader policy-making context by widening the focus of central government studies and applying a range of conceptual and theoretical approaches to the core executive, disclosing the fluid and relational nature of power through observing how the power of actors has changed in the process of state transformation. Elsewhere, exploring the change of governance in regulation directly relates to the state's political and institutional capacity to steer vis-à-vis the interests of other influential actors. As a key concept within the study of regulation and governance, the concept of the regulatory state examines the state–society relationship by analysing regulatory traditions and unfolds how the Japanese state has changed its scope and power in relation to society. With its significant role in the state's transformative process vis-à-vis markets, the increasing usage of regulation as an administrative tool to steer markets and society has characterised the reconstituted state (Peters 1996: 6; Vogel 1996; Sorensen 2004: 31–9; Richards 2008: 121–2). Therefore, exploring regulatory development in specific cases reveals the key characteristics of the reconstituted state.

This chapter first considers the concept of the core executive as key to explaining the system of governance and analysing the transformation of the Japanese state. The chapter then focuses on the concept of the regulatory state and governance, aiming to analyse the relationship between the state and society. The following two sections pay specific attention to regulatory development in the UK and New Zealand as examples of the regulatory state within different political traditions. The final section pulls the considerations of this chapter together, heeding the political tradition of Japan and beyond.

The core executive and state transformation

Although the significance of the concept of the core executive in the study of governance is evident, my approach to this concept seeks to establish a flexible scope for this study and beyond. As the concept has been shaped by debate since the 1990s,[3] revisiting relevant key ideas will help when considering the nature of the concept. The influential functional definition of the core executive was developed by Rhodes (1995: 12), who defines the core executive as 'all those organisations and procedures which coordinate central government policies, and act as final arbiters of conflict between different parts of the government machine'. His characterisation states that:

> In brief, the 'core executive' is the heart of the machine, covering the complex web of institutions, networks and practices surrounding the Prime Minister, cabinet, cabinet committees and their official counterparts, less formalised ministerial 'clubs' or meetings, bilateral negotiations and interdepartmental committees. It also includes coordinating departments, chiefly the Cabinet Office, the Treasury, the Foreign Office, the law officers and the security and intelligence services. (1995: 12)

The scope of the core executive is outlined by Smith (1999: 5), who adds departments to the core executive for the following two reasons: 'they are the core policy-making units within central government; and they are headed by ministers who are key actors within the institutions of the core executive'.

Behind this concept is a different perspective on power and the intention of bringing institutions back into the debate. The former is that 'Power has to be seen as fluid and relational, not static. In that sense, power does not lie anywhere within the system because it is everywhere – all actors have resources, and the outcomes need to be negotiated' (Smith 1999: 14). Power under this concept is based on resource-dependency; any actor in the core executive needs resources from others to achieve its goal because none of them monopolises resources. The idea behind this view is that power is relational between actors, fluid and unpredictable; power is determined through negotiations within the complex nexus of the core executive, in which many causes and interactions will affect outcomes (Smith 1999: 35–6). This view on power regarding the core executive contrasts with power between the core executive actors and societal actors. The key to understanding the difference is the concept of networks within the system of governance. The core executive since the 1980s has operated through networks within and between various elements of the state and civil society rather than formal institutions. The nature of networks between the core executive and society is different from that within the core executive (Smith 1999: 251):

> When we are analysing a closed policy community between a department and a pressure group, we are often looking at a particular power relationship. This type of network is a mechanism for excluding certain groups and defining policy issues in a particular way. Therefore, the policy community is constituting a particular power relationship and the nature of the relationship can explain policy outcomes.

Elsewhere, networks within the core executive comprise interdependent relationships between various actors and institutions within the central state; because the actors in the core are playing by certain rules of the game, they cannot be excluded from the network in most cases (Smith 1999: 251). Therefore, the nature of power is analysed not through the network but through the degree of resource-dependency between actors (Smith 1999: 251). Consequently, what is important is not membership of networks within the core executive but the nature of the dependency between actors within the networks; this makes networks within the core executive fluid (Smith 1999: 251). This framework offers the view that the core executive has asymmetric relationships with society based on power relations, while the relationship within is fluid and resource-dependent. It is dominant in relation to societal actors, and resource-dependent internally. The latter is understood as analysing the core executive in terms of structure and agency. The fluid nature of structure and agency enables researchers to capture the fluid nature of the state. A dialectic relationship can be observed between structure and agency; actors reproduce structures, whereas structures are created by agency.

The concept of the core executive, while originally developed and applied to the British case, has subsequently been applied to analyses of countries outside the UK (Peters et al. 2000; Elgie 2011: 64). An example that applies the core executive model to other countries is Itō (2006), who employs this concept for the Japanese case in the 1990s and 2000s. According to him, the core executive model suits the Japanese case because the government's decision-making system is composed of two closely connected arenas, the incumbent party arena and the executive arena, both of which are decentralised and interdependent (Itō 2006: 11). Analysing the LDP administration, what Itō highlights is the degree of power commanded by the LDP politicians outside the Cabinet together with their counterparts in the Cabinet, and the close interaction between these two groups within the LDP administration. Based on the definitions of Rhodes (1995) and Smith (1999), Japan's core executive in his analysis includes the Prime Minister, the Cabinet ministers and senior civil servants in the government, together with factions, three key positions (the secretaries general, the General Affairs Council chairperson, and the PARC chairperson), and the LDP's *Zoku gi'in*.[4] Elsewhere, Kamikubo (2010) explores the comparative politics of international monetary policy-making in Japan and China, based on the analytical framework of Rhodes (1995) and Smith (1999). His core executive in Japan is composed of the Prime Minister, the responsible Cabinet ministers (the finance ministers and the Cabinet ministers responsible for monetary issues), civil servants (the MOF, the Financial Services Agency), the Bank of Japan and key LDP figures (Kamikubo 2010: 5–6). Kamikubo's core executive in Japan can be viewed as a variation of Itō's, specialising in the international monetary sector. The approach by Itō and Kamikubo employs the concept of the core executive based on their understanding that Japanese state actors are decentralised and interdependent. They do not simply apply the analytical framework from British political science to the Japanese case without consideration of Japan's specific political contexts – so avoiding accusations of 'conceptual stretching' (Sartori 1970); rather, they transfer the concept of the core executive to the Japanese case based on their analysis of Japan's political tradition.

In pulling the above together, what emerges is the generalisability of the concept of the core executive. The concept effectively addresses the fluid power relations between actors and the interactions between structures and agency with a suitable scope for the case of research. Rhodes (1995: 12) defines the components of the core executive as the Prime Minister, Cabinet, Cabinet committees and their official counterparts, and coordinating departments such as the Cabinet Office, the Treasury, the Foreign Office, the law officers and the security and intelligence services. Taking account of the fact that some policies do not involve all the members of the government, this definition is rather crude and inflexible; for instance, policies related to the National Health Service (NHS), one of the UK's key domestic policy areas, will barely involve the security and intelligence services. Instead, the UK Department of Health is heavily involved in policy-making together with the Treasury. Elsewhere, Smith's (1999) definition allows more flexibility to include relevant actors by embracing departments in the core executive.

To respond to the case-specific characteristic of the core executive, one must recognise its polymorphous nature. Some important actors in one field (e.g. intelligence services in counter-terrorism) have few roles in other fields (e.g. the NHS, domestic anti-monopoly regulation). An example can be found in Kamikubo (2010), whose core executive includes specialised public organisations (the MOF, the Bank of Japan) together with the core of the core such as the Prime Minister.

This book defines the core executive and includes what the above fail to offer: it constitutes all those organisations and procedures that

Table 2.1 Membership of the core executive

ICT regulation	Anti-monopoly regulation
• Prime Minister • Responsible Cabinet ministers and other politically appointed officials • Civil servants (MPT/MIC) • key party politicians, e.g. the LDP's *Zoku gi'in*	• Prime Minister • Responsible Cabinet ministers and other politically appointed officials • Chairmen and commissioners (JFTC) • Civil servants (JFTC) • key party politicians

Note: Japan's Ministry of Post and Telecommunications was responsible for ICT issues until 2001, when it was reorganised into the Ministry of Internal Affairs and Communications.

coordinate central government and act as final arbiters of conflict between different parts of the government machine, the exact scope of which is determined by the specific nature of the targeted sector. The scope of the core executive includes the core machine of central government, with its polymorphous nature responding to the specific conditions of the focused sector; to explain with a concrete example, Japan's National Police Agency is a member of the core executive in Japan's anti-organised-crime policy, but is not a core executive member in its consumption tax policy. Table 2.1 reveals what is actually meant by the core executive in the case study chapters.

Politically appointed officials, namely the Prime Minister, Cabinet ministers, parliamentary vice-ministers,[5] senior vice-ministers and parliamentary secretaries, are in a position to be involved with policy-making, although to what extent is dependent upon the context, resources and personality. The JFTC chairmen and commissioners are in a similar position to politically appointed officials. Civil servants responsible for the fields (ICT regulation, anti-monopoly regulation) are key actors involved in policy-making and implementation. Other important actors are key party politicians outside the Cabinet. Because internal examination of important policy issues such as government bills was a norm under Japan's LDP regime (Beeman 2002: 174), key party politicians, those in the LDP in particular, obtained significant influence over policy-making. I set up the framework drawn from the concept of the core executive specifically aiming at the case studies, so that the framework can explain the nexus of regulatory policy-making in Japan, embracing the political arenas within the state at a macro level. In particular, the framework addresses the transformative processes of the state in the case studies in response to challenges resulting from the change of governance. In so doing, it reveals the nature of governance in Japan.

Evolving regulation and the state

Conceptualising regulation and the state has been contentious, despite its significance in the evolution of governance. The concept of the regulatory state remains a problematic notion. It can be referred to at the national level (e.g. Moran 2003 regarding the British state), and also at the supranational level (e.g. Majone 1996 regarding the European Commission). It is significantly affected by the structure (e.g. the characteristics of the specific sector, the context of the cases – i.e. multiple modes of regulation can coexist – existing institutions and national contexts) (Jordana and Levi-Farr 2004: 9). One element of the literature (Scott 2004) regards the regulatory state as the next mode of the state to the welfare state, and in so doing proposes regime change models. Others offer more complex accounts; for example, Moran (2003: 179–80) describes the emergence of the British regulatory state as an incomplete project of modernising the old British state that is confrontational to traditional elites. Braithwaite (2000) tries to solve this complexity by proposing the term 'new regulatory state', which employs rule-based regulation that keeps regulatees at arm's length by decentring the state and relying on self-regulatory organisation, enforced self-regulation, compliance systems, codes of practice and other responsive techniques that substitute for direct command and control (Levi-Faur 2012: 19).

Contention about the exact nature of the regulatory state may be sustained because many countries have been in the process of shaping their respective regulatory states since the 1980s. What most scholars recognise is the emergence of new state forms that sometimes extend their sphere of influence beyond those which operated in an area of the modern state. Given the fact that regulation has been a traditional administrative instrument, I pursue the permanent, flexible and generalisable nature of regulation in relation to the state. Therefore, my functional definition of the regulatory state is one that employs regulation to administer a sector through direct or indirect rule-making, monitoring and enforcement. At the same time, this book attempts to consider how the differences between each regulatory state can be explained in generalisable terms. For this purpose, the next two sections sketch the nature of regulation and the regulatory traditions of the UK and New Zealand. In so doing, in comparative terms, they offer potential insights for studying the Japanese case, particularly with regard to the perceived exceptionalism associated with the Japanese regulatory tradition. Here, the UK offers a comparative fit with Japan; both countries have significant but not dominant economies and started privatising the ICT sector in the 1980s. Their anti-monopoly regulation emerged after 1945. These similarities contribute to revealing potential generalisable features alongside the different political traditions of these two countries, although importing one political framework to another requires the consideration of respective political conditions. The example of New Zealand offers another reference, with its radical approach to deregulation in the 1980s, called the 'New Zealand experiment' (Kelsey 1995: 1).

The British regulatory state

In the UK, the regime of anti-monopoly regulation offered a prototype for the regulatory framework in other sectors, including ICT, as the Office of Fair Trading (OFT) became a model for regulatory organisations. Restrained by its tradition of business regulation, what emerged in this regulatory sector was an outcome of the compromise between the UK's political tradition and gradually increasing demands for anti-monopoly regulation (Moran 2003: 95–123). This tendency is shared by Britain's approach to regulation after the 1980s as a whole. It was significantly affected by the regulatory reforms initiated by the Conservative government in the 1980s, whose key privatisation projects, including British Telecom, which shaped a widely copied regulatory template, proceeded in an ad hoc fashion under intense time pressure. They were mobilised by the fact that the significantly unresponsive public ownership prompted the proponents of regulatory reform to choose a radical choice; the state's fiscal crisis in the early 1980s compelled the government to raise revenues through privatisation so as to fund its increased state spending, after it had committed to reducing state spending (Moran 2003: 100–1). The resulting regulatory regime was characterised by

> a distinctly modernist attempt by Littlechild to create an open, transparent world of non-discretionary regulatory decisions guided by fixed rules; and the very different attempt by the official creators in Whitehall to replicate as much as possible of the old discretionary and informal world that had privileged insiders in the club system. (Moran 2003: 120)

This contradictory set of characteristics created the following challenges. First, Littlechild's price formula (RPI − X)[6] created a new problem of how X should be set, and whether and how additional '+ Y' should be set; this provoked a political dispute, which the formula was intended to avoid, and resulted in a shift to a more open, formal system of politics, as described by Thatcher:

> The closed regulatory game of the pre-privatization era has given way to a more open and public one, with more participants, a higher degree of formalization of decision-making processes, greater public availability of information, more open conflict and complex manoeuvres involving

ministers, the DGs, former monopolists, new entrants, consumer bodies and the MMC (Monopolies and Mergers Commission, UK). (1997: 139 in Moran 2003: 109)

The impact of emerging regulators has been significant. With a wide range of regulatory institutions emerging from privatisation, this growth created a new community of regulators (who tended to share bureaucratic concerns), and the development of regulatory institutions produced regulators to prioritise social obligations such as universal service, marginalising the initial object of economic efficiency (Moran 2003: 109–13). Elsewhere, the practical politicisation of regulation, that is, the dominance of ministers, can be observed in spite of Littlechild's initial intention. An example can be found in the analysis of the water industry by Maloney (2001: 631), in which the Secretary of State decides whether or not the MMC's recommendations regarding the regulatees' complaints about the regulator's decisions on price setting would be accepted. Another example is the two British railway regulators (the Strategic Rail Authority and the Office of the Rail Regulator), which were marginalised in the decision-making process during the financial crisis of Railtrack in 2001:

> Perhaps the most remarkable feature of the way the crisis was tackled in the autumn of 2001 was the extent to which both were left on the sidelines. Although the dispute surrounds the actual terms of a critical meeting between the Secretary of State and the Rail Regulator when the Secretary had decided to put Railtrack into receivership, what is undisputed is that the Rail Regulator had simply no control over this decision: he was just told of it after the event. The same was true of the Strategic Rail Authority. Indeed, the Head of the Authority believed that the notion of an independent regulator had become fiction: 'almost every breath we draw has to be cleared by Ministers'. (Moran 2003: 117)

This is an example of politicisation in the form of the dominant position of party politicians in the key decision-making process of the crisis.

Overall, Britain's regulatory state since the 1980s can be characterised by the growth in regulatory bodies mobilised by privatisation. 'The privatisation movement in Britain ... provided the main impetus for the growth of economic regulation in the last two decades of the twentieth century and the early years of the twenty-first century' (House of Lords 2007: 16). As of 2010 11, fifty-six national regulators were on duty in the UK (Department for Business, Innovation & Skills 2013). Based on the institutional framework in anti-monopoly regulation (OFT) and ICT regulation (Office of Telecommunications, Oftel), the British regulatory state has deployed a roster of independent regulators as the key tool.

Britain's independent regulators have also adapted to the challenges; they have become transparent and open and developed a significant level of outreach. Their relationship with politics has been awkward; critics highlight their nature as a cosseted bureaucracy that lacks accountability (e.g. Norton 2004; Williams 2009). Also, the nature of independence seems to be under the ministers' implicit discretion; the practical politicisation of regulation has been observed in the form of ministers' domination. The case of Britain's regulatory state exhibits an adaptation by the core executive through setting out a contradictory set of approaches, often in a piecemeal manner, including establishing independent regulators. This has enabled Britain's core executive to retain its dominance in the sphere of regulation.

The 'hands-off' model? New Zealand

New Zealand offers an example of a significant scale of deregulation in the 1980s. Its reforms reflect one of the most comprehensive programmes of economic retrenchment in OECD countries of the period (Evans et al. 1996: 1860). The impact of New Zealand's reforms significantly changed its ICT regulation and anti-monopoly regulation by merging the two with the privatisation of the Telecom Corporation of New Zealand, which was formed as a state-owned enterprise through the separation of the former telecommunications department of the New Zealand Post Office in 1987. New Zealand relied on general competition law to regulate the telecommunications industry, including resolving disputes regarding the telecommunications network interconnection charge, which were dealt with by sector-specific regulators in many other developed countries. Because of its atypical regulatory approach, referred to as 'light-handed regulation'[7] (Evans et al. 1996; Patterson 1998; Howell 2008, 2010), analysing the case of New Zealand offers an unusual example shared by few developed economies.

The key tool here is the Commerce Act, which oversees both anti-monopoly regulation and ICT regulation. What is exposed is the New Zealand government's distrust of regulation as a tool to control industry, and reliance on Telecom's good will with few preconditions. The 1975 Commerce Act retained the provision that prioritised a group of aims such as consumer welfare and public interest; this provision was simplified to 'an Act to promote competition in markets' in 1986. The implementation of anti-monopoly regulation was lenient to business. The key ideology for New Zealand's anti-monopoly regulation in the reform period, that is, the 1990s, was the 'contestability approach', which was described by the then Commerce Commission member and Fletcher Challenge director Kerrin Vautiers: 'Various collusive or contractual arrangements may be necessary to compete efficiently in a market, especially in view of information and transaction costs under conditions of uncertainty. The risk that such arrangements may diminish consumer welfare is minimised in reasonably accessible markets' (Kelsey 1995: 90). The approach of light-handed regulation reliant on the good faith of big business faced a significant challenge in the 1990s. What emerged in New Zealand's telecommunications markets was not competition but integrated dominance, with an approach regarded as 'hands off' rather than light-handed, resulting in network interconnection regulation reliant on the incumbent operator's good will, with no mechanism to resolve disputes; under this framework 'the network owner becomes the de facto regulator, and the policy can rightly be described as a monopolist's charter' (Patterson 1998: 150).

The 2000s saw a change in New Zealand's regulatory policy trend. The 2001 amendments to the 1986 Commerce Act by the Labour-led government challenged the previous efficiency-oriented approach by reintroducing a consumer welfare approach to competition law. The enactment of the Telecommunications Act 2001 and the subsequent establishment of the Telecommunications Commissioner within the Commerce Commission exemplifies New Zealand's policy change from the framework based on the 1986 Commerce Act to re-regulation (Carter 2008: 46). The 2001 Telecommunications Act introduced a new framework in which the new regulator administers interconnection disputes – a major topic of telecommunications regulation debates in the 1990s.

The major impetus mobilising New Zealand to economic reform can be explained by three points: the emergence of elites influenced by the US Chicago School of Economics, the electoral system in which a single majority party could easily dominate political processes and the economic crisis before 1984. Key government organisations in New Zealand such as the Treasury and the Reserve Bank were significantly influenced by the Chicago School from the 1970s (Kelsey 1995: 54–5). A key characteristic of US influence in New Zealand was that theories and applied economic research of a particular school of economics tended to be directly introduced, with little filtering by New Zealand's own economic researchers (Easton 1989: 88; Kelsey 1995: 53–4). Achieving the dominance of the Chicago School of Economics within key government organisations was the major driver of economic reform (Kelsey 1995: 50–1). Through the change of government from National to Labour in 1984, key government organisations achieved a consensus on the need for economic reforms (Kelsey 1995: 53). The perspectives of the elites in government organisations were put into practice through New Zealand's political system in the 1980s: the single-house, first-past-the-post, two-party system, under which the election winner controls policy. The Cabinet could dominate decision-making in the caucus by having a strategic ratio of Cabinet ministers to MPs, together with a party whips system, which directs the MPs in line with the party executive's view: 'A small number of ministers dominated the Cabinet, the Cabinet dominated the caucus, and the caucus dominated the Parliament' (Kelsey 1995: 42). Under this framework, key proponents of economic reform such as Roger Douglas and Ruth Richardson pushed their reform policy.[8] Another factor prompting New Zealand to introduce economic reforms was the economic crisis before the government changed in 1984.[9] This crisis prompted elites in New Zealand to think that radical reform was necessary to revitalise their country (Kelsey 1995: 29).

In pulling the above together, what emerges is the atypical nature of New Zealand's regulatory state. After 1984 it prioritised economic efficiency, regarding regulation as a problematic tool of control that distorted the economy and markets rather than as a new approach to the economy. New Zealand's elites employed a strategy of stripping the state's regulatory instruments, letting private firms operate and reducing state power. The state was perceived to be hollowed out in regulation. The result was the emergence of a private monopoly in sectors such as ICT, in which the failure of this light-handed regulation emerged through network interconnection disputes. The power of the core executive has been dominant. Key government officials have led the economic reform initiatives. Party politicians steered the implementation processes of reform programmes that were not always popular. Under the asymmetric dominance of the core executive, New Zealand has realised the true retreat of the state from the regulatory front in anti-monopoly regulation and ICT regulation, an approach different from others (Patterson 1998: 151):

> It was once said that New Zealand led the world in deregulation. This was a theme trumpeted by the Commerce Commission in media releases such as 'Australians look to New Zealand experiences in competition law', 'British organisations see New Zealand competition law as outstanding' and 'Principles of New Zealand competition law increasingly used by others'. However, to be a leader others must follow, and as the Privy Council noted, 'New Zealand has taken a different course'; no other country has adopted New Zealand's 'hands-off' model.

The making of regulation and governance, Japanese style

The examples of the other regulatory states reveal different variations. What is common in the cases of the UK and New Zealand is the dominance of the core executive in shaping their regulatory states. The rise of the UK's regulators and deregulation led by elites in government organisations in New Zealand offer examples of the core executive's dominance. Another key characteristic is the extent to which respective political traditions have worked in shaping regulatory policies. The British regulatory regime can be characterised by regulators with a fragmented background: more politicised, open, but undemocratic in the fact that they are at arm's length from elected officials' control; they emerged as a result of the politicised nature of Britain's regulation and the influence of a traditional approach in which a closed community (the club world) takes control using opaque processes. The British regulatory state reveals the rise of a new form of institution, that is, regulators not formally either in the executive branch or the private sector, under the informal dominance of ministers. It is efficient in the fact that British regulators are required to be less accountable to party politicians and have more authority to implement policy programmes without legislation than government ministries. Elsewhere, the fragmented nature of the British regulatory system produces criticism about the accountability of the regulator.

New Zealand's case offers an unusual example of a regulatory state drawn from the unstable political machine as its political tradition. The significant influence of the Chicago School of Economics to its elites and its single-house, first-past-the-post, two-party system in the 1980s facilitated comprehensive policy reforms through the occupation of key government posts by proponents of economic reform. New Zealand's case could be the most atypical with its radical retreat of the state from regulation. Its economic reforms and its reactions offer an example incomparable to any other country's in the developed world.

These different examples can be compared to the case studies in this book. The two Japanese cases of regulation are of a similar nature to the UK's and New Zealand's – the sustained dominance of the core executive, with fluid changes of power within its community – but with strikingly different development and characteristics. Indeed, the specific development of the respective sectors exhibits the unusual characteristics drawn from Japan's political tradition, with fluidly changing power relations and structures within the core executive in response to the challenges of the time. Explaining this set of complicated characteristics requires a holistic approach to policy-making and implementation that embraces a range of relevant actors and structures, rather than one highlighting the specific aspects of the case. Regulation and governance in Japan has not seen a holistic framework that explains its nature and political development, aimed at relevant key state actors engaged in policy-making and implementation and structures. The set of frameworks set up by this chapter addresses this lacuna by covering the core nexus of the state with a specific focus on regulation. In so doing, it presents an account that explains the nature and transformation of governance in a Japanese context. The

32   Conceptualising the Japanese state and governance

following chapters will demonstrate the change of governance with this set of analytical frameworks through an exploration of the case studies of specific regulatory sectors.

Notes

1 The 'reconstituted-state' thesis is an approach that accepts that forces such as globalisation, marketisation and New Public Management have transformed the nature of the state, but argues that the asymmetrical, structural position of the core executive, relative to other actors in the policy process, ensures that it is strongly placed to respond to these forces. See Marsh et al. (2001; 2003: 248) and Richards (2008: 97–8) for details.
2 The Anglo-Governance School is a group of scholars whose position is affected by R. A. W. Rhodes's idea that the concept of governance be integrated 'into a conceptual model of contemporary government, its evolution and its relationship to political and wider social processes' (Marinetto 2003: 594).
3 The concept of the core executive emerged in critiques of the Westminster model within British political science literature. See Dunleavy and Rhodes (1990).
4 *Zoku gi'in* [tribe members of the Diet] are LDP members of the Diet specialising in particular fields such as postal and telecommunications affairs. They have not only a specialised knowledge of the field but also often special connections with other interest groups such as private firms (I'io 2007: 95). Inoguchi and Iwai (1987) offer a detailed study of this issue.
5 The parliamentary vice-ministers in Japan's government ministries were abolished in January 2001 and replaced by the upgraded senior vice-ministers, together with the newly established junior rank parliamentary secretaries.
6 RPI − X is the function employed by the price cap system, whereby telecommunications rates could not rise by more than RPI minus a certain percentage (X). Under this system, prices on a defined basket of regulated services would be allowed to grow at the rate of inflation (expressed by RPI) minus X percentage points (Spiller and Vogelsang 1996: 108).
7 The New Zealand government's policy statement on telecommunication in December 1991 succinctly explains its approach to light-handed regulation in the telecommunications industry (Patterson 1998: 135).
8 Roger Douglas was, as the Minister of Finance (1984–88) under the David Lange Labour government (1984–89), the most prominent promoter of New Zealand's economic reforms in the Cabinet, whose policy was called 'Rogernomics'. Ruth Richardson was the Minister of Finance (1990–93) under the Jim Bolger National government (1990–97), who played a similar role to Douglas's, with her economic policy called 'Ruthanasia'.
9 For details of New Zealand's economic crisis before 1984, see Evans et al. 1996: 1860.

Part II

Evolving regulation and governance

3

The evolving core executive in response to burgeoning ICT

The move to more liberalisation within markets after the 1980s marked a significant disjuncture in many economic sectors. In the case of the ICT sector, where market liberalisation has had a significant impact in many countries, liberalisation has meant a distinctive change from monopoly (often by the state/state corporation) to market-driven competition.

The case of Japan's ICT sector offers a potentially useful example because of its history of market competition dating back to 1985, when the privatisation of a state corporation monopoly had a significant impact on the telecommunications market. The former monopoly company (NTT)[1] has remained dominant, yet this position has been challenged by emergent new entrants (new common carriers: NCCs). Regulatory functions were not assigned to a newly created independent regulator but to a government ministry, the Ministry of Post and Telecommunications (MPT), which lacked experience and expertise in implementing this new task in its early stage (Tsuchiya 2003: 77). This chapter analyses the impact of this liberalisation, which was a complicated process of transformation in Japan's ICT sector, looking at the power and role of party politicians including those in the LDP outside the Cabinet, Cabinet ministers, civil servants in the MPT/MIC (Ministry of Internal Affairs and Communications) responsible for regulation in the ICT sector, and NTT as the strong former monopoly carrier.

After the 1980s Japan's ICT sector saw significant disjunctures including liberalisation and changes of government, which resulted in challenges to the core executive of the sector. Exploring this sector offers a case study in which the core executive has pursued regulatory policies to respond to the challenges; the evolutionary process of the core executive in the ICT sector is the issue that this chapter explores.

This chapter comprises the following sections. The next section reviews the development of Japan's ICT sector after the 1980s, starting from telecommunications liberalisation in 1985, which was an early example of a telecommunications reform, alongside the US and the UK.[2] It aims to reveal the development process of the regulatory framework. Understanding how the regulatory framework has developed shapes the basis on which the following sections establish their analysis. This review is followed by an exploration of power relations between key actors including those within the core executive. This section pays attention to how power relations have changed among core executive actors. Two issues emerge in the analysis: first, the relationship between Cabinet ministers and party politicians outside the Cabinet, including those in the ruling party. The significance of this issue stems from the understanding that the latter (sometimes referred to as *Zoku gi'in*) had widely recognised powers over the policy-making process (Inoguchi and Iwai 1987; Tsuchiya 2003: 73–4; I'io 2007: 94–7). The second issue is the partisan confrontation between the LDP and the DPJ. With the 2009 change of government, this confrontation had a significant impact on the relationship between party politicians including Cabinet ministers and civil servants. The third section explores how the core executive in the ICT sector has transformed its internal power relations by considering key actors – Cabinet ministers, party politicians outside the Cabinet and civil servants – and structures within the core executive after telecommunications liberalisation in 1985.

The development of Japan's ICT sector and the involvement of the core executive

Japan's ICT sector can be categorised as having undergone three key phases after the 1980s: the privatisation of the state corporation, NTT, in 1985; the reorganisation of NTT in 1999; and the transformation of the regulatory approach from ex ante to ex post[3] that gradually emerged in the 1990s and 2000s. These junctures have dismantled the previous regime of state corporation monopoly (Figure 3.1).

The 1980s was a striking period for Japan's ICT sector, commencing with the telecommunications regulatory reform in 1985. This reform was underpinned by two key events: the privatisation of NTT and the liberalisation of value-added networks[4] (Vogel 1996: 145). The former offered a significant opportunity for analysis of the Japanese state (Kalba 1988; I'io 1993; Vogel 1996). The telecommunications regulatory reform in 1985 was implemented as part of a wider administrative reform under the initiative of the Second Provisional Commission on Administrative Reform (*Rinji gyōsei chōsakai*: *Rinchō*), an independent council supported by Prime Minister Nakasone (1982–87) (Vogel 1996: 54). The administrative reform was one of Nakasone's prioritised projects

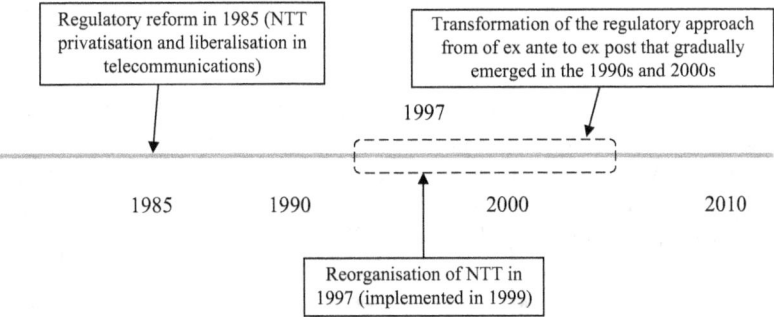

Figure 3.1 Timeline of the development of Japan's ICT regulation since the 1980s

(Vogel 1996: 57); he was the director general of the Administrative Management Agency responsible for this reform, before being promoted to Prime Minister. This administrative reform was a response to various challenges that Japan faced in that period. Vogel (1996: 54–6) summarises these as:

- Devolution: the effectiveness of the highly centralised system, which had characterised Japan's governing system up to this period, began to be questioned by party politicians and business elites. They, unlike their counterparts in bureaucracy, saw the *Rinchō* and its administrative reform as a vehicle to decentralise political authority away from the traditional system, in which 'lead' government ministries principally managed their respective sectors (Vogel 1996: 55).
- Spending cuts: as economic growth became sluggish after the first oil crisis, Prime Minister Kakuei Tanaka's (1972–74) public spending boost in the early 1970s created fiscal problems. This problem motivated the MOF and the business community to pursue spending cuts. In particular, the latter resented corporate tax increases and felt the government's attitude was irresponsible while private firms were struggling to cut their costs.
- The LDP's electoral strategy: the rising electoral power of the urban middle class and the declining rural population became a significant challenge to the LDP, as the party traditionally depended on its dominance in rural areas. To cope with this challenge, the LDP sought to liberalise the economy to appease the emerging urban middle class. The LDP also avoided accepting the blame as the principal planner of the change by employing an outside actor, the *Rinchō*, as the initiator of the administrative reform. At the same time, the LDP permitted its members in the Diet to work to protect their traditional interests in order that the LDP could retain its vote by taking the credit as a

protector of the interests of their traditional rural supporters such as farmers and small business owners.

The cooperation of civil servants, those of the MOF in particular, was vital for the *Rinchō* to achieve administrative reform. Indeed, this negotiation between the *Rinchō* and civil servants shaped the administrative reform into 'an exercise in limiting government spending and privatizing public corporations' (Vogel 1996: 57–8).

A key target of the reform was the telecommunications sector, which was monopolised by two state-sponsored corporations: NTT (the state corporation for domestic telecommunications) and KDD (the state-sponsored private corporation established by law for international telecommunications). Under the previous system, NTT attained the dual remits of nationwide direct dialling in 1977 and universal service in 1978 (Vogel 1996: 141; Kojima 2004: 302–19; Takahashi 2009: 142–3). The supervisory section of the MPT, the regulator of NTT since 1952, was marginalised by NTT, because the MPT had concentrated on running the postal services, leaving its telecommunications regulation section, the Telecommunications Inspectorate, unable to fulfil its responsibility (Vogel 1996: 139–42; Takahashi 2009: 107). The Telecommunications Inspectorate was staffed by only a small group of thirty or forty officials headed by two inspectors (*Denkitsūshin kanrikan*), one of whom was seconded from NTT with a two-year tenure (Vogel 1996: 142; Takahashi 2009: 107). NTT's status as a public corporation gave party politicians significant leverage over it. The Diet approved NTT's annual budgets and major amendments of its service provision, and reviewed its corporate investment plans (Vogel 1996: 139; Takahashi 2009: 105–8). This wide scope of authority prompted party politicians to intervene in NTT's activities. According to Vogel (1996: 142), ruling LDP members 'intervened in telecommunications policy selectively, when they saw political advantage in getting involved'. He observes that they were more interested in bringing services into their constituencies than in debating telecommunications policy (Vogel 1996: 142). Although the LDP's long rule (1955–93) marginalised its opposition, including the Social Democratic Party of Japan (SDPJ), the *Zendentsū* (*Zenkoku denkitsūshin rōdōkumi'ai*) [Japan Telecommunication Workers Union], which was NTT's union and a strong ally of the SDPJ, had a significant influence over Japanese politics (Vogel 1996: 142).

The creation of the privatised NTT alongside the institutional changes transformed the structure and major actors of the ICT sector. While the privatised NTT began concentrating on its business operations, major regulatory functions were transferred to the MPT (see Table 3.1). The MPT emerged as the dominant regulator after the 1985 regulatory reform. According to Vogel (1996: 161): 'the dominance of NTT within

Table 3.1 Primary authority before and after the 1985 telecommunications regulatory reform

Item	Primary authority before 1985	Primary authority after 1985
Telecoms business regulation		
Entry	Diet (NTT designated the monopoly service provider)	MPT
Prices	Diet (basic services prices set by law; NTT free to set prices on certain items)	MPT
Services	Diet (basic guidelines set in law; items not covered subject to MPT approval)	MPT
Technical standards	NTT (set by NTT for network; set by MPT for customer equipment)	MPT (set by MPT's Telecoms Council)
NTT regulation		
Budget	Diet (requires Diet approval)	NTT (business plan requires MPT approval; budget must be attached)
Personnel	Diet (subject to Diet approval through budget process; certain guidelines written into law)	NTT

Source: Vogel 1996: 157.

the old regime has been replaced by the dominance of the MPT within the new regime'. The role of the MPT in policy-making significantly expanded.

Elsewhere, a key factor characterising ICT regulation was a group of party politicians with specialism in the sector, including the group called *Yūsei-zoku*[5] (the post tribe) in the LDP. In light of the fact that the LDP dominated government for most of the post-war era up until 2009, the significance of *Yūsei-zoku* was evident (Muramatsu 1991: 289; Tsuchiya 2003). *Yūsei-zoku* played a key role in regulatory policy-making in ICT by preliminarily examining bills in the LDP's PARC Communications Division (Internal Affairs and Communications Division after 2001); as members of the division, *Yūsei-zoku* could examine key policy issues such as draft bills with discretion and prevent their endorsement if necessary (Inoguchi and Iwai 1987; Muramatsu 1991; Vogel 1996; Tsuchiya 2003). *Yūsei-zoku* used the PARC and its Communications Division as their key tool to influence policies by controlling debates in the Division and stopping policy-making processes if necessary. Subsequently, under the LDP/LDP-led Coalition governments, the LDP established a custom of preliminary examination within the LDP for government bills before their formal submission to the Diet (I'io 2007: 83–8). Since laws are significant governing tools for Japan's government ministries, and the LDP administration established a custom whereby bills without the ruling parties' internal authorisation would not be adopted, the ruling parties' preliminary examination had a significant impact on policy-making processes (George Mulgan 2005: 14–8; I'io 2007: 123–6).

In the case of ICT regulation, the LDP's preliminary examination was handled by *Yūsei-zoku* in the PARC and its Communications Division. Given that *Yūsei-zoku* had leverage in the preliminary examination within the LDP, its influence was significant. In addition to *Yūsei-zoku*, older and senior LDP politicians exercised significant influence over important policy decisions (Inoguchi and Iwai 1987). This is a dynamic flagged up by Vogel (1996: 154–5) in his description of the key moment of NTT privatisation:

> [The LDP's] Tanaka faction, the largest and most powerful, played the pivotal role in formulating the LDP's approach to the reform. Kakuei Tanaka himself, like the other top LDP leaders, had committed his support to the *Rincho*, although he reserved the right to differ on specific issues. In July 1983, Tanaka faction elder Shin Kanemaru devised a shrewd way to coerce the more conservative LDP Communications *zoku*. He announced a proposal that they could readily accept, a minor revision of NTT's status to that of 'public organisation.' Kanemaru designed the proposal to fail, as it did when the MOF and the LDP leadership overwhelmingly condemned it. This way, Kanemaru was able to tell the *zoku* that he had tried to convince them to accept a bolder proposal. ... On September 6, 1983, Ryutaro Hashimoto, chairman of the LDP's Committee on Administrative Reform, abruptly announced an eleven-point proposal. The proposal favoured the privatization of NTT but not its breakup.

The power of the ruling parties' politicians had a significant effect in shaping key decisions within ICT regulation. A further example can be identified in the debate over the break-up of NTT which emerged as a key issue after the 1985 NTT privatisation. The debate on the NTT break-up dominated the period between 1985 and 1999. This idea was first proposed by the *Rinchō* in the debate on privatisation, but was postponed in the regulatory reform of 1985 because NTT and its union lobbied interested parties to block the idea (Vogel 1996: 155). This question, also called 'the reorganisation of NTT', involved party politicians including LDP members, the MPT, NTT itself and its unions.

The NTT Law, which was formulated in the 1985 regulatory reform, stipulated that the government would examine the status of NTT five years after privatisation and take appropriate action. Following this provision, the MPT started its policy deliberation by consulting on this issue with the Telecommunications Council in October 1989.[6] The Council's report recommended the break-up of NTT, but this was not accepted by the government, because significant opponents such as the MOF and *Keidanren* emerged both within and outside the government (Vogel 1996: 158–9; Tsuchiya 2003: 82). The government decided only to separate the mobile division from NTT, and postpone the break-up of its long-distance communications division.

The second round of this debate was launched in April 1995, when the MPT again consulted with the Council about the status of NTT. In February 1996 the resulting report (Telecommunications Council 1996a) recommended dividing NTT into three parts: the long-distance communications division, the east regional communications division, and the west regional communications division. This recommendation was again not implemented, because significant opponents emerged in the ruling coalition of the day,[7] including the SDPJ backed by the *Zendentsū* (Tsuchiya 2003: 83–4; Takahashi 2009: 213). The MPT announced in December of the same year that NTT would be transformed into a holding company group that would control a long-distance communications company and two local communications companies. The nature of this debate on the NTT break-up was characterised by fierce confrontation between two groups. The MPT and new entrants to the ICT sector strongly supported the break-up of NTT, with NTT and its union in opposition; the contention between these two groups divided party politicians influential over ICT regulation (Tsuchiya 2003: 77, 83–4).

The central issue of the NTT break-up was its bottleneck monopoly of the regional communications networks. This led to 'a situation whereby almost all of the telecommunications services cannot be provided without the monopolistic regional communications network' (Telecommunications Council 1996a: ch. 3.2(8)). The Telecommunications Council recognised that NTT had a 99 per cent market share in regional communications markets. The negative impact stemming from NTT's monopoly of regional communications networks included the monopolist's potential to emasculate competition by exercising its dominant market power; the lack of any competitive incentive to pursue efficient management and a more competitive price structure; and the power commanded by a monopoly supplier to cross-subsidise its equivalents in competitive markets with the resulting emasculation of competition in telecommunications markets (Telecommunications Council 1996a; see also Table 3.2).

The NTT break-up plan drew on the experience of the break-up of AT&T in the US in 1984. Focusing on competition within domestic

Table 3.2 Problems resulting from NTT's dominance in local landline telecommunications networks

1. The continued existence of a bottleneck monopoly will cause the following problems:
   a. there will be no incentive for NTT to improve management efficiency
   b. the development of fair and effective competition will remain limited
   c. as a result, there will be no increase in incentive to provide consumers with better services and reduce rates
2. Policies for promoting competition that rely solely on such non-structural measures as issuing administrative orders are limited in terms of effectiveness, and the time and costs required for regulation may become extensive.
3. More specifically, while NTT faces a reasonable degree of competition in the long-distance communications markets in regions such as Tokyo, Nagoya and Osaka, it still retains a more than 90 per cent share of the overall communications market in Japan. This is an impediment to the business dynamism associated with competition.
4. Restrictions on the business of NTT are inevitable if it is to enter such competitive markets as international communications while maintaining its existing company structure, because issues relating to fair and effective competition that we currently see in the long-distance communications market will appear in other markets as well.
5. Change in the corporate management environment is likely to be even more rapid in the future. However, if NTT remains in its present form as a giant management organisation, this will run counter to its own objectives, namely to take full advantage of its management resources, establish more mobile management and enjoy the 'economies of speed'.

Number of employees in major companies in the private sector (financial year 1994)

NTT	194,721
JR East Japan	79,709
Hitachi	76,679
Toshiba	73,463
Toyota	69,748

Source: Telecommunications Council 1996a.

telephone networks, local telephone networks in particular, the proponents of the NTT break-up (e.g. the MPT, NCCs) argued that the plan would stimulate competition within the ICT sector (Tsuchiya 2003: 77, 83–4). NTT and its union strongly opposed the break-up plan, highlighting its potential negative impact on NTT's business. NTT argued that the negative impact of the break-up could result in the decline of its universal service within Japan and research and development (NTT 2013). The confrontation between the two sides was settled through arbitration by a group of party politicians.

The evolving core executive in response to ICT 43

After the Telecommunications Council issued a report in favour of the NTT break-up in March 1990, the first round of the debate was resolved by the five-year postponement decision of Tsutomu Hata, the chairman of the relevant LDP committee, with the delegation of senior LDP politicians in the same month (Vogel 1996: 159). The second round was arbitrated by LDP secretary general Hiromu Nonaka in December 1996, following the ruling parties' (LDP, SDPJ, New Party *Sakigake* [New Harbinger Party]) decision in favour of a one-year postponement in March 1996.

What is revealed here is the dominant power of the ruling party politicians outside the Cabinet in decision-making. Both cases highlight the MPT's failure to achieve its original goal of completely breaking up NTT, because a group of ruling party politicians opposed the MPT's plan and supported NTT's view (Tsuchiya 2003: 82–4). The key decision-makers here were the group of ruling party politicians. Being divided between the MPT's supporters and NTT's supporters, the LDP's *Yūsei-zoku* was unable to control the debate regarding the NTT break-up alone; rather, a broader group of ruling party politicians outside the Cabinet (e.g. Tsutomu Hata, Taku Yamazaki and Hiromu Nonaka), including some members of *Yūsei-zoku*, collectively arbitrated the debate (Tsuchiya 2003: 82–4). The arbitration in 1996 did not aim to resolve the policy challenges identified in Table 3.2 but to seek compromise and conciliation between the two sides. The arbitration divided NTT into three, which was in line with the Telecommunications Council's recommendation in 1996. At the same time, these three companies were established under a holding company; this meant that NTT's unity was retained. The nature of the arbitration can be regarded as highly political rather than policy-oriented, because the arbitration aimed not to pursue a policy-oriented goal such as developing a new competition framework but to appease both sides by trying to adopt some of their proposals (Tsuchiya 2003: 84). The debate around the NTT break-up offers an example of the weakness of the power of civil servants through their failure to obtain the ruling party politicians' collective support.

The transformation of the regulatory approach from ex ante to ex post was characterised more by piecemeal evolution than a sudden disjuncture (Kushida 2006: 133). The key events of this transformation included the deregulatory measures summarised by Kushida (2006: 136–7):

- Japan's signing of the WTO Telecoms Agreement in 1997. This removed most restrictions on foreign ownership of carriers and infrastructure.
- The abolition of most licensing requirements for market entry and price changes in 1998, while relaxing restrictions over the scope of

the carrier's business activities. In particular, the MPT changed most regulatory requirements on Type I[8] carriers to notifications from permissions.
- The abolition of most of the classification, registration and notification requirements. The MIC removed the Type I and Type II carrier classifications altogether in 2003.

While these deregulatory measures were intended to relax ex ante regulation, newly introduced regulatory measures can be understood as ex post oriented. The key components of these new regulatory measures were the development of the rule for interconnection between telecommunications operator networks and the establishment of the Telecommunications Dispute Settlement Commission (TDSC).

The initial telecommunications regulatory framework introduced by the 1985 reform made only a simple provision for the dispute settlement of telecommunications network interconnection between operators (Kushida 2006: 135). The terms and conditions of interconnection were determined between interested parties, and the MPT intervened when no agreement could be reached. The MPT's interventions included issuing orders by the minister and arbitration (Telecommunications Council 1996b: 1). This system prompted significant problems and resulting disputes between NTT and the new entrants, which can be summarised as follows (Telecommunications Council 1996b: 2–3):

- Prolonged interconnection negotiations: some interconnection negotiations between new entrants and NTT, in particular those related to NTT's local networks, became significantly prolonged. After long-distance NCCs requested interconnection with NTT concerning the virtual private network service in September 1989, it took more than five years to reach an agreement. 'During that period, the long-distance NCCs requested the Minister of Post and Telecommunications to issue an order to connect in November 1994, which the Minister issued to [the] NTT in December of the same year. An agreement was finally concluded in April, 1995.'
- The costs base for calculating interconnection charges: a dispute arose over the appropriate base for calculating interconnection charges. The NCCs negotiated with NTT regarding the scope of costs for NTT local network interconnection charges for four years from 1993. In November 1995 the NCCs and NTT agreed to exclude NTT's sales activities expenses, but still continued to negotiate other items including research and development expenses.
- Network modifications for interconnection: NTT's network needed to be modified to connect with other telecommunications networks,

because 'it was not necessarily designed for interconnection'. The modification required two years on average. Also, NTT requested that NCCs bear the modification costs, which was a significant burden for small NCCs.
• Interconnection with Type II carriers: there were also disputes between NTT and Type II carriers about technical issues, such as network–network interfaces and unbundling NTT's network components for lease.

These problems prompted the MPT to revise the Telecommunications Business Law to establish clear rules for interconnection in 1997 (Kushida 2006: 135; Takahashi 2009: 239). This amendment obliged NTT to lease its local network, calculate its interconnection charge in line with the MPT's formula dictating the prices that NTT was allowed to charge, and establish the interconnection accounting system (Kushida 2006: 135–6; Takahashi 2009: 239).

Another regulatory measure that can be regarded as ex post is the establishment of the TDSC in 2001. The MIC transferred its responsibilities as the coordinator and mediator of the dispute between telecommunications operators to the TDSC, which is located within the ministry but is in principle an independent, third-party, deliberative organisation. The members of this commission are appointed by the Minister of Internal Affairs and Communications after endorsement from the Diet (TDSC 2016a). Although the actual impact of the TDSC does not appear significant – it issued sixty-six mediations (forty-three resolved, nineteen withdrawn/terminated, four dismissed), three arbitrations (all dismissed), nine inquiries/reports, and three recommendations between 30 November 2001 and 31 March 2016 (TDSC 2016b) – the creation of this commission can be understood as showing the government's intention to change its mode of ICT regulation.

This set of changes, aimed at rule-making and dispute resolution, contributed to shaping the development of the sector. As a result, broadband services rapidly grew. Ida (2011) argues that the impact of the debate on the NTT break-up prompted the significant development of broadband communications services within Japan by compelling NTT to allow its competitors access to its networks and to invest in broadband infrastructure, attracting new entrants and retaining NTT as a single incumbent developing broadband infrastructure. Indeed, the period after the 1990s saw a significant surge in broadband services together with mobile communications services; 2008 saw 80 per cent of Japan's households able to access broadband services and more than 100 million mobile communications subscribers accessing the Internet and developed data services (Ida 2011). The development of wireless networking technology led to the rise of a new business model based on wireless Internet services. The emergence of new business models and cost structures prompted by technological development (e.g. broadband technology, mobile phones) and competition development has presented challenges to the Japanese regulatory state. The significant development of these new businesses indicates that the Japanese regulatory state has successfully managed them. An example is the MIC's policy statement 'New Competition Program 2010', which focuses on setting and revising rules on key issues, such as opening networks, promoting mobile communications businesses including introducing new fee plans explicitly separating terminal prices from service charges, and reviewing the current interconnection framework on NTT's networks (MIC 2007).

However, the traditional decision-making framework within the core executive did not change in ICT regulation under the LDP/LDP-led Coalition governments before 2009. Key decision-making processes were dominated by party politicians outside the Cabinet after the debate regarding NTT. A typical example of the dominant party politician groups under this framework was the LDP's *Yūsei-zoku*, who exercised power in their political arena: the LDP's PARC Internal and Communications Affairs Division. Tsuchiya (2003: 86–7) reports a case in which the MIC's trial to introduce asymmetric regulation, by which NTT's regional communications divisions (NTT East and NTT West) and mobile division (NTT Docomo) were to be designated as carriers with significant market power, was opposed by *Yūsei-zoku* in the PARC Internal Affairs and Communications Division in March 2001. The MIC was left with no other option but to weaken its original regulatory proposal. Kawabata (2006: 176) does not regard this change as outright, for most original policy measures remained; it was possible because the LDP politicians generally supported the MIC's approach to promoting Internet-related services. The MIC could realise policy measures as long as its LDP counterparts supported them.

Elsewhere, challenges to this traditional framework also emerged in the 2000s under the LDP-led Coalition government. First, this can be seen in the impact of the administrative reform implemented in January 2001 which enhanced the Cabinet by explicitly recognising the Prime Minister's leadership in law and strengthened the Prime Minister's staff (e.g. giving stronger power to the Cabinet Secretariat and establishing the Cabinet Office) (I'io 2007: 195). Second, replacing the previous parliamentary team within a ministry (a Cabinet minister and one or two parliamentary vice-ministers) with the *Seimu sanyaku* (three political officers), a team of parliamentary senior officials comprising a Cabinet minister, senior vice-ministers and parliamentary secretaries (Neary 2002: 126–7) in January 2001, strengthened the power of individual Cabinet ministers within their respective ministries (I'io 2007: 196). In addition to these institutional changes, Jun'ichirō Koizumi's approach

Table 3.3 The major elements of Jun'ichirō Koizumi's approach to strengthening the Cabinet

- Appointed Cabinet ministers without reference to other key LDP politicians; this significantly strengthened Koizumi's political authority.
- Gave Cabinet ministers explicit instructions in writing; this contributed to forming policy unity in the Cabinet.
- Refrained from frequent Cabinet reshuffles and instead moved ministers from one post to another; this contributed to Cabinet ministers' longer tenure and the continuity and unity of the Cabinet.
- Formulated an appointment system for senior vice-ministers and parliamentary secretaries and obtained the confirmation of respective Cabinet ministers who would supervise the appointees; this enhanced the unity of the *Seimu sanyaku*.
- Employed the Council for Economic and Fiscal Policy as an arena of key policy debates and made decisions himself after debate between Cabinet ministers.
- Scapegoated the LDP's *Zoku gi'in*, *Yūsei-zoku* in particular, as the enemy of his reform policies and expelled LDP politicians who opposed his post office reform, many of whom belonged to *Yūsei-zoku*, from the LDP in 2005. Koizumi's landslide victory in the subsequent general election gave him unchallengeable authority within the LDP and the power of *Zoku gi'in*, *Yūsei-zoku's* in particular, significantly declined.

Source: I'io 2007: 195–201.

summarised in Table 3.3 also contributed to further enhancing the power of the Cabinet and Cabinet ministers in the 2000s.

Power relations within the core executive, which can be characterised by the rise of Cabinet ministers under the LDP government in the 2000s, encountered another significant disjuncture in 2009. The change in government from the LDP to the DPJ following the 2009 general election led to the dismantling of the power of LDP *Zoku gi'in* as key ruling party politicians. Here, power relations within the core executive in Japan's ICT regulation can be seen to enter a new phase in which the DPJ's framework now shaped the decision-making process. An example can be found in the debate surrounding the 'Path of Light',[9] in which DPJ MIC Minister Kazuhiro Haraguchi strongly promoted his policy project, including the possible break-up of NTT, by launching an 'ICT Policy Taskforce for a Global Era'. This project was, however, promptly emasculated after Haraguchi's departure in 2010, with the taskforce recommending a halt to breaking up NTT, a reduction of NTT's interconnection charge on its fibre optic cable networks and a postponement of the target of accomplishing 100 per cent broadband coverage (Kushida 2013: 272).

Elsewhere, the evidence suggests that competition in Japan's

ICT sector significantly increased. For example, the number of telecommunications operators in the sector rose to 16,784 in March 2014 from one in 1985: this highlights significant growth of the sector from that under the state corporation monopoly (MIC 2016). Elsewhere, in terms of pricing, a call using NTT from Tokyo to Osaka cost 400 yen/3 minutes in April 1985; NTT East now charges 8 yen/3 minutes not only for a call from Tokyo to Osaka, but for any call to anywhere in Japan (MIC 2013; NTT East 2016).

Throughout this process, it is evident that a significant change of power took place between actors in the sector. Direct management through a state corporation changed to principal–agent regulation through the executive branch. The regulatory approach was changing from interventionist or ex ante oriented to ex post oriented. Party politicians changed their approach from direct commitment through approving NTT's management issues to more subtle influence through the MPT/MIC. The MPT emerged as an influential regulator after privatisation, although its regulatory approach has also evolved in response to the development of competition and ICT. Elsewhere, the relative strength among private-sector actors has been volatile; although NTT has retained its dominant position, the evolution of the market has enabled new entrants to challenge it. The state has withdrawn from the direct management of telecommunications service provision, and instead introduced new regulatory measures such as rules for telecommunications network interconnection.

If these changes are drawn together, what emerges is the extent to which the ICT sector has seen a significant change in both its actors and structure. The impact of this evolution on the core executive is one of the crucial topics explored in this book. The following section focuses on how the core executive has changed through adaptation to its external challenges.

Transforming power and roles within the core executive

The post-privatisation period

The privatisation of NTT proved a contentious issue for the core executive. Despite its significant impact on the telecommunications sector, this policy project did not have a clearly elaborated goal. Interviews reveal that there was no clear vision among either party politicians or civil servants on how the newly liberalised markets would be developed. For example, one retired senior civil servant argued that

> First of all, nobody had an image of how the competitive environment would be developed and what kind of competitive conditions would be

realised. Logically, 'no monopoly after privatisation', 'must engage in competition', but, under the condition that no facility [other than NTT's], nothing, no [alternative] operators existed, everybody was concerned whether competition was possible. (interview with a retired MIC senior civil servant)

This view was not uncommon among former civil servants: 'It started from zero. Civil servants and politicians had zero. And it was a very new growing industrial field so we could say various things' (interview with a retired MIC senior civil servant). A retired senior party politician (former secretary general) who witnessed the 1985 telecommunications reform as a Liberal Democrat also noted: 'Not many people [party politicians] have been deeply involved with and studied telecommunications policy.' This account is in line with Inoguchi and Iwai's (1987: 204) description: 'Policy contents are highly specialised whether postal saving or information and communications. Policies were completely decided by MPT officials and *Yūsei-zoku* rarely intervened in the MPT's policy decisions.' The accounts from those in key positions in the core executive in the mid-1980s indicate that policy-makers did not have a clear long-term future plan about how competition should be introduced in telecommunications after privatisation. This is also supported by a government official's explanation in the Diet in 1984:

In reality, the immediate emergence of such carriers [NCCs] after the enactment of this law is not likely because telecommunications markets require a significant extent of investment and technological expertise; but we expect this framework [liberalised telecommunications markets] will enable NCCs to emerge, so we are drafting the bills of this framework. (The House of Representatives 1984a)

Elsewhere, liberalisation created a significant and immediate impact. Vogel (1996: 161) highlights the transfer of a significant proportion of responsibilities from NTT to the MPT. This inexperienced ministry did not have any expertise at the beginning of the post-privatisation period, while NTT had both knowledge and experience as a state corporation. As a member of the Information and Communications Council revealed:

Initially, the MPT's communications policy was completely controlled by NTT ... Before privatisation, in the 1970s. The MPT wasn't capable of making arguments. I suggest they didn't know what to do ... it was common in the 1970s that NTT quickly smashed whatever the MIC [MPT] did. (interview with a former member of the Information and Communications Council)

This account is similar to Vogel's (1996: 141): 'NTT officials handled most of the "politics" of telecommunications policy, i.e. relations with the Diet'. Such a situation was evidenced in the continuing supremacy of NTT despite the significant disjuncture caused by its privatisation. The initial phase of NTT privatisation, therefore, saw the coming together of a powerful and experienced ex-state actor and an emerging but embryonic state actor. The latter was not powerful in the policy-making arena; key decisions were made by party politicians, Liberal Democrats in particular, and the MPT was subject to the decisions of party politicians. The relationship between party politicians and civil servants was as follows:

> The first half of the 80s saw privatisation; the precondition of liberalisation was protecting NTT or NTT's functions. In simple terms, it [the party politicians' role] was like the PTA (Parent–Teacher Association). However, since many [party politicians] thought the ICT industry needed something, their approach gradually changed from the PTA to reform oriented. Elsewhere, they thought the overexpansion of the MPT's authority problematic and began checking [the MPT]. ... leaving aside whether it was good, the politicians' role could be called not 'leadership' but checks to [the undesirable activities of] civil servants. (interview with a retired MIC senior civil servant)

This account parallels Johnson's (1982: 315) analogy about the relationship between Japanese politicians and their bureaucratic counterparts: party politicians functioned as a 'safety valve', meaning that politicians oversaw bureaucracy and acted to control it when necessary, such as when bureaucrats tried to draft a law that the majority of the nation opposed. The key points here are:

- party politicians' power in the decision-making process was stronger than that of civil servants;
- the significant institutional power of the regulator (the MPT);
- the regulator's lack of expertise resulting from the fact that the operational functions of the state were privatised and moved to the private sector.

Unusual factors such as the regulator's lack of expertise resulted in the emergence of a dominant private-sector actor (NTT) in the market and the temporary retreat of state control in the initial phase of the post-privatisation period. However, the MPT's increased institutional authority stipulated by law and its response to the new environment changed the nature of the relation between actors, including the MPT and NTT. This is noted by Vogel (1996: 161–6), who points out that the

The evolving core executive in response to ICT   51

emergence of the MPT as a strategic regulator was a distinctive characteristic of the post-privatisation period. This enhancement of the MPT is alluded to by a retired senior civil servant:

> The MPT's power was strengthened by various factors emerging together, which worked together and transformed the MPT from a mere operational ministry to a so-called policy ministry ... liberalising the market and separating the operator from the regulator prompted the MPT to consolidate its position through coping with its challenges in the 1990s, with the dominant tide initiated by the *Rinchō* [meaning market-oriented policies], the break-up of the US incumbent operator called by us 'Communications Big Ban', and the confrontation with rival ministries including the MITI (Ministry of International Trade and Industry). (interview with a retired MIC senior civil servant)

The MPT's power was described as the establishment of the regulatory institutional framework in his view: 'Between the end of the 1990s and the beginning of the 2000s most of the competition policy framework was accomplished ... communications liberalisation through the transformation from the NTT's monopoly to its reorganisation has enhanced the MPT's regulatory role' (interview with a retired MIC senior civil servant).

The enhanced MPT exercised detailed regulatory measures, which Vogel (1996: 161–6) describes as 'micro management'. Civil servants described this approach (interventionist regulation by the MPT in the early post-liberalisation period) as a response to the uncertainty of the newly liberalised ICT market. A civil servant commented:

> What is astute in ICT is that very specific regulations, which should be left to operators, have been eliminated, while those such as ensuring safety, ensuring quality and securing connections have been retained. In this way, I suggest, regulation hasn't been completely dismantled. Simply unnecessary regulation has been eliminated and truly necessary regulation has been retained. At the beginning of liberalisation, because nobody knew what would happen, everything must have been covered, or, anything dropped could result in trouble; such an idea existed. I suggest the ministry gradually got to understand what measures could be left to operators and eliminated what measures could cause trouble if something happened. (interview with an MIC civil servant)

One senior civil servant offered an interpretation that micro-managed regulation could be understood as a relaxed mode of regulation compared to the previous mode, under which many operational decisions needed Diet approval because operations were managed by a state corporation:

> Some parts of the framework were strict. To elaborate in the simplest terms, tariffs and services could be offered through application and admission. And facility-based careers [Type I] needed permission for market entry ... after twenty years now, I guess this system had both a flexible part and a difficult part. What I thought at that time was, things started from the world of monopoly, in which minor tariff changes needed more than admission, [because they were] legally determined. Therefore, regarding legally determined tariffs, whether tariffs drop or rise, such fundamental things were decided by law. And such things became more flexibly determined without debate in the Diet. Opportunities to change the law are limited: once a year or so. We thought at that time no system was more relaxed than this one; that fundamental services such as telephony, in our understanding, could be freely determined, was unimaginable. (interview with an MIC senior civil servant)

His account is in line with Moriya Koyama's, the chief of the MPT Telecommunications Policy Bureau, parliamentary explanation of the regulatory framework after NTT privatisation:

> Hitherto the legal framework hasn't permitted public telecommunications business except for NTT's and KDD's. In terms of regulatory permissions and approvals, everything has been prohibited so far. The present bill can be understood not as the introduction of new regulatory permissions and approvals but liberalisation within the framework of the regulatory permissions and approvals. In short, we'd like you to understand that this set of permissions and approvals opens the previously prohibited business activities and the permissions and approvals are the leverage of this process ... [Telecommunications] regulation should be minimum, in our view. (The House of Representatives 1984a)

Another account explained this as the result of a deliberate effort to create competition in the telecommunications market: 'The government tried to deliberately create competition in the markets, which isn't an idea based on legally justifiable approaches. Therefore, it was unavoidable that such approaches [micro management of the market based not on law but political power] produced "conflicts"' (interview with a retired MIC senior civil servant). These accounts highlight how the MPT evolved from an inexperienced and powerless regulator to an established one.

The evolving core executive in response to ICT   53

Power relations between the MPT/MIC and party politicians and the change in the regulatory approach

The MPT's expansion of its regulatory power did not have a significant impact on its power relations vis-à-vis party politicians. According to an MIC senior civil servant: 'It [politicians' power after telecommunications liberalisation] hasn't changed so much'. Another civil servant revealed that 'the final decision's been made by politicians. Because politicians pass bills, they've actually dominated a significant portion of decision-making processes.' This view is shared by I'io's (2007: 91) analysis of civil servants and party politicians; Japan's civil servants need party politicians' cooperation to pass bills in the Diet. What has changed between party politicians and civil servants is the approach of the former to the latter. In the early phase of the telecommunications post-liberalisation process, party politicians intervened in regulatory matters administered by civil servants, as the following account revealed: 'Suddenly in response to the claims from politicians [the MPT] instructed "call rates are expensive so drop them". Such things happened several times, and this wasn't based on law' (interview with a retired MIC senior civil servant). As regulatory approaches to operators changed, party politicians' interventions also changed. One senior civil servant argued that the change in the regulatory approaches from ex ante oriented ones such as market entry permissions and tariff change approvals to ex post oriented ones such as network interconnection regulation made it difficult for party politicians to intervene:

> In the first five years [from NTT privatisation], during the debate over the NTT break-up, issues such as call rate reductions and tariff competition between NTT and the NCCs needed official approval, and politicians frequently intervened in them, even about tariffs. For example, let the NCCs drop their charges more, or, on the contrary, from politicians supporting NTT, let NTT drop its charges more. Such interventions were so frequent that I didn't feel party politicians retreated from involvement. And as competition in telecommunications markets wasn't effective enough, probably politicians contacted industry in various ways and required the government to develop something like competition policies. (interview with an MIC senior civil servant)

This overt intervention from party politicians was based on strict regulation, called micro management by Vogel (1996). The call for deregulation, therefore, undermined the basis on which party politicians intervened and changed their role in regulation:

> Politicians exercised their influence through government permission and approval. As deregulation stripped the government of the authority for

permission and approval, such politicians' role was forced to change. Therefore, leaving aside whether this was good, if specially commented, I can say they undermined their own power base ... But I guess formulating a regulatory framework in response to how effective competition is in the market is very rational, and through such a process the politician's role has changed. And this happened under the LDP administration, so this had nothing to do with the administration's ideology. (interview with an MIC senior civil servant)

This interviewee elaborated further on the relationship between the change of regulatory approach and the party politicians' approach to ICT regulation:

It is very hard for politicians to intervene in and be involved with network interconnection regulation and ex post regulation for consumer protection. Therefore, taking such a meaning, politicians' approaches which I described as 'politicians didn't retreat' became very difficult to sustain because regulatory approaches changed [from ex ante regulation such as market entry permissions] to new ones [such as network interconnection regulation and other ex post regulation].[10] (interview with an MIC senior civil servant)

This account is supported by an LDP politician, who argued that deregulation and the change of regulatory approach significantly transformed the role of politicians. This transformation came with a change in the relative strength within the community of party politicians:

Traditionally, *Yūsei-zoku*, which was part of the Tanaka/Takeshita faction,[11] had power and it is true that they had a significant influence over the decision-making of ICT policies. This situation continued until the juncture period from telephony to the Internet, but gradually this policy-making mechanism, in which *Zoku gi'in* decided policies, changed to another in which operators negotiate with each other and the Ministry plays a role as a referee, as networks have become more open. And naturally regulation has been relaxed, and politicians and laws have fewer places to be involved. (interview with a member of the House of Councillors)

If one reviews the above accounts, what emerges is how the state's regulatory mode changed. Its initial approach was as an ex ante regulator whose major tools included market entry permissions and tariff approvals. This approach was mobilised with the idea that markets needed the introduction of competition. Politicians significantly intervened in the process of ex ante regulation. The interviews also highlighted a change to the ex post oriented regulatory mode. This change was explicitly recognised by a senior MIC official in the Diet: 'The newly introduced framework will facilitate competition and allow new competitive entrants to enter the markets; and it is basically ex post oriented' (The House of Councillors 2003). An emerging new mode based on ex post regulation made the MPT act as a referee during disputes between operators rather than as an ICT sector strategist; an example of this approach can be found in the 'New Competition Program 2010'.

The growing significance of Cabinet ministers and the 2009 change of government

Another factor emerging from the interviews is the decline in power of party politicians outside the Cabinet and the rise in power of Cabinet ministers including the Prime Minister. This changed the relative strength between Cabinet ministers and those outside the Cabinet in favour of the former:

> The post office privatisation wiped out *Yūsei-zoku* in the LDP, or diminished their power within the LDP through its process. In concrete terms, Mr Nonaka [a significant *Yūsei-zoku* member in the 1990s and early 2000s] retired, most of the people [LDP politicians] who co-ordinated regulatory policies with the MPT lost the election, or left the LDP even if they carried it. In such a situation, politicians' power in ICT regulation significantly declined. (interview with a member of the House of Councillors (LDP))

The impact of this turmoil within the LDP was also witnessed by another LDP politician, who was close to the MPT and left the LDP during the process of post office privatisation:

> Regarding *Kantei* (the Prime Minister's Office), it wasn't Mr Koizumi but Mr Takenaka[12] [Minister of State for Economic and Fiscal Policy of the day]. His open policy or liberalisation policy confronted us ... after his lead in the CEFP,[13] the government and the party [LDP members outside the Cabinet] frequently conflicted ... at that time, Mr Nonaka resigned after a big fight with Mr Koizumi. After that, there was the turmoil of the postal services [the 2005 postal privatisation]. And those specialised in ICT like me, Mr Furuya and Ms Seiko Noda were kicked out. After that, the remaining Mr Kawasaki and Mr Den Sato needed huge efforts [to cope with the situation] ... So the party's [LDP politicians outside the Cabinet] power quickly waned and regulatory issues were dealt with under Mr Takenaka's leadership. (interview with a member of the House of Representatives)

56 Evolving regulation and governance

The change in the power relationship between Cabinet ministers and politicians outside the Cabinet is also noted by a retired MIC senior civil servant: '[the LDP's policy councils such as the PARC] became weaker after Koizumi. Became weak and, that's it [nobody has taken over].'

The 2009 change of government from the LDP to the DPJ also had an impact on the relationship between party politicians and civil servants, although its significance is contested. The highlighted points regarding the DPJ were:

- The lack of key party politicians: the DPJ did not have key figures with significant expertise and influence over the sector. Many of its powerful politicians were in the Cabinet. Because of this, Cabinet ministers under the DPJ government were increasingly empowered.
- The Cabinet ministers' short tenure: like their LDP counterparts, the DPJ Cabinet ministers had a short tenure,[14] rendering their power weaker, as it was not certain if their initiatives would last long.

On the first point, the lack of key DPJ politicians outside the Cabinet was witnessed by several interviewees. For example, an MIC senior civil servant offered the following interpretation:

> If asked whether the power relations between politicians and civil servants have changed and whether the power relations between one particular group and other groups have changed, the answer could be yes. And if asked whether the political factors of the policy-making process have become stronger, the answer will be 'it hasn't changed so much'. (interview with an MIC senior civil servant)

In his view what changed were the power relations within the core executive, such as between party politicians, civil servants and political groups. Elsewhere, he denied an increase in the influence of political factors over policy-making processes with the following comment:

> What has been changed by the DPJ is, in simple terms, the party itself hasn't been involved in policy decisions. That is to say, major politicians, for instance, have joined the Cabinet, and if asked whether the DPJ party machine has developed alternatives to the ideas of the Cabinet, the answer will be no. Regardless of sectors such as Land and Infrastructure, Welfare and Labour, etc., there are few things like that. This is because it's the DPJ's policy, and it also doesn't have those called *Zoku gi'in* in it. (interview with an MIC senior civil servant)

The reason why the DPJ did not have *Zokugi'in* was, in short, that it had not been in government:

In other words, the LDP's long tenure created a large group of ex-Cabinet ministers and ex-parliamentary vice-ministers. They weren't in the Cabinet but influential in their sector. If the DPJ stays in power for twenty years and creates their equivalent, the party's [DPJ politicians outside the Cabinet] influence may become stronger. We don't know it now. No such group is in the DPJ at this point. (interview with an MIC senior civil servant)

This interpretation was shared by a DPJ politician who was previously in the civil service:

Under the LDP governments, NTT and civil servants lobbied key people in the ICT sector for twenty years, such as ex-Cabinet ministers, the chairpersons and principal directors of the Diet Internal Affairs and Communications Standing Committee and their OBs. Such key persons were identified, and things were decided around them. Since the DPJ government started, no such key person has been there. (interview with a member of the House of Representatives)

This was described by a former DPJ Cabinet minister:

Almost all of it [the influence of party politicians outside the Cabinet] has disappeared, because the DPJ has unified the government with the party. And lobbying the party needs the secretary-general's authorisation. This stops lobbying politics and leads to the destruction of the guild. But two years after the change of government, some may try to do a similar thing again. We need to make [policy-making] processes more transparent and ensure the freedom of information so that we can watch and stop such a trial. (interview with a former Cabinet minister)

These accounts indicate that the 2000s saw a rise in the Cabinet ministers' power. The ICT sector experienced a significant change: Koizumi's post office privatisation debate in 2005 brought most of the LDP politicians previously influential over the sector out of the LDP. The DPJ government from 2009 adopted a policy of unifying the government with the party. Few DPJ politicians outside the Cabinet were powerful enough to exercise influence over the MIC and the ICT sector. These factors have undermined the power of party politicians outside the Cabinet. This observation coincides with the data collected by Michio Muramatsu and his associates (Krauss and Pekkanen 2011: 242):

Longitudinal data from Michio Muramatsu and his associates indicate that between 1987 (under the '55 system) and 2002 bureaucrats themselves clearly saw a major increase in the prime minister's influence over their own ministries and decline in the influence of *Zoku giin* and PARC and of the ministries and their advisory councils.

Data from this same survey also indicate that, within a ministry itself, between 1987 and 2002 the perceived relative influence on the bureaucracy of the upper levels of the bureaucracy (the bureau chief) and the cabinet ministers changed greatly; whereas in 1987 the bureau chief was perceived to have two to three times the influence of the minister, by 2002 the minister was perceived to have almost double the influence of the bureau chief.[15]

The same survey highlights the decline of party politicians outside the Cabinet. In 1987 their influence was considered to be most important by almost 40 per cent of civil servants, but this number significantly declined to a little more than 20 per cent in 2002 (Krauss and Pekkanen 2011: 243). This set of findings seems to support the analysis revealing the decline of party politicians outside the Cabinet and the rise of Cabinet ministers.

Whether or not DPJ Cabinet ministers actually obtained a dominant role in policy-making is a different question. Indeed, the short tenure of Cabinet ministers, which characterised the LDP governments (I'io 2007: 24), was also common among their DPJ counterparts. The impact of this short tenure was described by a senior lobbyist of a telecommunications operator:

> I suggest what MIC Minister Haraguchi did after the change of government [September 2009] is typical of a politician's leadership ... And replacing him in September [2010] changed everything. And I wonder if not only civil servants but also politicians need continuity and if the change of a minister is adequate [after a short period] ... if such things happen, it will be difficult [to accomplish policies], because without a minister's long tenure, things won't be done to the end. Under such circumstances, officials won't react so much if a minister says something ambitious, because that minister may be replaced any time. (interview with the General Manager of the President's Office of a telecommunications operator, a former member of the House of Representatives (DPJ))

This concern was shared by a consumer group leader who has participated in the policy-making process of the ICT sector:

> It's very problematic that, in a way, themes [given by ministers] have popped out frequently like thoughtless ideas but haven't been implemented to the end partly because initiating ministers were replaced. About MIC ministers, probably Minister Haraguchi and present Minister

The evolving core executive in response to ICT   59

> Katayama have very different kinds of interest, so in spite of the strong slogan of 'Path of Light', its goal has gradually changed to around 2025 from the previously stated 2015. The goal is getting much farther away. In such a way, it [the short tenure of ministers] is very influential [over policy-making and implementation]. (interview with a consumer group leader)

Similarly, a civil servant shared these concerns:

> In the case of the DPJ, who determined the fundamental principles such as [equivalents to post office] privatisation is unclear. Just decided like those based on the previous cases, or, simply, in the case of Mr Haraguchi, launching something somewhere with no substantial coordination; but because ministers' tenure isn't very long, whether such policies will be accomplished is doubtful. Based on such things, the *Seimu sanyaku* tend to proceed on their own, hardly trying to form a consensus through bureaucracy. But such an approach doesn't mobilise things. (interview with an MIC civil servant)

These accounts highlight the problems stemming from Cabinet ministers' short tenure: it significantly reduces the incentive to accomplish policies initiated by Cabinet ministers because the initiating minister is likely to leave soon. Also, the interviewees reveal an awkward relationship between DPJ Cabinet ministers and civil servants. The emergent challenge for DPJ Cabinet ministers was mobilising the bureaucratic machine, which needs a stable relationship between ministers and civil servants. Cabinet ministers' short tenure destabilises such a relationship. All accounts pointed out that this short tenure contributed to discouraging civil servants from engaging in policy implementation. It can be regarded as a significant reason why the Cabinet minister did not emerge as a new dominant actor in decision-making.

Drawing these analyses together, after the 1985 NTT privatisation, the core executive, in which power changed fluidly between actors, sufficiently retained control over the ICT sector with the supremacy of party politicians, including those in the LDP. The change of resources within the core executive after the 1980s exemplifies its fluid nature. The emergence of the enhanced state actor (the MPT) coincided with the transfer of NTT from the state sector to the private sector, together with its resources. The key decisions were made by party politicians, and their dominance in policy-making processes was based on their authority to approve bills in the Diet. The power of the MPT depended upon party politicians' support for a bill drafted by the MPT. The LDP's one-party rule gave power to its informal process. This situation gave party politicians outside the Cabinet power to control policy-making processes. The

Table 3.4 Relative strength of the actors in the ICT sector

	Before 1985	From NTT privatisation to 2000	2000–
The Cabinet and the *Seimu sanyaku*	large	large	enhanced further
Party politicians outside the Cabinet (*Zoku gi'in*)	large	large	declined
The MPT	small	enhanced	large
NTT	large	large	large

MPT took the position held by NTT and the party politicians supervised the transition process. With significant expertise and the capacity to lobby party politicians, NTT retained significant power after privatisation in 1985. However, NTT's power also depended upon party politicians; persuading them was NTT's method of influencing policy-making processes, that is, the core executive enjoyed a dominant position. The LDP's internal changes had a significant impact on the decision-making mechanism but have not changed the strength of party politicians as a whole relative to their bureaucratic and private-sector counterparts. The 2009 change of government exacerbated this internal change of party politicians by eradicating the LDP's *Zoku gi'in*. What has emerged is a power vacuum; while party politicians are reorganising their internal structure, civil servants and private-sector actors have not filled the gap (see Table 3.4).

This set of processes after the 1980s prompted by the fluid change of resources and power within the core executive offers a different story to the British core executive depicted by Smith (1999: 115–30). The key difference is the impact of the ruling parties' internal rules resulting from the LDP's long dominance within the administration. The ruling parties' internal rules are not formal; they have been established within the political parties outside the formal institution of the state. The impact of informal rule by the ruling parties, in particular the LDP, can be exemplified by the existence and power of party politicians outside the Cabinet (*Zoku gi'in*). The power of this group of party politicians gradually waned as Cabinet ministers and their teams gained more power. This trend was intensified by the change of government in 2009. This change of power offers an example of fluid change within the core executive, with the strength of party politicians significant.

The rise of the new regulatory ministry (MPT/MIC) reveals another case of the change of power. The analysis of this book concurs with the argument of Vogel (1996) highlighting the rise of the MPT after 1985, which resulted from another example of the fluid change of power: the privatisation of NTT offered the MPT an opportunity to enhance its power and authority. This can be understood as transformation of state power from the service provider to the regulator.

A key characteristic of ICT regulation since the 1980s has been a significant degree of discretion by ruling party politicians. They have been lobbied by both civil servants and industry and have steered the sector. Together with the emerging regulatory function of the MPT, the core executive has exercised a discretionary approach to regulation. The tools of its discretion include rule-making capacity such as legal amendments.

The above analysis reveals the dominance of the core executive through discretion. The changes have taken place under the supervision of party politicians. The discretion of the core executive, including party politicians, has worked to maintain their dominance in policy-making. Policy-making has involved the inner community of the core executive: ruling party politicians and the relevant government ministry. This set of analytical results offers an example of the core executive's dominance through its discretionary approach to regulation.

One of the important questions in exploring this transformation is how this evolving core executive has affected the institution of Japan's ICT sector. The next chapter addresses this. To elaborate, it examines the lack of an independent regulator in Japan's ICT sector, which is a distinctive institutional characteristic. Indeed, Japan is atypical in having only a few independent regulators that supervise regulatory implementation, such as the JFTC (OECD 2004: 46). Examining how a government ministry has retained its regulatory function offers an example of the process of shaping a particular structure and actors' concomitant views.

Notes

1 NTT used the same acronym before and after privatisation. It only slightly changed its name (in English as well as in Japanese) after privatisation. Before privatisation it was Nippon Telegraph and Telephone Public Co.; after privatisation it was Nippon Telegraph and Telephone Co.
2 The break-up of AT&T was decided in 1984, and resulted in the end of AT&T's regional monopoly. In the UK, British Telecom lost its monopoly in 1984. After the duopoly by BT and Mercury, a new entrant, between 1984 and 1990, the UK's telecommunications market became open to other new entrants in 1991.
3 This typology is based on a proposal by an MIC civil servant during the interviews.
4 A value-added network is a type of public network that leases basic transmission facilities from incumbent telecommunications operators, adds features

62 Evolving regulation and governance

5 *Yūsei-zoku* is a group of *Zoku gi'in* specialised in postal and telecommunications affairs in the LDP.
6 The Telecommunications Council was a Policy Deliberation Council which was consulted over key policy issues by the MPT minister. The resulting reports could become the basis for government bills in the respective field. This council transformed into the Information and Communications Council in 2001.
7 The LDP formed a coalition government with the SDPJ and the New Party *Sakigake* from 1994 to 1998.
8 Telecommunications operators that had their own facilities were classified as Type I carriers by Japan's Telecommunications Business Law, while those without their own facilities were categorised as Type II carriers (MPT 1998: 5–6).
9 'Path of Light' (*Hikari no michi*) was a policy project initiated by MIC Minister Haraguchi (September 2009–September 2010), through which broadband services would be enhanced through competition and service promotion measures including opening ICT networks, supporting broadband services in various sectors including medical care, and restructuring the NTT group (ICT Policy Taskforce for a Global Era 2010). The scope of debate to formulate concrete policy measures includes the reorganisation of the NTT group, which could lead to an NTT break-up.
10 In this context, 'ex ante regulation' means regulation focusing on issues that emerge before firms act, that is, what firms will do. An example is market entry regulation, which aims at firms' access to markets rather than their actual business activities in existing markets. In a similar way, 'ex post regulation' means regulation focusing on issues that emerge after firms have acted, that is, what firms do in existing markets. An example would be regulating dispute settlements between firms and consumers.
11 The Tanaka faction was the LDP's internal faction headed by Kakuei Tanaka (Prime Minister, 1972–74). In 1987 the majority of its members left the Tanaka faction and formed the Takeshita faction, which was headed by Noboru Takeshita (Prime Minister, 1987–88).
12 Heizō Takenaka was a Cabinet minister in the LDP Koizumi government (April 2001–September 2006). He was Minister of State for Economic and Fiscal Policy (April 2001–October 2005; concurrently served as Minister of State for Financial Services, September 2002–September 2004) and Minister of Internal Affairs and Communications (October 2005–September 2006; concurrently served as Minister for Postal Services Privatisation, October 2005–September 2006 2006).
13 The CEFP is a council in the Cabinet Office that deliberates on important issues of economic and fiscal policy as an instrument to establish the Prime Minister's substantial supervision on these issues. Established in 2001 as part of the administrative reform, it is chaired by the Prime Minister and composed of core Cabinet members and key private-sector figures (business leaders and academics) (Cabinet Office of Japan 2012).

14 None of the DPJ MIC ministers had a tenure longer than a year. See also Appendix 1.
15 The analysis of the survey results is based only on the first choice of answering options in the questionnaire.

4

Regulatory state transformation with an unusual approach

This chapter examines the specific characteristics of Japan's ICT regulation after the 1980s. The chapter first considers the impact of state transformation through the institutional characteristics of the ICT regulator as a ministry and the lack of an independent regulator. The impact of the collective view and power relations between state actors regarding issues such as regulatory organisations exemplify the development of state transformation. Japan offers an unusual example in which only a limited number of independent regulators have been established. This reflects Japan's political tradition as well as a path-dependent history. The analysis of this characteristic reveals how the core executive has shaped its perspectives on the independence of the ICT regulator within its political tradition. The chapter then turns to the state capacity of the sector. The second section looks into the capacity of the state in ICT regulation and its transformation. The last section considers the nature of Japan's state transformation in ICT regulation after the 1980s, pulling together the analysis hitherto.

Retaining the status quo with evolving regulation

Although several countries have established independent regulators in ICT, the response of interviewees in Japan was striking; few expressed a positive view about the establishment of an independent regulator, reflecting instead disapproval. As an example, an LDP member of the House of Councillors cast doubt over the establishment of an independent regulator, pointing out the complex nature of the US Federal Communications Commission (FCC), in which regulatory functions are combined with implementation functions:

> I don't think creating independent regulators will offer a significant benefit. Everyone often refers to an FCC type organisation, but the FCC

also has a political characteristic. Its commissioners are selected by the President. Its regulatory functions tend to work with its implementation functions, so regulatory functions are integrated into implementation functions. So I wonder with concern if separating the regulatory functions from implementation functions will work only in Japan. (interview with a member of the House of Councillors)

This concern over the creation of an independent ICT regulator was shared by another LDP politician, who drew attention to the state tradition of Japan's public policy-making: 'Since Japan's policy-making model is coordination based and consensus based, so directly introducing models like the FCC's will probably prompt resistance and opponents, in my view' (interview with a member of the House of Councillors). Elsewhere, there was a concern that an independent regulator similar to the JFTC might fail to retain the MIC's current regulatory capacity and could become an incompetent regulator of NTT. Such concern over the competence of an independent regulator was disclosed by a retired senior businessman, who was strongly committed to the idea of a powerful ICT regulator, having been an NCC executive officer for years: 'Whether the independent supervisory commission, the Japanese FCC, can take decisive measures, do various things, and properly supervise is not clear. So, I hesitate over whether creating the Japanese FCC is good' (interview with a retired executive officer of a telecoms operator). Similar concern was expressed by a senior civil servant, referring to the case of independent administrative commissions introduced by the Supreme Commander for the Allied Powers (SCAP) just after the Second World War:

> Independent administrative organisations were introduced under the administration of the SCAP, but it's doubtful if they strongly worked. So, I suggest, the regulatory authority's power will decline when it's transformed to a commission. If it needs to implement determined things in determined ways, it may work, but governing requires something creative in Japan, so it's not clear whether such creative activities can be done by a commission. The JFTC has a clear mission, which is supervising competition in markets, so if the mission is clear, a commission can work. But I wonder if a commission can create its own mission. (interview with a senior civil servant)

This next interviewee also cast doubt on the benefit of creating an independent regulator:

> It is debatable whether regulation and policy can be separated from each other. But it will create both benefits and problems. It is theoretically possible that creating policy will be done by a different organisation and only

implementation will be done by the commission ... but we haven't done it in such a way so far and I doubt we will get benefits by employing such an approach [creating an independent regulator]. (interview with a senior civil servant)

His view concurred with the MPT's official paper from 1997: 'The information and communications sector requires comprehensive, strategic, and timely responses. This kind of sector does not suit an administrative commission based on collective decision-making with the independent authority of the Cabinet' (MPT 1997).

The doubts cast over the creation of an independent ICT regulator can be summarised as:

- uncertainty over how effective an independent regulator can be;
- concern about the democratic governance of the independent regulator; and
- the possibility of addressing conflicts of interests between the regulator and developmental policy through a different method other than creating an independent regulator.

The first point is implicit rather than explicit, as expressed in the above accounts. A group of interviewees from the core executive pointed out the political nature of the American FCC, and argued that changing an organisation to an independent regulator has a limited or even negative impact on regulatory capacity. Interviewees from business were particularly clear on this point. They expressed concerns over whether or not an independent regulator could confront and substantially regulate incumbent operators such as NTT. Elsewhere, an interviewee from a consumer organisation argued for the creation of an independent regulator because independence might offer coherent regulation, although she showed no analysis on how workable such an organisation might be.

The second point can be understood as a type of state tradition. Independent agencies in the form of commissions which mushroomed in Japan after 1945 were in most cases abolished after the Allies' occupation ended (Harada 2011: 15). The report to the Shigeru Yoshida[1] government (1948–54) by the Government Orders Amendment Consultation Committee (*Seirei kaisei shimon i'inkai*), which examined what adaptations were necessary after the peace treaty with the Allies in 1951 and subsequent Japanese independence, set out the following reasons for abolishing most of the independent administrative commissions (Harada 2011: 15):

Because our social and economic conditions did not originally require them [independent administrative commissions], their organisations expand without aim; when it is unclear where the responsibility lies in their administrative tasks regarding which aims should be actively pursued, and therefore they are not adequate for efficiently achieving their tasks, they shall be abolished in principle. However, they shall be simplified and retained when they mainly deal with passive tasks which require careful decisions.

Harada (2011: 15) also points out that the committee's view was established during a period when a significant reduction of the civil service was required to cope with the aftermath of the Second World War. A civil servant highlighted this point by disclosing his understanding that the government's perspective on this period has been sustained and affected its response to creating independent regulators:

> Historically, in simple terms, it's Shigeru Yoshida. In other words, when Japan became independent, they said 'No independent commission', to say, well, the executive is the Cabinet. 'It's wrong that organisations for which the Cabinet is not responsible have remits in particular fields'; this describes everything. This leads to an idea that politicians should be responsible, like the politicians' leadership [*Seijishudō*] by the DPJ today. Therefore, things were decided at that moment, 1952, and after that they have just followed those decisions. (interview with a civil servant)

This account reveals an element of path-dependent, institutional decision-making (Thelen 2009: 474–5). Drawing on Thelen (2009: 474), it can be argued that 'the historical trajectories' have flowed from the legacies that the 'critical juncture' in 1952 produced. This path-dependent preference can be identified as a significant factor contributing to the emergence of negative views towards independent regulators.

Elsewhere, another civil servant illuminated the technical difficulty of creating an independent organisation in Japan:

> Independent regulators are required because regulators need to be fair, neutral and free from political interventions. When we refer to the US, Congress makes the law, which is enforced by the independent regulator, the FCC. In Japan, a significant difference is that most bills are put forward by the Cabinet. And what is the nature of the independent organisation if it's independent from government? For instance, the JFTC is usually regarded as a highly independent organisation, called an Article 3 organisation, but it still belongs to the Prime Minister under the parliamentary system. Therefore, from what the independent organisation is independent is important. (interview with a civil servant)

He argued that this different institutional background gives the JFTC a different type of independence from that which US independent commissions have:

> The model of an independent regulator is the JFTC, in my view. It's generally understood in such a way, and I also think so. But from the viewpoint of [Japan's] National Administration Organisation Law it is within the Cabinet, so it's not independent. Because it is a player in the government, it's not independent from the government. Because it's a player of the government, its status is different from independent commissions of other countries like the US. (interview with a civil servant)

Third, interviewees from the core executive rejected the view that establishing an independent regulator is the key to addressing conflicts of interest between industry development and regulation. This understanding led them to argue that the issue is not organisational independence but ensuring the neutrality of regulation. As another civil servant observed:

> Another issue to emerge is over the independence of competition policy from industrial/promotional policy prompted by conflicts of interest. Large private corporations like NTT play a significant role, for example, in the deployment of broadband communications networks. This leads the government to employ promotional policies favourable to NTT. Yet the government's regulation tends to be unfavourable to NTT, for it tends to focus on dominant operators. (interview with a civil servant)

With his experience in the US, he also highlighted the political nature of the US independent commissions, referring to the case of the FCC:

> I think the government has to avoid mutual influence between these two policies. In the US, the FCC is under the auspices of Congress. In other words, it's independent of the federal government and belongs to Congress. Its major financial source is the licence fee. Spending this money requires Congress's approval. Can we call this system independent of politics? I don't think it's truly independent of politics; the current majority of commissioners are three democrats, together with two republicans. (interview with a civil servant)

He concluded that the key is not the organisational framework but the neutrality of policies:

> Taking account of such facts, I think what the government needs isn't organisational independence but the neutrality of policies such as

competition policy. The point is, establishing the legal framework of independent regulators is very difficult, and if the point isn't independence from politics, the regulator's institutional framework doesn't have to be scrutinised, provided that the fairness and the neutrality of competition policy are ensured. (interview with a civil servant)

The above accounts reveal that the challenges to the modern state have not had a significant impact on the institutional framework of Japan's ICT regulator.

This set of views may relate to the fact that Japanese law only permits legal provisions to have narrow scope and interpretations with limited flexibility compared to their British counterparts. A senior civil servant revealed a detailed observation of the difference between Japanese law and that of the UK:

I thought that Japanese law was inconvenient and that the system of English communications law, in which nothing is written, in other words significant discretion was given to the administrative organisations, the organisations focus their discretion and can implement conditions like no regulation, was very convenient. The reason why it's convenient is that policy can be flexibly changed by the executive branch. When we write in law, we can't go back. Therefore, I thought such a system was very rational. It's probably based on the court system, in particular in the US. The abuse of discretion by the executive branch is expected to be stopped in court.

This comparison of technical aspects of Japanese law and the UK's was further elaborated:

When I read English laws, I found surprising provisions such as that 'all telecommunications facilities in the UK need licences', and the government's authority to operate the licensing system has little limitation. In such a case, for example, policy goals, which greatly change as society changes, can easily shape rational regulation such as 'such a thing is necessary so such a regulation will be implemented', in line with the principles, such as the legal provisions. But Japan's Cabinet Legislation Bureau is extremely strict about this point, so they say 'you want to operate the system in such a way, but the law doesn't say such things, so you can't do that', so I envied the English system. It is very inconvenient. But legal infrastructure including the legal system and the judicial system are different, so it's not easy to do that in Japan. I envied that, but it [the flexible operation of law] has not been realised so far.

Rapid changes to the rules require legal amendments in Japan. This means that regulators frequently need to consult with party politicians.

In the UK, laws such as the 1984 Telecommunications Act provide regulators such as Oftel with a broad degree of discretion (Spiller and Vogelsang 1996: 82). This stems from the UK's legal tradition that regulators were not required to explain their decisions in detail or face judicial reviews until the mid-1990s; instead, the UK judiciary restrained government discretion in the form of contracts (Spiller and Vogelsang 1996: 82). Contracts between the regulator and operators in the form of licences are based on the courts' robust tradition of upholding contracts among private parties: 'so it is not surprising that utility regulation has been implemented through licences, which can specify both substantive restraints on regulatory discretion and restraints on changing the regulatory system as well as the regulatory incentives structure' (Spiller and Vogelsang 1996: 82).

In the case of Japan, the law plays an important role in making regulators more dependent on the political process and party politicians. This in turn makes it difficult for them to be separated from the Cabinet. Also, the nature of Japanese law gives the executive ministries limited discretion and requires frequent legal amendments in policy-making processes. This necessitates a greater involvement of politicians than other legal systems such as the UK's. There is the possibility that independent organisations outside government might encounter a problem in policy-making processes because their limited access to politics prevents them from formulating necessary policies via legislation and the Diet's approval. Beeman (2002: 174) raises this point as a challenge to the JFTC as an independent administrative commission, drawing from his examination of anti-monopoly regulation.

Elsewhere, interviewees outside the core executive offered different views. An official of a major business organisation recognised that the ICT sector needs intimate cooperation between promotional (developmental) policy and regulatory policy, although establishing an independent regulator is an option:

> ICT needs both regulation and industry promotion, so [whether it needs an independent regulator is] not clear, but I suggest it's a possible option that the MIC intervenes in the sector [directing promotional policy] while an independent regulator supervises it. (interview with a *Keidanren* official)

This specific characteristic of the ICT sector, the necessity of close cooperation between industry promotion and regulation, was recognised by a retired academic involved in policy-making for many years:

> The ICT sector changes so quickly and this rapid change is the basis of international competitiveness. And if a commission concentrating on

regulation is established, the result will be a disaster. For example, the FCC not only regulates the sector but also, in my view regarding radio regulation, formulates new rules to promote technological development. Therefore, an organisation which doesn't promote but only regulates industry will create no benefit. (interview with a former member of the Information and Communications Council)

This argument was supported by a retired senior civil servant: 'What I've experienced is promotion and regulation ... If regulation and promotion fail to [co-work and] generate synergy, things won't work in ICT industry and policies' (interview with a retired senior civil servant).

Creating an independent ICT regulator was more openly supported by an interviewee from a consumer group. She hoped that an independent regulator could fend off influence from politicians and realise more coherent regulation:

> We said that a third party organisation [an independent organisation] was necessary, an independent organisation with a substantial capacity for data collection and authority was necessary, in the opinion of a consumer organisation. The MIC's current approach conflates industry promotion and regulation including competition policy and consumer protection. For example, users can't use the equipment of a previously used version. This [version-up] comes too quickly, but when I say this, others say things like 'don't stop development' and 'international competitiveness is necessary'. To think about the balance between these conflicting aspects and make decisions, a substantially independent organisation is necessary, in our view. (interview with a senior official of a consumer organisation)

Although this account shows a preference for independent regulation at arm's length from industry promotion, it does not suggest how such an organisation could be established.

In pulling these arguments together, the following are reasons why an independent ICT regulator has not been created:

- An embedded perspective among the core executive resists the notion of the independent organisation introduced by the SCAP after the Second World War: an independent regulator is regarded as an American product and has been thought of as an organisation suitable for passive policy implementation. Interviewees from the core executive argue that an independent regulator is not suitable for creating policy.
- Technical difficulties such as that of the Constitution: the Constitution of Japan stipulates: 'Executive power shall be vested in

the Cabinet' (Article 65). This provision expects all administrative organisations including regulators to be under the jurisdiction of the Cabinet. Such an institutional framework limits the independence of regulators, because they are subject to the control of the Cabinet.

- The lack of benefits: an interesting feature to emerge from the core executive interviewees was that there was no mention of any benefits in creating an independent ICT regulator. Instead, their focus was on the relationship between the existing institutional framework and an independent regulator, which they regarded as a US-style commission, and the view that creating an independent ICT regulator was not suited to Japan's political tradition. Also, the core executive interviewees concentrated on arguing that they could avoid problems such as conflicts of interest between industry promotion policies and regulatory policies within the current institutional framework. What emerges then is that party politicians did not think that taking responsibility for highly technical issues such as ICT regulation was a risk; and the core executive interviewees thought that current ministerial regulation implemented by generalist civil servants could develop sufficient expertise regarding the ICT sector. These views are indifferent to the possible benefits of an independent regulator. For example, OECD (2002: 95) highlights the benefits: 'to shield market interventions from interference from captured politicians and bureaucrats', improved transparency, more stable regulation, improved conditions for business, and the possibility of improved accountability if an independent regulator has explicit objectives and a specific reporting system to the government or parliament. None of the core executive interviewees expressed an interest in such benefits; some of them rather argued that these benefits could be obtained even if a government ministry has regulatory functions.
- Developmental approaches using regulation as a tool for industry promotion: a group of interviewees argued that regulatory independence could undermine the close cooperation between regulation and industry promotion. A similar idea was revealed by the MPT's official document:

> Specifically separating 'information and communications industry development activities' is not in line with an international trend of retreat from promotional and protective approaches to specific industries ... the approach that pursues 'promotion' and 'regulation' together achieves policy goals efficiently and effectively. An example can be found in the spread and development of mobile communications services. (MPT 1997)

This idea is based on two premises: that outdated ICT regulation could jeopardise the development of ICT as did the monopolistic regulation before privatisation, which significantly hampered the development of telecommunications networks; and that regulatory independence could undermine the necessary interaction between industry promotion and regulation.

If the above points are contrasted with the risks of independent regulators shown in Table 4.1, according to the OECD (2002: 95–6), the first point (the risk of slowing structural changes) and the third point (the risk of inadequate democratic accountability) are the characteristics that can be observed in Japan's ICT regulation. The first point responds to concerns that an independent regulator could jeopardise close cooperation between industry promotion and regulation. Some interviewees emphasised the nature of the ICT sector, which continually faces rapid technological developments. They argued that such challenges require the ICT sector to frequently change its regulatory measures. In relation to the third point, executive oversight and regulatory independence conflict with one another. All executive organisations are under the Cabinet in the Japanese system. This inevitably allows party

Table 4.1 Risks associated with independent regulators

Independent regulators may slow structural changes, losing potential gains to consumers. Regulators are often established on sectoral lines and may tend to obstruct convergence between sectors and the emergence of new business models. Similarly, as regulators proliferate, institutional rigidities may increase.

The risk of capture is reduced but not eliminated if the regulator faces structural weaknesses, particularly with sectorally defined regulators lacking resources. Similarly, over-regulation may result where static institutions wish to guard their *raison d'être*.

Democratic accountability may be inadequate. Independence needs to be balanced with accountability mechanisms to avoid creating 'governments in miniature'. Accountability must be maintained through well-designed statutes, including executive oversight and powers of direction, strict procedural requirements, reporting mechanisms, public consultation and substantive judicial review.

Independent regulators may contribute to the fragmentation of governmental policies and actions, in particular in the case of competition policy. As sectors restructure and become more competitive, sector-specific issues become less important vis-à-vis general competition issues. But inertia and resistance from the regulator is likely to impede transfers of power to the overarching competition regulator. Weaknesses in the judiciary and/or legislative branch also have an impact on the overall performance of the independent regulators.

Source: OECD 2002: 95–6. Emphasis in original.

politicians to intervene in a regulator's activities. In addition, the nature of Japanese law, which allows only narrow interpretation, requires frequent amendments. This offers party politicians opportunities to intervene in regulation.

The case of creating an independent ICT regulator is an example where traditional structures significantly contributed to an unusual outcome. The abolition of US-style independent administrative commissions has significantly impacted the core executive's perspective on an independent regulator. Institutional characteristics such as the constitutional framework and the inflexible nature of Japanese law also result in significant obstacles to an independent ICT regulator. The Constitution requires all executive organisations to be under the supervision of the Cabinet. The inflexible interpretation of existing laws limits the possibility of the executive branch making policies within its own jurisdiction. It requires frequent consultations with the Diet through legal amendments, which offers opportunities for party politicians to intervene in policies. Legislation as a key element of the state's resources contributing to the asymmetric dominance of the core executive plays a significant role here (Marsh et al. 2001: 248). The lack of clear benefit in creating an independent regulator, in the view of the core executive, however, could be one of the most significant reasons why Japan has not established such a regulator. No actor will be motivated to contemplate a project with uncertain benefits. In addition, some interviewees revealed their concern that regulatory independence could jeopardise close interaction between regulation and industry promotion, including information-sharing regarding technological development. This concern among elites, including the business community as well as the core executive, could further have contributed to a negative view regarding an independent ICT regulator.

What has influenced the choice of a ministerial regulator is Japan's political tradition rather than power relations within the core executive. The core executive actors have collectively chosen to retain their regulatory functions within the government ministry. This demonstrates that no endogenous incentive to change has emerged within the core executive. The disjuncture following privatisation in 1985 did not offer an opportunity to debate the independent implementation of regulation and the establishment of an independent ICT regulator, as was the case in a number of European countries. The lack of effective endogenous incentives and exogenous pressures, together with Japan's political tradition, contributed to retaining the regulatory approach through a government ministry.

Whether or not this negative view of an independent ICT regulator has affected the regulatory capacity of the state in the ICT sector is a different question. The next section explores how it has been transformed.

Regulatory state capacity and the transformation of a regulatory ministry

Observing state capacity can contribute to explaining how the state has been transformed. If one turns to the regulatory aspects of the state, the transformation of the state's regulatory capacity will offer useful information about how the regulatory state has been shaped. In relation to the state capacity of ICT regulation, most interviews focused on the bureaucratic machine as key. Those interviewees expected another core executive actor, party politicians, to steer the machine. Only a few referred to external factors such as the relationship with industry. The extent to which regulatory capacity has been transformed is contested. Although Vogel (1996: 161–3) describes the privatisation of NTT and the emergence of the MPT as significant, it can also be understood as a decline in the capacity of the Japanese state: the whole telecommunication management function of the state was transferred to the private sector. Taking account of the significant power of NTT as a public corporation before privatisation, the growing power of the MPT can be understood as a form of resurgence of the state through filling the gap created by privatisation. What followed was the reduction of the MPT's statutory authority as deregulation removed ex ante regulation.

The perspectives drawn from the interviews regard the regulatory capacity of the MPT/MIC. Several interviewees emphasised the development of the ministry's capacity after NTT's privatisation:

> The regulator has a sufficient number and quality of staff. In the past, they had to ask NTT, and before that, NTT sent their officials when it was a public corporation, but it's not the case now. The MIC has obtained clear responsibilities including dispute settlement through law amendments and developed its own staff, so it's competent enough to satisfy its responsibilities. (interview with a member of the House of Councillors (LDP))

What emerges here is how the responsible government ministry has developed, based on the understanding that it represents the regulatory state capacity. This view was shared by a retired senior civil servant highlighting the organisational growth of the ministry:

> Communications liberalisation, through NTT break-up [reorganisation], significantly enhanced the MPT's role as a regulator from 1985 to 2000, for fifteen years, if compared with the Telecommunications Inspectorate. Such a rapid enhancement enabled three bureaus to be left in the ministry [MIC] after post office privatisation, which stripped postal services from the ministry. The ministry's regulatory power has been strengthened by this. (interview with a retired senior civil servant)

Elsewhere, the CEO of an incumbent telecommunications operator concurred with this view, revealing his explicit recognition of the remarkably augmented capacities of the regulator – not just crude enforcement power but other aspects such as various types of expertise.

An ex-politician elaborated on the detail of bureaucratic capacity, admitting its piecemeal growth: 'More people [officials] are needed … I guess the ministry has been short of staff … as an organisation it needs to establish the framework in which it collects information from private firms' (interview with a member of the House of Representatives (DPJ)). Staff shortages were also commented on by another civil servant and a consumer group leader; the latter mentioned this problem together with the impact of the short tenure of civil servants:

> I suggest that the MIC wants more staff. And in government offices outcomes depend heavily upon assigned officials' ability. They leave their positions after a two-year tenure even when things worked very well. Establishing consistency under such a system is a significant challenge; most good jobs by officials aren't continued and accomplished by their successors … Sometimes I think it's wasted. Despite their efforts, they leave when their project actually starts moving. Two years is such a [short] period [to accomplish a project]. (interview with a consumer group leader)

A senior civil servant offered a different view that the MIC was not so understaffed compared with its British counterpart:

> I don't know now, but Oftel's personnel resource was limited when I was there [in 1993]. A significant number of people were there, but most of them were in the consumers' call centre. Those assigned to regulation were very limited, and the number of fast streamers was very different from that of the MPT's Telecoms Business Department … I don't know how Ofcom (Office of Communications) is now, but I suggest Japan's MIC has assigned a significant number of people with a certain quality level. (interview with a senior civil servant)

The official suggested that the capability of the staff in the ministry has been key, and he stated: 'In the past a significant number of such people [able officials] were in the civil service.'

Elsewhere, a retired civil servant highlighted the decline of the power of civil servants:

> [The state's capacity to mobilise the ICT sector] has significantly declined … because it's getting more difficult to use policy tools with no legal authority like administrative guidance, and more preferable to restrain officials from exercising their legal authority … and there is no

Regulatory state transformation with an unusual approach 77

guiding administration, what the MITI [METI][2] calls guideline administration, in which the ministry proposes a vision and gets responses [from private firms]. The MIC can't create such a vision. (interview with a retired senior civil servant)

This decline of the MIC's regulatory function was described as a type of transformation by a civil servant: 'The necessary part [of regulation] has remained and the unnecessary part has disappeared, so I suggest whether regulation of the NTT has been enhanced or reduced is not the case.' A senior lobbyist of a telecommunications operator (a former DPJ member of the House of Representatives) highlighted the importance of the political will to take strict action. This view highlights the extent to which Cabinet ministers have had their power curtailed:

> If we create a regulatory organisation in Japan, we need to empower it so that it can do its duty. But even when the regulator gets such authority, it won't exercise it in the end, will it? Including the MIC. In such cases, politicians have the regulator exercise its power, in theory. It's difficult for civil servants to exercise such power. So politicians sometimes need to show the power is exercisable ... politicians also aren't familiar with governing and control yet ... Just exercise legal authorities once or twice. Without this, nobody will get shocked. (interview with the General Manager of the President's Office of a telecommunications operator)

Two views emerge in identifying the reasons behind the decrease in the government ministry's power. The first focuses on the emergence of the 'smart regulator', arguing that the state has eliminated unnecessary regulation and adapted its regulatory framework. The second is that the decline of the state's regulatory authority has created a power vacuum, which has not been filled by other actors, including party politicians. When this decline of civil servants became distinctive remains contested. One account argued that it started during the Koizumi government (2001–06), while another highlighted the disjuncture caused by the change of government in 2009. These two views suggest that since the 2000s a decline of civil servants' power has occurred.

The transformation of regulatory capacity can be understood as the rise and decline or the adaptation of responsible civil servants through shaping a variation of the Japanese regulatory state in ICT regulation after the 1980s. The MPT's approach just after liberalisation can be characterised as strategic/discretionary, with a wide range of legal responsibility to exercise draconian regulation, such as strict market entry examination. It was a response to the transformation of state power in the sector from the service provider to the regulator. These approaches were transformed to more specific ones with a more detailed and limited legal basis, such as dominant carrier regulation and ex post regulation, while deregulation removed the previous wide range of legal responsibilities such as those related to market entry. At the same time, civil servants enhanced their knowledge and expertise. The 2000s saw the decline of strategic management by civil servants, while no new actor has taken over this role. This loss of civil servants' function came with the weakening of party (in most cases LDP) politicians outside the Cabinet. Cabinet ministers obtained opportunities to control policy-making processes, but their short tenure and lack of experience have been significant obstacles. This can be understood as the result of the change of power within the core executive; party politicians outside the Cabinet have seen their power eroded, while the opposite has occurred in relation to Cabinet ministers. What party politicians have done so far is to undermine the strategic function of civil servants without creating any substitute. Attempts to create a strategic role have resulted in instability rather than a settled order replacing the previous function played by officials. The change of state power in ICT regulation can be understood as the process of shaping the Japanese regulatory state under the dominance of the core executive, within which fluid and complicated changes of power took place.

The dominance of the core executive

The ICT sector has experienced an array of regulatory reforms including liberalisation mobilised by technological development. Since Japan liberalised the telecommunications sector and introduced competition in 1985, its experience of liberalisation has been significant. Examining this process reveals a gradual transformation of the Japanese state in the ICT sector.

Telecommunications liberalisation is often framed in the context of deregulation and a neoliberal approach to the economy (Collins and Murroni 1996: 5–6; Vogel 1996: 77, 151; Jordana and Levi-Faur 2004: 1). It is sometimes regarded as the start of the shrinkage of the state within the sector. Others interpret telecommunications liberalisation as a process of reconstituting the state. Sorensen (2004), for example, argues for a transformation of the modern state in which state power has adapted to cope with changing circumstances. In this view, the state has retreated in some areas (e.g. direct service provision in areas such as telecommunications) and enhanced its power elsewhere (e.g. telecommunications regulation). In Japan's ICT sector, the service provision implemented by the state corporation before 1985 moved to the private sector. The government organisation strengthened its regulatory capacity after 1985. Between the 1980s and 2000s, the state in the sector retreated in service provision and enhanced its power in principal–agent regulation. State power in regulation also changed from ex ante oriented to ex post oriented. This set of changes can be understood as the reconstitution of the state.

What emerges in Japan's ICT regulation after the 1980s is a variation of state transformation. The incumbent telephone operator was transformed from a state actor to a private one. A new type of state power emerged to fill the vacuum created by privatisation; the MPT as the responsible regulatory ministry emerged as a new state actor with significant authority. Another state actor, party politicians, has dominated the key decision-making process, although their role in the detail of regulatory policies has been limited, like that of British ministers in Smith's (1999: 125) analysis. The retreat of the MPT/MIC from strategic decision-making in the 2000s created a gap, which was not filled by the emerging power of party politicians in the Cabinet. The increase in their power has resulted in an unstable situation rather than the emergence of a new order. This can be understood as a dynamic reconstitution process of the state with the fluid change of power between the core executive actors.

The key to analysing the transformative process is power relations within the core executive. Fluid changes of power within the core executive have led to the adaptation of the state to changing circumstances. Prioritising principal–agent regulation as a key tool to control the ICT sector came with the rise of the regulatory ministry. Another example is the change of power within the group of party politicians, that is, the weakening of ruling party politicians outside the Cabinet and the rise of Cabinet ministers. Together with the change of government in 2009, the lessening of power within the group of party politicians resulted in an unstable situation with no strategic actor. However, as the key decision-makers, party politicians have successfully retained control of the ICT sector. The relationship between party politicians and civil servants in Japan's ICT sector is analogous to Smith's (1999: 125–8) analysis of the interdependence of the civil service–minister relationship. According to him:

> Ministers and officials need each other because of their different resources and different structural positions. Ministers need officials to reproduce the Whitehall game and its constitutional foundations. Officials need ministers to act and to provide legitimacy, political support and finance for the work of the department. The different structural positions produce different advantages. Officials do have control over the bureaucratic machinery and have the time to control most of what goes on in a department. Ministers can only pay attention to a limited number of issues. Therefore, officials have the discretion to act where the ministerial light does not shine. However, once a minister pays attention to an issue it is extremely

difficult for the civil service to thwart him or her, and indeed there is more prestige in achieving the minister's goal.

A similar relationship can be observed between party politicians (both outside and inside the Cabinet) and civil servants in the MPT/MIC. The significant regulatory authority obtained by the MPT after 1985 required legitimacy and political support from ruling party politicians. In line with Smith's analysis, MPT/MIC officials could exercise significant discretion (Vogel 1996) as long as ruling party politicians did not pay attention. However, once ruling party politicians took heed of an issue, preventing them from intervening was difficult. The power change within party politicians (from those outside the Cabinet to Cabinet ministers) did not have a significant impact on this interdependence between party politicians and civil servants. Rather, it can be understood as party politicians' flexible response to circumstantial change; they have retained their dominance by changing the key actors within their group.

The question of the independent regulator offers an insight into the Japanese state's development. This chapter has disclosed two major reasons why the core executive rejected setting up an ICT regulator: significant resentment towards the independent commissions formed in the late 1940s in Japan and the importance of the party politicians' role in policy-making processes. The failure of most independent administrative commissions to embed themselves in Japan's political tradition led to their abolition in the 1950s, shaped a negative perspective towards independent administrative commissions within the core executive, and created a significantly negative outlook towards independent regulators, among civil servants in particular. Not only the interview accounts but also the MPT's paper in the 1990s (MPT 1997) demonstrate the impact of the perspective of the Government Orders Amendment Consultation Committee under the Yoshida government (1948–54), by disclosing either direct or implicit reference to the committee's view. This can be understood as a negative view created by a path-dependent sequence, in which the impact of the independent administrative commissions' failure in the 1940s and 1950s played the role of the initial event that shaped the successive sequence of events. The resulting preference for avoiding an independent regulator among the core executive actors contributed to Japan's approach to ICT regulation.

Elsewhere, mobilising the Diet is vital in Japan's public policy-making, in which a significant proportion of regulatory policies need to be written in law (Beeman 2002: 174). Under this mechanism civil servants regard as crucial a strong connection with party politicians, who play a key role in policy-making processes. Party politicians have also imposed their will on specific issues, some of which contribute to their own self-interests rather than those of the public. The internal change of power relations within the group of party politicians from key non-Cabinet members to Cabinet ministers has not eroded the power of party politicians as a whole. Instead, this change of power relations has created a different impact in the regulatory policy arena. The emerging power of Cabinet ministers has rendered the situation unstable rather than resettled in a new order, because they have not taken over the role previously played by civil servants, including strategic decision-making.

Other factors such as Japan's legal tradition and the lack of a clear benefit in establishing an independent ICT regulator also contributed to retaining ministerial regulation. Given that a significant extent of veto has existed among the core executive actors – all of the core executive interviewees showed negative views towards the idea of establishing an independent ICT regulator in Japan – it has been natural for the responsible government ministry to retain its regulatory function. This has affected the capacity of the regulator. The views of many interviewees focused on the capacity of the government ministry and its civil servants. This understanding creates a strong association of civil servants with regulatory capacity. Therefore, the decline of the capacity of civil servants can be directly regarded as a decline of regulatory capacity. As the growing power of the *Seimu sanyaku* as elected officials in bureaucracy has not filled the vacuum created by the retreat of civil servants, the resulting situation was unstable; the *Seimu sanyaku* have failed to consolidate their resources and exploit the opportunity of taking over the role of civil servants as a result of two obstacles: their short tenure in office and lack of experience.

It is within this complex environment that significant contention emerges in evaluating how the capacity of the state has been developed in ICT regulation. A group of interviewees composed of party politicians, a senior incumbent operator official and some civil servants argued that significant regulatory capacity has been developed, mainly in the government ministry and based on a newly established bureaucratic power base. Another group of interviewees, including senior officials of NCCs, a senior consumer group official and a number of civil servants, highlighted different aspects of regulatory capacity; their view suggests compromised regulation resulting from the inconsistent approach of civil servants stemming from their short tenure, the retreat of the government ministry's legal authority, and the lack of political will to impose strict measures. The process of regulatory capacity-building in ICT can be viewed as the adaptation of the core executive to the regulatory challenges of the period. That the issue of regulatory capacity has been determined within the core executive (planned by civil servants and authorised by party politicians) implies that the core executive has retained a significant degree of discretion on this issue.

What emerges is a transformative process from a well-coordinated state corporation monopoly to competitive markets managed by a regulator with a principal–agent relationship with party politicians. Although party politicians have had significant power to control the sector, they have not exercised their influence (LDP) or had sufficient capacity to accomplish goals (DPJ). The distance between party politicians and civil servants adds a characteristic to this situation in Japan. Throughout the interviews, all the party politicians and civil servants regarded political parties and bureaucracy as independent of one another; none of them had a strong sense of the state. Party politicians viewed their own role as key decision makers. The internal transformation among party politicians (the decline of those outside the Cabinet and the rise of Cabinet ministers) may affect this situation, although no change has been observed yet. The overall picture of how the respective power of these actors within the core executive has been transformed is summarised in Table 4.2.

The analysis in this chapter has revealed that Japan's ICT regulation since the 1980s has similar governance characteristics to the governing structure of the UK analysed by Smith, despite different political traditions. To explain the Japanese case, 'ministers' as actors in Smith (1999: 118) can be rephrased as 'key party politicians' (Cabinet ministers and party politicians outside the Cabinet). Power relations within the group of key party politicians and civil servants have been fluid; the dominance of ruling party politicians was replaced by that of Cabinet ministers in the 2000s; civil servants enhanced their influence in the 1980s and saw further transformations in the 2000s. The nature of the relationship between the core executive actors has been interdependent. Both party politicians and civil servants needed other core executive actors' resources. Elsewhere, the core executive has been dominant in the sector. Key decisions have been made by ruling party politicians throughout the period. Unlike civil servants, societal actors such as telecommunications carriers have not had the resources that the core executive crucially

Table 4.2 Changes in the core executive actors' power

State actors	Function	1980s–1990s	2000s
Cabinet ministers	decision-making	weak	enhanced but unstable
	strategic management	weak	enhanced but unstable
Non-Cabinet members	decision-making	strong	declined
	strategic management	weak	weak
Civil servants	strategic management	strong	declined
	legal capacity to regulate	strong	declined
	knowledge and expertise	weak	enhanced

needed. This point differentiates the MPT/MIC from societal actors. Even the strongest telecommunications carrier (NTT) has had limitations; although NTT has had significant funds and information about the industry, its power has depended upon decisions by party politicians. Party politicians have primarily depended not upon NTT but on the MPT/MIC as the government machine governing the ICT sector. Although NTT demonstrated significant power to stop its break-up in 1990 and 1996, it did not have the resources that party politicians vitally needed. This means that NTT could successfully fend off its break-up but was dominated by core executive actors such as party politicians. Other telecommunications firms and societal groups have been in weaker positions than NTT in terms of resources, such as funds and lobbying power.

A group of party politicians has retained the key decision-making position in Japan's ICT sector. In the 1980s and 1990s key decisions were taken by party politicians outside the Cabinet; some of them sought the possibility of getting benefit through regulation and their influence on civil servants and the former state corporation. Party politicians outside the Cabinet exercised their power through the party machine such as the LDP's PARC Division. Their power was based on the oversight processes of these bodies, their legitimacy as members of the Diet (i.e. representatives elected by their constituencies), internal seniority (many of them had experience in the government ministry as Cabinet ministers and/or parliamentary vice-ministers), and the LDP's internal tradition (internal examination was regarded as a precondition for governmental legislation) (I'io 2007: 87–8, 99–102). The fact that their legitimacy was not based on formal institutions including law but on informal custom indicates that the foundation of their legitimacy was not established but unstable. Also, the informal nature of their legitimacy made their approach to regulatory policies discretionary rather than rule-based.

The efforts to enhance the powers of Cabinet ministers by both LDP and DPJ administrations have significantly changed this landscape. The replacement of the parliamentary vice-ministers by the new *Seimu sanyaku* system by the Keizo Obuchi government (1998–2000) can be regarded as a significant effort to enhance the power of Cabinet ministers (Neary 2002: 126–7; I'io 2007: 196). The Koizumi government further enhanced the power of Cabinet ministers through several measures, including making their tenure longer together with stopping frequent Cabinet reshuffles; establishing a system of selecting the *Seimu sanyaku*; and obtaining Cabinet ministers' endorsement before selecting senior vice-ministers and parliamentary secretaries (I'io 2007: 196). The stronger influence of Cabinet ministers became intensified by the change of government to the DPJ in 2009, which declared that parliamentary officials including Cabinet ministers and other *Seimu sanyaku* members would substantially plan and decide policies in government

(DPJ 2009: 5). The resulting rise of Cabinet ministers, whose legitimacy to govern is based on law, undermined the capricious legitimacy and power of party politicians outside the Cabinet. This is a process in which the power of the core executive actors has fluidly changed.

Elsewhere, the power or weakness of civil servants in the ICT sector can be explained by referring to Vogel's (1996: 161–6) claim in addition to the analysis of this chapter. The MPT's 'heavy-handed' approach to regulation based on political discretion rather than law can be understood as a weakness of the MPT rather than a strength, because it would not have to employ coercive means if it had a cooperative relationship with operators. The decline of the MPT's role as a strategic manager and its legal responsibilities transformed the nature of its power together with its increasing expertise. Its approach to the ICT sector has become more rule-based and ex post oriented.

What emerges from the above is that fluid changes of power within the core executive have shaped the power of the state at a macro level. In the ICT sector, the embedded structure in the 1980s and 1990s was a coalition of party politicians (typically the LDP) and civil servants in the government ministry (MPT/MIC); the former oversaw and the latter realised regulatory policies in detail. The power of the state at a macro level draws from the fact that party politicians are elected by their constituencies and bestow their support on civil servants. The new political mode dominated by the Cabinet minister has the potential to change the previous mode's logic of power. The Cabinet minister is appointed by the Prime Minister and has legal authority to control the relevant government ministry. This new structure, however, has yet to be firmly embedded. Whether this situation is intermediate between one set of equilibria and another or is a more permanent condition is a question for future research. Throughout the process the core executive has steered policy-making as the key decision maker with a superior position to its societal counterparts. State power in the sector has changed in response to fluid changes of power within the core executive. It is a more universal form of state power, based on legitimacy through formal institutions, electoral processes and popular support, rather than the intimate relationship between the state and private-sector actors such as the governed interdependence mode (Weiss 1998: 38), which is a type of close relationship between strong public actors and their strong private counterparts, referring to the case of the MITI. The power of the actors has waxed and waned within the group of the core executive. State power at a macro level has asymmetrical dominance to society based on fluid changes of power within the core executive. As a result, the core executive has successfully retained its steering capacity, setting the mode of the ICT sector, even under the more unstable conditions since the 2000s. It has been the core executive's discretionary position to formulate and implement regulatory policies that has enabled it to dominate the ICT sector.

Focusing on the state at a macro level reveals the core executive's asymmetric dominance based on what Marsh et al. (2001: 248) describe as the government's 'unique set of resources – force, legitimacy, state bureaucracy, tax-raising powers and legislation – which are unavailable to other actors'. The complex power changes within the core executive in ICT regulation since the 1980s can be understood as a process of reconstituting the state within ICT regulation, which has resulted in shaping a variation of the regulatory state in Japan. The reconstitution process of the state in ICT regulation presents an example of how the Japanese state has been transformed since the 1980s, in a field where distinctive state transformation has been reported (Sorensen 2004; Smith 2009). The next two chapters explore the case of anti-monopoly regulation as a contrasting case to ICT regulation.

Notes

1 Shigeru Yoshida was the Prime Minister (1946–47, 1948–54) who signed the peace treaty with the Allies in 1951.
2 The Ministry of Economy, Trade and Industry (METI) took over the responsibilities of the Ministry of International Trade and Industry (MITI) in 2001.

5

Piecemeal transformation: anti-monopoly regulation

Anti-monopoly regulation, which is sometimes referred to as 'antitrust' regulation, initially emerged in the US but grew internationally after 1945. This process provoked a contention between indigenous states' traditions and the American approach; the spread occurred 'within a contested cross-cultural public discourse that recognized Americanization as an active element primarily in relation to indigenous factors already constituting capitalist systems' (Freyer 2006: 1). The development of anti-monopoly policies caused a significant transformation in countries outside the US, which assumed before the Second World War that 'anticompetitive collaboration through cartels among business, government, and producers was necessary to preserve social order at home and competitive advantage abroad' (Freyer 2006: 3). This transformation prompted the emergence of anti-monopoly regulators as state actors in countries outside the US. At the same time, because traditional sentiment in favour of state–business collaboration existed in those countries, the introduction of an approach in favour of competition and anti-monopoly regulation was contested.

This book focuses on the Japanese case of this emergent regulation, exploring the response of the state to the specific challenges it presents. A characteristic of the Japanese case includes significant influence from the US; Japan's anti-monopoly institution was designed under the initiative of the SCAP on its establishment in 1947. This direct import from the US provoked a contest with the traditional approach. The subsequent revision of Japan's anti-monopoly regulation in 1953 significantly weakened the system, leaving the responsible JFTC as one of the weaker government organisations until the 1970s.

The second turning point emerged in the form of a legal amendment in 1977, enhancing the JFTC. The subsequent Structural Impediments Initiative (SII) between the governments of Japan and the United States offered a significant turning point for Japan's anti-monopoly policies.[1]

Piecemeal transformation: anti-monopoly regulation   87

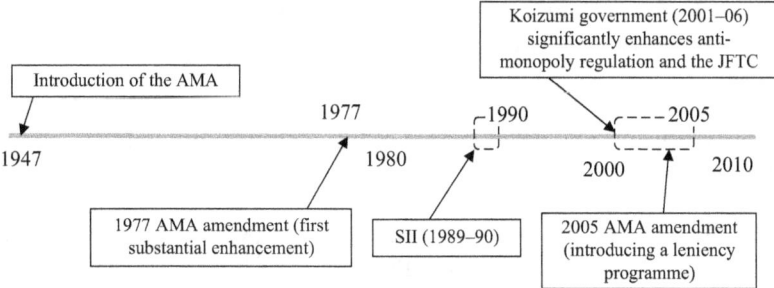

Figure 5.1 Timeline of the development of Japan's anti-monopoly regulation

The impact of the SII resulted in prioritising the enhancement of the JFTC and anti-monopoly regulation (see Figure 5.1).

The transformation of Japan's anti-monopoly regulation has had a gradual impact on the core executive in this field. With its independence of authority, the JFTC has not only fended off party politician intervention but also successfully protected itself against opponents such as other government ministries. The influence of party politicians has concentrated on policy-making processes, typically in the form of endorsing infrequent law amendment bills. More active policy-making after the SII has increased political processes such as legal amendments. The 2009 change of government from the LDP to the DPJ accelerated this tendency, since the DPJ government started assigning new Cabinet ministers responsible for the JFTC.

This transformation has affected the JFTC's status as an independent regulator. As the JFTC strengthened its power and organisation as the responsible agency for anti-monopoly regulation after the 1990s, its independent status has faced challenges such as a demand for more democratic accountability (Beeman 2002: 174) and the decreasing need for protection from its opponents such as other government ministries. Such circumstantial changes have affected state capacity in anti-monopoly regulation. The JFTC has been significantly enhanced in terms of its organisational size and budget since its establishment in 1947 (in particular after 2001 under the LDP's Koizumi government). However, the fact that the number of professionally trained staff is still small could indicate that the commission's professional expertise is insufficient.

This chapter examines Japan's anti-monopoly regulation since the 1980s. The next section reveals how anti-monopoly regulation emerged and developed in Japan. The review starts with the JFTC's establishment in 1947, and pays attention to the period after the SII between 1989 and 1990. How the core executive actors transformed their power and roles is explored in the following section. Together with the next chapter, this chapter explores how the Japanese state has responded to the challenges of governance in anti-monopoly regulation.

The emergence and development of Japan's anti-monopoly regulation

The introduction of the Anti-monopoly Act (AMA) (*Dokusenkinshihō*) in 1947, officially the Act on the Prohibition of Private Monopolisation and Maintenance of Fair Trade, which was originally drafted by the SCAP as an improved version of the US antitrust laws, launched Japan's anti-monopoly regulation (Yamamura 1967: 9; Schaede 2000: 14).[2] This new competition framework was not regarded as embedded by commentators such as Hadley (1970: 107–8),[3] who states that almost all Japanese government officials, excluding those of the JFTC, appeared to consider that economies of scale should continue indefinitely, partly because they did not have the empirical economics studies to refute this idea and partly because they had no 'antitrust tradition'. Yamamura (1967: 173) also argues that the SCAP's economic policies, including the formulation of the AMA, ignored their potential impact on economic recovery and growth. It was therefore unsurprising that the AMA faced amendment pressures after its enactment in 1947 (Hadley 1970: 197; Schaede 2000: 78). The Treaty of Peace with Japan (the Treaty of San Francisco) in 1951 and the abolition of the SCAP were significant turning points for the AMA. The amendment to the AMA in 1953 substantially changed the nature of the 1947 AMA, the key points of which are summarised in Table 5.1.[4]

Yoshikawa (1983: 496) draws attention to the fact that until 1974, the JFTC's major weakness was its lack of support from party politicians including those of the LDP; the LDP supported the MITI during its major disputes with the JFTC:

> For example, when the FTC persistently refused to approve the merger plan of Yawata Steel and Fuji Steel in 1968, the LDP attacked the FTC. It even threatened to 'reorganize' the Commission. Unlike most of the other administrative agencies, the FTC, taking as a model the independent administrative agencies in the United States, is granted status and authority independent of the Cabinet, and the Commissioners enjoy guarantees against discharge and reduction of salary. In advocating the reorganization of the FTC, influential members of the LDP declared that such provisions were unconstitutional since they violated Article 65 of the Constitution which provides that executive power rests with the Cabinet. It was under such political pressure that the merger was eventually approved by the FTC with certain changes in the original plan. (Yoshikawa 1983: 496–7)

Table 5.1 The key points of the 1953 AMA amendment

1. **Admission of recession and rationalisation cartels**
   Cartels and other collusive activities became legal in those cases where the competent minister deemed it necessary on the grounds of averting a recession or for the purpose of rationalisation. Any competent ministry, as well as any industry group, might initiate the action, though when it was initiated by an industrial group, concurrence of the competent ministry was required. In either case the consent of the JFTC was also required.
2. **Relaxation of stockholding regulation**
   According to the amended Articles 10 to 16, interlocking directorship, mergers and mutual stockholding became legal, except when they conflicted with Article 9 (prohibition of holding companies) or Article 2 (limitation of stockholding by a financial institution), and when the result of these activities did not limit competition in a market substantially.
3. **Redefinition of unfair competition**
   Unfair competition and the catch-all clause of the original Article 2-7, which read in part lessening of 'competition which is contrary to the public interest', were amended to apply only in six specified cases of 'unfair business practices,' as indicated in the amended Article 2-7.
4. **Admission of retail price maintenance**
   Article 24-2 permitted an entrepreneur 'who produces or sells a commodity which is designated by the JFTC and the identical quality of which can be easily recognised' to maintain retail prices provided that these commodities were 'not used daily by the general consumer'.
5. **Modification of the definition of unreasonable restraint of trade**
   The original Article 4, which forbade entrepreneurs from entering into agreements with other entrepreneurs on prices and output, restraint of technology and investment, was eliminated. The reason was that Article 3, which states that 'no entrepreneur shall effect private monopolisation or shall undertake any unreasonable restraint of trade', covered the areas that came under Article 4 previously.
6. **Total elimination of two articles**
   Article 5 (prohibiting the establishment of or becoming a party to a monopolistic organisation) and Article 8 (prevention of substantial disparities in bargaining power) were completely deleted from the Act.
7. **Abolition of the Trade Association Act**
   The Trade Association Act, which significantly restricted the activities of trade associations, was abolished. Its three clauses, which specified illegal activities on the party of trade associations in the amended Trade Association Act of 1952, were incorporated into the AMA.

Source: Yamamura 1967: 57.

This trend to suppress the impact of anti-monopoly regulation was substantially countered by the 1977 AMA amendment, which was the first amendment to strengthen the statute since its enactment in 1947 (Sanekata 1986: 393; Schaede 2000: 78–97).

The 1977 AMA amendment originated from the economic turmoil of the oil crisis in 1973, which prompted significant inflation in Japan; it raised wholesale prices by 40 per cent and consumer prices by more than 30 per cent (Schaede 2000: 97). Private firms exploited this opportunity by increasing their profits through restricting production and holding back products until they could be sold at higher prices through collusion (Schaede 2000: 98). The JFTC addressed this situation by proceeding against sixty-six cases in 1973 and fifty-eight cases in 1974[5] as AMA breaches, the highest since its establishment in 1947. This period also saw the first criminal cartel case since the end of the SCAP administration in 1952: the oil cartel case (Schaede 2000: 99).[6] This case, whose chronological detail is shown in Table 5.2, was an incident in which twelve petroleum companies were prosecuted for collusion as an AMA breach by the JFTC in 1974 and found guilty by the Supreme Court in 1984. Corporate behaviour in this period, including this cartel case which was in court and therefore in the media for years and generated an immediate impact on the revision of the AMA, galvanised public demand for enhancing the AMA (Sanekata 1986: 393; Schaede 2000: 100).

The JFTC revealed its proposals for a possible AMA amendment in early 1974, the major points of which were as follows (Yoshikawa 1983: 499; Schaede 2000: 101):

- to empower the JFTC to order the break-up of dominant firms, oligopolies or conglomerates;
- to abolish price cartels;
- to increase penalty provisions such that a criminal fine was a meaningful threat, and to introduce a new administrative surcharge (*Kachōkin*) to cream off the profits made by companies over the duration of a cartel;
- to lower the requirements of what constitutes 'sufficient evidence' for a cartel to be prosecuted;
- to strengthen disclosure and accounting rules for large firms, including cost data;
- to strengthen the rules on unfair trade restrictions; and
- to limit stockholdings in one corporation by banks and trading companies.

Although the proposals were not immediately taken seriously by the ruling LDP, they were picked up by Prime Minister Takeo Miki (1974–76) as a tool to regain popular support (Sanekata 1986: 94).

Table 5.2 The chronological sequence of the oil cartel case

1960s–1971	The PF (Petroleum Federation: *Sekiyu ren'mei*), the leading trade association of Japan's petroleum industry, repeatedly received cease-and-desist orders from the JFTC.
November 1972	The PF's 'Demand and Supply Committee' (*Jukyū i'inkai*) established crude oil processing quotas for all members.
May–November 1973	Twelve companies met five times in the PF's conference room and agreed on price increases in all of the various categories of oil (light, heavy, etc.).
May 1973	Most of the twelve arranged for a 'gasoline *Kachōkai*' (gasoline division chiefs meeting) and agreed on monthly sales restrictions (i.e. volume quotas) for each cartel member in each region of Japan to support the price agreement.
February 1974	The JFTC filed criminal charges against the PF, twelve companies and their seventeen top representatives.
May 1974	The Tokyo Police Department began collecting evidence from the companies and the trade association.
1980	The Tokyo High Court acquitted the PF but held that the twelve oil companies and their executives were guilty of price fixing. It sentenced the executives to from four to ten months' imprisonment (although the sentences were suspended) and imposed fines ranging from 1,500,000 to 2,500,000 yen.
1984	The Supreme Court supported most of the verdicts of the Tokyo High Court.

Source: Yoshikawa 1983: 499; Schaede 2000: 99–100.
Note: In Sanekata's (1986: 382) assessment: 'The JFTC won on theory but lost on enforcement.'

When Miki took over the premiership, the LDP's reputation had been significantly damaged by the scandals of his predecessor, Kakuei Tanaka (Sanekata 1986: 394; Schaede 2000: 101). The new Prime Minister promised a revision of the AMA as well as swift clean-up action in his inauguration speech (Schaede 2000: 101). According to Schaede (2000: 102), the debate on the AMA amendment can be characterised by the confrontation from 1975 to 1977 between LDP politicians lobbied by the MITI and its business allies which were trying to dilute the JFTC's proposals, and the opposition group composed of opposition parties, consumer groups, and economics and law academics. In 1977 the amendment bill was finally adopted under the strong initiative of then Prime Minister Takeo Fukuda in the Diet. This amendment significantly enhanced the AMA.

A key actor to emerge in 1975 during the process of the 1977 AMA amendment was the LDP's AMA Examination Committee (Hayashi 2008: 314). Located within the LDP's PARC, the impact of the AMA Examination Committee can be compared to the PARC's other divisions (*Bukai*). The interests and arguments represented by LDP politicians became the LDP's view through the process of debating policy issues in the committee; its function was similar to the PARC's divisions (Inoguchi and Iwai 1987: 99). The committee exercised its power typically by examining AMA amendment bills; its examination was vital for bills to be put before the Diet between the 1980s and 2000s.

The LDP's AMA Examination Committee was also the arena where Sadanori Yamanaka (1921–2004) emerged as a key figure in anti-monopoly regulation. The relationship between the JFTC and the ruling parties in the 1980s and 1990s can be described as a support network that surrounded him. Having first been elected to membership of the Diet in 1953, he had a long career in politics, affording him the opportunity to exert significant influence over the LDP. In the field of anti-monopoly policies, he was chairman of the LDP's AMA Examination Committee between the 1980s and 2000s (The House of Representatives 2004; interview with an LDP member of the House of Representatives). The informal nature of Yamanaka's influence makes it a feature that is difficult to identify in the official documents. Even his memorial address offered only a brief reference to his contribution to anti-monopoly regulation:

> Since the period of the Miki Cabinet in 1974 as the Anti-monopoly Act Examination Committee Chairman he was involved with the Anti-monopoly Act amendment whose enhancement was urgent for establishing the fundamental rule of a liberal economic society, tirelessly addressed opposing views in and outside the LDP, continued pursuing an agreement, finally led the amendment bill to be unanimously adopted, and opened a new era in Japan's anti-monopoly policy. (The House of Representatives 2004)

In the process of the 1977 AMA amendment, Yamanaka chaired the committee and led the debate within it; he worked hard on the amendment bills, addressing most of the major issues raised by the bill, and personally lobbied major politicians opposing it (Hayashi 2008: 335–6). On the day before the session of the committee, he often studied issues relating to the bill all night with a JFTC official as part of his commitment to seeking a consensus (Hayashi 2008: 335–6). It was claimed that the result of debates within his AMA Examination Committee became the basis on which the government's bill on the AMA amendment was shaped (Hayashi 2008: 318).

Yamanaka's dominance was not continuous. His appointment as the MITI minister led to his resignation as the chairman of the AMA Examination Committee and so sidelined his role in anti-monopoly regulation. His revival as the AMA Examination Committee chairman did not last long, as Yamanaka's failure in the general election in January 1990 kept him out of politics until 1993. His return to politics following the 1993 general election revived his influence in anti-monopoly regulation. He retained this influence until 2004 when he died in the middle of his tenure as chairman (Shiozaki 2013a, 2013b).

Yamanaka's approach was a variation of *Zoku gi'in*'s (Inoguchi and Iwai 1987); his key tools of power were specialist knowledge obtained through experience and the PARC. As a witness, Hayashi (2008) reports Yamanaka's efforts to understand issues related to anti-monopoly regulation and the AMA. This shaped the foundation through which Yamanaka was able to persuade opposing LDP politicians during the process of the 1977 AMA amendment. Another key tool was his position as the chairman of the AMA Examination Committee. He presided over the meetings of the committee. This position conferred on him the power to select and shape the policy agenda, lead debates, persuade opponents and seek out consensus. The importance of the post of chairman is shown by the fact that the influence of Yamanaka significantly decreased in the mid-1980s when he was out of the AMA Examination Committee and not politically active (interview with a former secretary general, JFTC). As the interviews below reveal, Yamanaka usually exercised his power through choosing policy agendas; he was informally briefed by JFTC officials on possible policy issues in anti-monopoly regulation. His endorsement in the informal briefing was crucial; without it, the issue could be rejected in the committee. Elsewhere, official sessions of the AMA Examination Committee also became the arena for choosing a policy agenda when Yamanaka wanted debates in the committee.

Yamanaka and the AMA Examination Committee retained their positions as key consensus makers on major issues in anti-monopoly regulation, such as important legal amendments. Until his death in 2004, the LDP's AMA Examination Committee, which was called the 'Yamanaka Committee', acted as the central arena for political coordination on anti-monopoly regulation. This framework was retained after Yamanaka's death. The committee continued to work as a central policy-making arena within anti-monopoly regulation until the 2009 change of government.

As the first substantial measure to enhance the AMA, the 1977 amendment, whose major points are summarised in Table 5.3, was a significant event in the history of Japan's competition policies and regulation, together with the turmoil of the 1970s. Whether or not this had a direct impact on the course of competition policies and regulation is

Table 5.3 The key points of the 1977 AMA amendment

1. **Eliminating 'monopolistic conditions' (Article 8-4)**
   The newly introduced Article 8-4 empowers the JFTC to order firm(s) in 'monopolistic conditions' to 'effect partial transfer of business or take other measures necessary for recovering competition in respect of the commodity or service' concerned.
2. **Imposing surcharges on illegal cartels (Articles 7-2 and 8-3)**
   The JFTC is empowered to levy a surcharge upon firms or trade associations that engage in unreasonable restraint of trade or conclude an international agreement or contract constituting unreasonable restraint of trade, which pertains to the price of a particular commodity or service, or affects the price by limiting the supply of the commodity or service in question. The amount of the surcharge is prescribed to be one half of the sum equivalent to 3 per cent of the amount of sales realised by the firms concerned during the period that the activity continued (4 per cent in the case of a manufacturing business, 2 per cent in the case of a retail business, and 1 per cent in the case of a wholesale business).
3. **Requiring reports on parallel price increases**
   The JFTC is authorised to ask for a report concerning 'alignmental price increases', which have the potential of cartels, from the firms concerned, under certain conditions meticulously defined:
   1. If such a price increase has occurred in an industrial sector where the total value of the commodity or service supplied during a defined one-year period exceeds 30 billion yen.
   2. If the total volume of the commodity or services supplied by the three largest suppliers constitutes more than 70 per cent of the total volume of the commodity or service supplied by the entire industrial sector.
   3. If two or more of the five largest entrepreneurs in that industrial sector (including the largest) have increased the price at the same or a similar rate during a three-month period.
4. **Restriction on shareholding by large corporations (Article 9-2)**
   Any large corporation, having capital of 10 billion yen or more or net assets of 30 billion yen or more, shall not acquire or hold shares in any domestic corporation if the aggregated acquisition price of all the shares in domestic corporations held by it exceeds the amount of its paid-in capital or the amount of its net asset, whichever is greater.

Source: Yoshikawa 1983: 500–2.
Note: The definitions of 'monopolistic conditions' are the following in summary, according to Article 2 Paragraph 7:
1. In the industrial sector, when the total value of a particular commodity or other commodities having a similar function or a particular service supplied in Japan during the last one-year period exceeds 50 billion yen, when the market share of an entrepreneur exceeds 50 per cent or when the total of the market shares of two entrepreneurs exceeds 75 per cent.
2. Circumstances exist under which other entrepreneurs have extreme difficulty in entering the market.
3. When, over a considerable period of time, there has been a remarkable increase in prices, or little reduction thereof, in light of the fluctuation of supply and demand and the costs of supplying the particular commodity or service, and entrepreneurs have acquired profits greatly exceeding 'average' rates of profit or expended sales and general administration expenses much greater than 'average' sales and general administration expenses.

a different question. Indeed, they encountered rigid resistance and did not significantly develop in the 1980s (Yoshikawa 1983: 503–4; Sanekata 1986: 388–91; Tsuruta 1997: 139–41; Schaede 2000: 103–6; Uesugi 2007: 122–38). The JFTC utilised the authority conferred on it by the 1977 AMA amendment 'to pursue administrative compliance rather than the more activist enforcement', epitomised by the oil cartel case (Freyer 2006: 203). According to Professor Hidekatsu Hirabayashi, a former JFTC commissioner: 'It turned out to be ineffective, except [the] surcharge system, because the amendment became too much a political issue' (and its detail was not elaborated) (Freyer 2006: 203). Enforcement by the JFTC in the 1980s can be described as law enforcement without impact (Uesugi 2007: 122–3). It tended to be administrative guidance oriented and lacked transparency; such an approach created no judicial precedent and it proved difficult to show actual examples of AMA breaches (Tsuruta 1997: 154).

Significant turning points in anti-monopoly regulation can be seen first in telecommunications liberalisation in 1985 and secondly in the SII. Telecommunications liberalisation was identified as a significant event by a retired senior JFTC civil servant. According to him, the JFTC, which had concentrated on enforcement of the AMA, was inspired by this liberalisation to get involved in policy issues:

> The JFTC didn't deal with policy issues so much; [on policy issues] it rather was compelled by other government organisations, like 'please make an AMA exemption law'; policy issues relevant to the JFTC tended to weaken the AMA and competition policies before the 1985 telecommunications liberalisation. Things that emerged after Mr Nakasone's telecommunications liberalisation in the 1980s were opposite [to such previous trends] and the policy debate was launched to strengthen the AMA ... An example of such things was the issue of NTT and telecommunications ... As far as I remember telecommunication liberalisation in the 1980s was the first time for the JFTC to pick up or get interested in policy issues. (interview with a retired JFTC senior civil servant)

The JFTC's interest in the 1985 telecommunications regulatory reform can also be found in a senior official's comment in the Diet: 'We recognise the introduction of competition in telecommunications and expect efficient and rational development there ... we consider these three bills [for telecommunications regulatory reform] significant from the viewpoint of competition policy' (The House of Representatives 1984b). This disjuncture between the JFTC's previous approach focusing on law enforcement and more latterly focusing on competition policy development became evident when the JFTC was involved with the second event: the SII.

Commentators agree that the impact of the SII created a significant disjuncture in Japan's anti-monopoly regulation (Tsuruta 1997: 149–50; Freyer 2006: 203, 216; Uesugi 2007: 146). Morita (1991: 800–2) summarises the proposals in its final report of June 1990 (Trade Compliance Center 2012) related to the Japanese government's commitment to anti-monopoly policies as follows:

- Enhance and increase enforcement of the AMA by implementing mechanisms which will:
  - require the JFTC to expand and enhance its investigatory function and increase its proof-collecting capacity against illegal activities. The JFTC will especially target price cartels, supply-restraint cartels, market allocations and group boycotts.
  - increase budgetary allocation to expand the number of personnel involved in violation detection and investigative functions.
  - raise surcharges against cartels in order to deter violations.
  - increase the use of criminal penalties for vicious and serious cases that impact on people's livelihoods and for repeat offenders. In conjunction with this policy, the Minister of Justice publicly requested all the chief prosecutors to cooperate with the JFTC by making available any information they might have uncovered relating to violations of the AMA. The chief prosecutors must also make special efforts to 'vigorously pursue' cases of criminal violation of the AMA.
  - increase the effectiveness of the damage remedy system for individuals provided in Article 25 of the AMA by reducing the plaintiffs' burden of proof for violation and damage. The JFTC, when submitting its opinion, will describe in detail its findings on the violation, the causal relationship between the violation and damage, the amount of damage and the measure used for its calculation. It will also append any necessary data or materials to its opinion.
  - ensure that its administrative guidance 'does not restrict market access or undermine fair competition'.
- Minimise the use of exemptions from the general rules of the AMA and review existing exemptions to ensure that they enhance competition and do not impede imports.
- Take steps to loosen *Keiretsu*,[7] including making a commitment to:
  - strengthen the JFTC's 'monitoring of transactions among members of the same *Keiretsu* groups with cross-shareholding ties to determine whether these relationships impede competition'. The JFTC shall also establish and publish guidelines for the enforcement of the AMA against *Keiretsu*-type group actions.

Violations resulting from cross-shareholding will result in the restriction or divestiture of shares.
• make the *Keiretsu* more open and transparent.
• issue a government policy statement affirming that the Japanese government will take steps to ensure that *Keiretsu* relationships do not impede fair competition and at the same time request the cooperation of the *Keiretsu* firms in achieving this policy.

These measures to enhance anti-monopoly regulation and the JFTC came with structural changes. Freyer (2006: 203–12) reports the change in Japan's traditional anti-monopoly approach as a result of the SII and the collapse of the Japanese asset bubble.[8] He highlights the LDP's need to form a coalition with smaller political parties such as the Social Democratic Party of Japan (SDPJ) and New Party *Sakigake* between 1994 and 1998 as a major reason why the LDP embraced deregulation and anti-monopoly measures, a different approach from that in the early 1980s.

The major opponents to anti-monopoly regulation also changed their views in this period. In the mid-1990s one of the largest business groups, *Keidanren*, stopped its opposition to the SII and publicised a deregulation programme that envisioned a capitalist market order (Freyer 2006: 203–4). This programme, set out in *Keidanren*'s 'Deregulation Promotion Plan', proposed the rigorous enforcement of the AMA, together with substantial deregulation in industrial sectors (Freyer 2006: 204–5). Two major factors prompted this change of opinion. First, *Keidanren* acknowledged through their market data that a significant number of consumers were dissatisfied with higher domestic prices resulting from protectionist policies in the prolonged recession of the 1990s (Freyer 2006: 206). Second, many larger multinational firms competing in global markets perceived that their profitability was constrained by subsidising their uncompetitive counterparts in protected sectors (Freyer 2006: 206). Indeed, '*Keidanren*'s deregulation reforms potentially benefited large firms competing in a global market the most' (Freyer 2006: 205).

The MITI, which had been an active advocate of business, also changed its standpoint. Its official pronouncements urged 'the FCT's vigorous enforcement of competition law' (Freyer 2006: 204). According to Freyer (2006: 206–7), a significant proportion of MITI officials argued for the MITI's shift from industrial policy to those focusing on deregulation, the reform of existing systems and the promotion of competition, although its internal critics retained their nostalgic sentiment for the old protectionist regime. This change on the part of *Keidanren* and the MITI coincided with the emergent role of lawyers (Freyer 2006: 207). Previously, Japan's private firms had little reason to seek advice from lawyers because they generally turned first to government officials for guidance (see Johnson 1982; Freyer 2006: 207). This traditional approach changed by the late 1980s; many large firms began consulting lawyers about industrial policy and the AMA, even before approaching civil servants. Freyer (2006: 208) suggests that this was because 'large multinational corporations wanted greater independence from industrial policy in order to operate efficiently in the competitive global market'. These corporate changes led in the 1990s to the expansion of the JFTC through its organisational upgrade and the relaxation of the holding company prohibition.

Strengthening the JFTC's enforcement structure became symbolically and practically important during the SII's implementation after 1989. Three significant actors supported this theme: the US government (the Department of Justice Antitrust Division), *Keidanren* and the ruling coalition of the day including the LDP (Freyer 2006: 216). The expansion of the JFTC was evidenced in the form of its upgrading. Promoting the rank of the JFTC senior staff (e.g. the secretary general from bureau chief level to vice-minister level) substantially enhanced the JFTC's negotiating power in bureaucracy, as well as its enforcement capacity (Tsuruta 1997: 182; Freyer 2006: 218).

Another significant issue emerged in relation to the relaxation of the holding company prohibition. Japan was unusual in supporting an outright ban on holding companies by Article 9 of the AMA as a measure to prevent the revival of the *Zaibatsu*,[9] despite their being permitted by other major industrial countries (Tsuruta 1997: 180; Freyer 2006: 217). However, this issue was domestically contentious. *Keidanren* and the MITI supported the relaxation, while a group of party politicians, including the SDPJ, opposed it (Freyer 2006: 223–4; Uesugi 2007: 200). The fact that this regulation prohibited all holding companies regardless of whether there was any actual anti-competitive behaviour implies that its nature was ex ante. Therefore, relaxing the holding company prohibition could be interpreted as a retreat from ex ante regulation.

The adoption of these two measures by the Diet is evidence of how much Japan's anti-monopoly policies have developed. They shifted from ex ante oriented to ex post oriented, focusing on AMA enforcement by the JFTC. The 2000s sustained this trend, as Prime Minister Jun'ichirō Koizumi (2001–06) pledged in his policy speech in May 2001 'to strengthen the organisation of the Fair Trade Commission and establish competition policies suitable for the twenty-first century'.

The impact of the Koizumi government was evident in the 2000s. One of the most significant events in anti-monopoly regulation during this period was the introduction of a leniency programme for surcharges in 2006[10] by the AMA amendment in 2005 (Table 5.4), together with the rise of surcharge rates. Japan's leniency programme is linked to the sur-

Table 5.4 The key points of the amendment to the AMA in 2005

1. **Surcharge rates increase**
   Surcharge rates imposed on AMA violators were increased from 6 per cent to 10 per cent of the related turnover for the large-sized enterprises, and the application of 50 per cent higher rates to repeat offenders was authorised.
2. **The awarding of criminal investigation authority to the JFTC**
   The JFTC was authorised to conduct criminal investigations in order to address serious violations in a more strict and effective manner, which was expected to enable the JFTC to file criminal accusations much more aggressively.
3. **The introduction of a leniency programme for surcharges (see note [??])**
4. **The transformation of the complaints system (Shinpan seido)**
   The JFTC's complaints system changed from a process whereby accused firms had an opportunity to submit their claims in writing before the JFTC's decision to one in which firms can file complaints about the JFTC's actions (typically the issuing cease-and-desist orders) afterwards.

Source: Takeshima 2007.
Note: Kazuhiko Takeshima was the JFTC chairman between July 2002 and September 2012. He spent most of his career in the Ministry of Finance after joining the ministry in 1965.

charge system, because its criminal law does not usually tolerate leniency in this manner (OECD 2004: 73). The introduction of a leniency system was expected to enhance the capacity of the JFTC by giving incentives to those involved in cartels to report to the JFTC. The actual number of applications in Table 5.5 suggests that this expectation was correct. The staff and budget of the JFTC discernibly grew in this period, as Table 5.6 and Figure 5.2 reveal. For example, the JFTC's budget grew by more than 1 million yen between 2001 and 2002 from 6,035,756,000 yen to 7,686,000,000 yen.

The governing framework within Japan's anti-monopoly regulation has a similar set of characteristics to that of ICT regulation. Indeed, at a broader policy level the JFTC worked within the framework of Japan's established public policy-making (Beeman 2002: 174). Until the 2009

Table 5.5 The number of applications to the leniency programme

Financial year (1 April–31 March)	2005	2006	2007	2008	2009	2010	2011	2012	2013	2014	Total
Number of applications	26	79	74	85	85	131	143	102	50	61	836

Source: JFTC 2011a, 2015a.

Table 5.6 The JFTC's staff numbers and budget

Financial year	Number of staff	Budget (mill. yen)	Financial year	Number of staff	Budget (mill. yen)
1947	284	10	1982	425	2,660
1948	327	36	1983	427	2,667
1949	323	42	1984	431	2,800
1950	316	55	1985	432	2,882
1951	305	65	1986	436	3,019
1952	240	72	1987	440	3,147
1953	237	94	1988	445	3,249
1954	237	95	1989	461	3,521
1955	237	98	1990	474	3,759
1956	237	102	1991	478	4,083
1957	237	102	1992	484	4,407
1958	237	108	1993	493	4,624
1959	237	123	1994	506	5,244
1960	238	122	1995	520	5,239
1961	245	145	1996	534	5,382
1962	245	162	1997	545	5,561
1963	251	186	1998	552	5,622
1964	266	222	1999	558	5,781
1965	277	259	2000	564	5,902
1966	307	306	2001	571	6,036
1967	336	359	2002	607	7,686
1968	341	415	2003	643	7,853
1969	346	470	2004	672	7,819
1970	351	572	2005	706	8,131
1971	356	653	2006	737	8,338
1972	358	815	2007	765	8,416
1973	363	970	2008	795	8,682
1974	369	1,131	2009	779	8,446
1975	392	1,557	2010	791	8,962
1976	399	1,795	2011	799	8,915
1977	405	1,963	2012	799	8,742
1978	416	2,199	2013	823	8,802
1979	422	2,315	2014	830	11,321
1980	422	2,393	2015	838	10,739
1981	423	2,493	2016	840	10,994

Source: JFTC 2011b, 2013a, 2013b, 2015b, 2015c

change of government, the key actor in shaping major decisions was the ruling party; the LDP's AMA Examination Committee had a significant role within the PARC. The committee offered an arena where a group of party politicians involved in issues related to anti-monopoly regula-

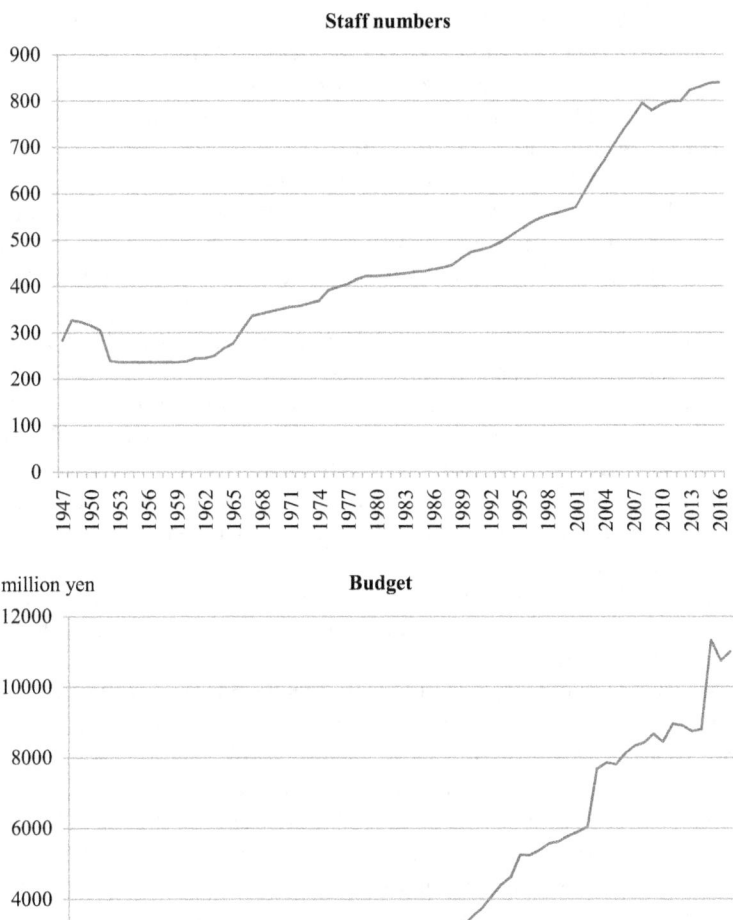

Figure 5.2 The JFTC's staff numbers and budget
Source: JFTC 2011b, 2013a, 2013b, 2015b, 2015c

tion such as Yamanaka shaped key decisions. In the 1990s the existence of the LDP-led Coalition government enabled coalition partners such as the SDPJ and their politicians to significantly influence policy-making processes, typically through negotiation with the PARC; for example, the negotiation between the LDP's PARC and its SDPJ counterpart was key in shaping both a consensus and the subsequent relaxation of holding company regulation in 1997 (Oikawa 1999: 256–305). Under the LDP/LDP-led Coalition governments, policy issues in anti-monopoly regulation such as AMA amendments were shaped within this framework, characterised by the significant influence of ruling parties' internal processes. The change of government in 2009 dismantled the framework by replacing the LDP and its coalition partner with the DPJ and its partners.

In addition to the group of politicians, the JFTC has been another major state actor. The period between the 1980s and 2000s saw the AMA and the JFTC significantly, if intermittently, enhanced in terms of authority and organisational scale. Although the AMA was first strengthened through its 1977 amendment, observers highlight the SII; its impact on Japan's anti-monopoly regime since the 1990s was regarded as significant by both US and Japanese anti-monopoly authorities with the following assessment: 'the FTC's enforcement record (since the 1990s) may be seen as relatively effective, though the paucity of private actions was a major problem in Japan' (Freyer 2006: 243). The commission's steady organisational development, shown in Table 5.6, indicates its significant quantitative expansion.

The development of Japan's anti-monopoly regulation reviewed in this section reveals a piecemeal institutional growth of the field with the JFTC's gradual organisational expansion. The JFTC's position as a rare independent regulator is formally meant to keep it at arm's length from political decision-making. At the same time, the Constitution of Japan requires government organisations including the JFTC to be under the control of the Cabinet through the provision of Article 65: 'Executive power shall be vested in the Cabinet'. Amendments to the AMA are put before the scrutiny of the Diet, like other legal amendments. These complicated circumstances surrounding the JFTC and anti-monopoly regulation offer a contrast to the case of ICT, where a government ministry headed by a Cabinet minister administers and regulates the sector.

Power relations within anti-monopoly regulation have gradually changed. Anti-monopoly regulation saw no significant change of actors until 2009. The MITI and *Keidanren* opposed stronger anti-monopoly regulation. The JFTC has been the key body responsible for implementing anti-monopoly regulation. Transformation emerged as the MITI and *Keidanren* changed their views and the JFTC was strengthened; this resulted in enhanced anti-monopoly regulation during the early 1990, when debates on the SII emerged. Party politicians retained their power and shaped key decisions in relation to the views of relevant parties such as the JFTC and *Keidanren*.

The actors and structures highlighted above did not change until the 2009 change of government. Similarly, the nature of state power in anti-monopoly regulation remained the same. However, the growth of the

JFTC as an anti-monopoly regulator led to the gradual enhancement of state power in anti-monopoly regulation within the traditional framework. This transformation was significantly inspired by the SII (Tsuruta 1997: 149–50; Freyer 2006: 203, 216; Uesugi 2007: 146). The disjuncture resulting from the SII launched a transformative process that continues to the present day. Taking account of the significant impact of this event, the next section focuses on the transformative relationships between the core executive actors in anti-monopoly regulation by analysing how they have changed their roles and power through their adaptation to challenges after the SII.

Independence and political control: the relationship within the core executive

The LDP/LDP-led Coalition governments

Japan's anti-monopoly regulation can be characterised by its relationship with politics. The JFTC is formally independent of politics, as the AMA (Article 28) stipulates that: 'the Chairman and Commissioners of the Fair Trade Commission shall perform their authority independently'. Often called 'the independence of authority', this provision ensures the independent investigation of each anti-monopoly case, free from interventions including those from party politicians and Cabinet ministers (interview with a retired JFTC senior civil servant). In return, what the interviews reveal is an indifference to anti-monopoly policies and the JFTC among party politicians. At the same time, the JFTC is under the supervision of the Cabinet as an executive organisation pursuant to the Constitution of Japan, Article 65. In practice, the JFTC has informally been shaped by political pressures as the evidence from the interviews reveals.

The relationship between party politicians and the JFTC under the LDP/LDP-led Coalition governments before 2009 was summarised by a JFTC civil servant:

> Before the DPJ government, since the AMA was under independent implementation, the JFTC was an independent administrative commission, and the independence of its authority was ensured, basically; I don't know the issues discussed behind closed doors but formally, politicians intervened only in legal amendments, when the JFTC contacted politicians. Of course, the chief Cabinet secretaries were responsible for the JFTC, but they weren't regularly briefed on what's going on in the JFTC. (interview with a JFTC civil servant)

Therefore, the JFTC did not contact party politicians when it had no legal amendments. In the *Showa* period (1926–89), when comparatively few substantial AMA amendments emerged, 'the Fair Trade Commission wasn't close to the ruling parties' (interview with a JFTC senior civil servant).

The relationship between the JFTC and the ruling parties in the 1980s and 1990s can be described as a network surrounding Yamanaka; almost all the interviewees, both within and outside the core executive, referred to him as crucial in terms of the relationship between the JFTC and party politicians in this period. Anti-monopoly policies in the 1980s and 1990s were formulated in the circle surrounding Yamanaka; according to a retired senior civil servant: 'For example, when we amended law, or raised surcharges through the amendment, or likewise, things were debated in the Examination Committee. Of course, beforehand we frequently briefed Chairman Yamanaka and let him understand the issue well' (interview with a retired senior civil servant). This account describes how crucial Yamanaka was in the policy-making process. Almost all the accounts obtained through interviews endorsed this view. For example, a law professor specialising in the AMA who had a long relationship with the JFTC stated:

> In the past, the LDP had the committee named the AMA Examination Committee and the politician named Sadanori Yamanaka was there. The JFTC said he was the 'don' for good or bad, and if he said 'yes', things worked very smoothly. But it is said that since his death no similar figure has emerged. (interview with a law professor)

This view is confirmed by another account by a retired senior civil servant:

> Before that [the emergence of the Koizumi government in 2001], a group of specialised politicians in the AMA surrounding Mr Yamanaka, about ten people, led and decided, like, how far the JFTC could go if it was allowed to move in one way; it seemed that not the general public but only that group was interested in the JFTC's policy. (interview with a retired JFTC senior civil servant)

The nature of Yamanaka's role is described as that of a mentor rather than a key man by a retired JFTC senior civil servant:

> Other executive organisations have to generate policies from time to time and in these processes somebody like a key man probably exists. In the case of the JFTC, it generates new issues not frequently but only at key turning points. Enforcing the AMA requires no key man, particularly if the

Piecemeal transformation: anti-monopoly regulation 105

independence of authority is considered. So, when the JFTC sometimes launches something, it needed to find a mentor, who was honourable Mr Yamanaka. (interview with a retired JFTC senior civil servant)

The description 'mentor' implies that Yamanaka did not closely cooperate with the JFTC but supported it at arm's length. This retired official further elaborated his account by employing a comparison between the JFTC and other government ministries:

> In an extreme description, the JFTC needs only such a man. Well, the AMA Examination Committee chairman was there, and he said 'OK, I'll do that' in preliminary briefings, then everything's all right. In this way, the JFTC probably doesn't need a key man equivalent to other government organisations. (interview with a retired JFTC senior civil servant)

These accounts highlight the nature of the relationship between the JFTC and party politicians. Focusing on AMA enforcement, the JFTC has not had a strong relationship with party politicians. It has mainly contacted party politicians in the process of AMA amendments. Such circumstances have created a weak relationship with politicians, compensated for by the relationship with Yamanaka. This observation is backed by a comment from a retired JFTC senior civil servant: 'If the JFTC didn't have people like Mr Yamanaka, it may have had to think about establishing a relationship with somebody like a key man, as disturbing interventions from politicians would probably try to stop things sooner or later' (interview with a retired JFTC senior civil servant).

If Yamanaka played such a significant role in policy-making processes, the nature of his role should be a topic of further exploration. The civil servants of the time, namely the period until 2004, expressed a discernibly positive view of Yamanaka, exemplified by the comment from a retired JFTC senior civil servant:

> He [Yamanaka] really thought with confidence how the AMA should be, and rejected things against his own ideas, even if they were from the Prime Minister. He had such resolution, and his presence was very important for the JFTC. If described in an extreme way, when the SII urged the enhancement of law enforcement and anti-monopoly policy-making, things worked well because of him. (interview with a retired JFTC senior civil servant)

A similar view was expressed by another retired JFTC senior civil servant:

> When Yamanaka's Examination Committee worked well, it gave civil

servants a sense of trust. Probably to other government ministry officials too, for he wasn't a mere JFTC sponsor. In short, he happened to be the chairman of the AMA Examination Committee, but wasn't 'the supporter of the JFTC: Sadanori Yamanaka'. He thought of Japan's economy and its people's lives, and happened to address the tax system or anti-monopoly as actual cases. He thought in such a way, at least said so. (interview with a retired senior civil servant)

The perspective of these former civil servants suggests that Yamanaka made decisions based not according to the demands of interest groups behind him but on his own judgement. Indeed, he was powerful enough to realise his own ideas in the political arena; Inoguchi and Iwai (1987: 242–6) depict Yamanaka's significant power through observing the MOF's failed attempt to abolish tax exemption for office automation (OA) facilities. In 1984 the MOF tried to abolish tax exemption for OA products to generate compensatory income to make up for income tax cuts (Inoguchi and Iwai 1987: 243). In its efforts, the MOF created a significant row with Yamanaka, who was also a key member of the LDP Taxation Committee: it tried to push this policy when diabetes prevented Yamanaka from attending relevant policy meetings (Inoguchi and Iwai 1987: 245). The sessions of the LDP Taxation Committee starting in December 1985 saw strong opposition to this new tax on OA products from LDP Diet members, who were lobbied by the OA industry (Inoguchi and Iwai 1987: 245–6). Backed by such a group, Yamanaka strongly opposed the new tax; in the end, the MOF and the core members of the LDP Taxation Committee including Yamanaka prevented its introduction (Inoguchi and Iwai 1987: 246).

Inoguchi and Iwai conclude that in the 1980s, a planned policy project would not come about if a very strong *Zoku gi'in* such as Yamanaka opposed it, even if he was alone. His dominant power was also evident in anti-monopoly regulation, as described by an outside observer: 'The LDP's AMA Examination Committee was a very mysterious organisation; it's only an organisation under the PARC, but under Mr Yamanaka's dictatorial influence ... Mr Yamanaka dictatorially decided AMA [related affairs] during the period of the Yamanaka Examination Committee' (interview with a *Keidanren* official). These accounts reveal the impact of Yamanaka's influence. His power drew in part from his seniority in the LDP and his long experience and expertise in the anti-monopoly field. Much of his power stemmed from his personal position. However, what allowed him to exercise his power was his internal position in the LDP and the LDP's status as the ruling party. The nature of Yamanaka's power was generated by his personal assets (experience, expertise, character, relationships with other politicians) as well as structural elements (his position as chairman of the AMA Examination Committee, and the LDP's position as the ruling party). It was a product of conflation between agency and structure.

In contrast to Yamanaka's strong power and influence, party politicians formally responsible for the JFTC did not exercise a significant influence over the JFTC and anti-monopoly regulation under the LDP/LDP-led administrations. The Prime Minister is formally responsible for the JFTC according to the provision of the AMA.[11] The actual responsibilities of the premier were assigned to the chief Cabinet secretary pursuant to the provision of the Act for Establishment of the Cabinet Office.[12] The impact of the chief Cabinet secretaries, who were formally responsible for anti-monopoly policies under the LDP/LDP led-Coalition governments, on policy was limited according to the account offered by interviews. A retired JFTC senior civil servant elaborated on the relationship between the JFTC and the chief Cabinet secretary:

> The relationship between the JFTC and the chief Cabinet secretary wasn't substantial at all ... the law gives the JFTC independence of authority untouchable even to Cabinet ministers; under such circumstances what remained to the Prime Minister and the delegated chief Cabinet secretary were only a few things. First, when the AMA amendment is put before the Diet, the government has to explain the bill in the Diet. The chief Cabinet secretary did that as a Cabinet minister. (interview with a retired JFTC senior civil servant)

The rest of the tasks borne by the chief Cabinet secretary were also ceremonial:

> After the bill is adopted in the Standing Committee, the responsible Cabinet minister stands up and says 'Thank you very much'. And sometimes the adopted bill gets an attached resolution. And usually the Cabinet minister says things like 'taking account of the resolution's intention the government will do its best'. These statements were made by the chief Cabinet secretary. Only a Cabinet minister can do this; the JFTC chairman can't, so the chief Cabinet secretary did such ceremonial, truly ministerial jobs, and said nothing like how some particular cases are or likewise. The chief Cabinet secretary never usually politically intervened in the JFTC's job. This was how things worked under the LDP administration. (interview with a retired JFTC senior civil servant)

The nature of the relationship between the JFTC and the responsible Cabinet minister was described as ceremonial, offering a possible interpretation that political control by the chief Cabinet secretary was titular and negligible under the LDP/LDP-led Coalition governments. This

108 Evolving regulation and governance

account is also supported by current JFTC officials.

In drawing the above accounts together, what emerges is the degree of control by a party politician outside Cabinet (Yamanaka) and titular control by the formally responsible Cabinet minister. Yamanaka's role was in decision-making based on the JFTC's proposals rather than active management, as the following reveals: 'Mr Yamanaka didn't actively give concrete instructions. Rather, we said "we want this", "we want that", and he sometimes rejected saying "you can't do that", or sometimes said "that's good. Interesting, do it". It's up to the cases' (interview with a retired JFTC senior civil servant). This description was endorsed by a senior *Keidanren* official: 'At that time it was called the Yamanaka–Hayashi regime, administered by Chairman Yamanaka and Head of the Secretariat Hayashi ... but in reality what Mr Yamanaka decided materialised from Mr Hayashi. Further debate was impossible after Mr Yamanaka said "this".' These accounts imply that the nature of Yamanaka's role was not managing but decision-making. What also appears here is the fact that power was not vested in formally responsible Cabinet ministers but in a key LDP politician whose authority depended upon the party and his personality.

Under the strong authority of Yamanaka, the JFTC had more freedom from party politicians' intervention. This was possible because the AMA gives the JFTC independence of authority. This legal framework gave JFTC civil servants more freedom from formal control by the responsible Cabinet minister, who did not supervise the implementation of anti-monopoly regulation. This offers a striking contrast to other government ministries, where responsible Cabinet ministers have the authority to supervise policy implementation. The implications of this system are a lack of democratic control and poor political coordination when the JFTC drafts legal amendment bills; because many policy-making issues emerge in the form of legal amendments, through which the Diet and party politicians exercise their power, active anti-monopoly policy-making activities force the JFTC to confront the challenges of democratic accountability and political coordination (Beeman 2002: 174).

The role the JFTC played in legal amendment processes offers a clue to figuring out the relationship between the JFTC and legal amendments. A lawyer specialising in the AMA offered the following observation from his experience in the LDP AMA Examination Committee and other relevant places:

> Ideas for AMA amendments originated from various places. For instance, from other developed countries in the anti-monopoly field which offered their opinions in places like the SII ... or from private firms and other government ministries. And the third one is the points the JFTC thinks

inconvenient. The final output is made by the JFTC. In the process of making outputs, the JFTC often insert their own view. (interview with an AMA lawyer)

He argued that the JFTC has infrequently offered a future vision for the anti-monopoly field, but has skilfully managed policy-making processes:

When we think about where the ideas for AMA amendments originated, I don't think the JFTC has created so much but it has adopted various outside opinions. I also think that the JFTC is good at adapting law amendments so that they can conveniently be implemented. (interview with an AMA lawyer)

His view reveals that the JFTC's approach to legal amendments has been based on process management and coordination. Another interviewee offered a more critical view on the JFTC, drawing on his experience in anti-monopoly policy-making up to 2004:

It [JFTC] is powerless; new reforms can't be done only by the JFTC. Therefore, various domestic conditions surrounding anti-monopoly regulation mobilise the policies, but it's doubtful if the JFTC has played the role of the main engine. (interview with a retired economics (industrial organisation) professor)

These accounts from anti-monopoly specialists outside the JFTC reveal that the nature of the JFTC's role has been as a coordinator. It has not been strategic, but has been able informally to assert its will regarding the detail of issues. Such an approach is different from other examples of Japanese government ministries offered by Johnson (1982) (MITI) and Vogel (1996) (MPT). A role such as the JFTC's could be described as bureaucratic management rather than strategic. The power of the JFTC stemmed from its institutional authority as an anti-monopoly regulator. Its power in legislation was not dominant and its scope was limited by the LDP's decisions, which the JFTC had no capacity to counter. What the JFTC did was manoeuvre the legislative process as well as monopolising its implementation. In summary, the nature of JFTC's power was policy implementation and a limited range of policy steering within the LDP's decisions.

A policy disjuncture resulting from the SII did not change power relations and roles among the core executive actors. Although enhancing the JFTC and the AMA became a policy priority, the concrete measures to materialise such a policy goal were deliberated and implemented under the supervision of the LDP's AMA Examination Committee. Those civil servants interviewed did not witness a significant disjuncture under the LDP administration between the 1980s and 2000s. Rather, a civil servant commented that business was as usual:

> I was just involved in the last part of the 2009 AMA amendment; we abolished the 2008 bill and remade it as the 2009 bill, and at that time [the bill was examined by] probably the joint LDP committee of the AMA Exam Committee and the Economy and Industry Division; the AMA Exam Committee was held, and I had a little odd feeling ... the policy authorisation process such as consulting with the LDP's PARC, and then the General Council was the same. (interview with a JFTC senior civil servant)

Her account implies that the LDP-led Coalition government retained its internal process with no explicit change of power relations until the 2000s. This observation was verified by another JFTC senior civil servant, emphasising the role of the AMA Examination Committee:

> The AMA Examination Committee was the most significant. In that way, the JFTC was an independent administrative organisation and implemented ordinary law enforcement alone, but things like legal amendments are naturally progressed by the government, so explanations and answers in the Diet were undertaken by the chief Cabinet secretaries; but rather than instructions from them, the debate in the AMA Examination Committee was the most influential over legal amendments. (interview with a JFTC senior civil servant)

These accounts by civil servants indicate that the institutional framework under the LDP/LDP-led Coalition administrations underwent few changes in terms of the process and power relations among actors until the change of government in 2009.

The change in the 2000s: Yamanaka's departure, the DPJ

Elsewhere, some interviewees highlighted the overt change of circumstances that emerged in the 2000s. In their view, such changes were prompted first by Yamanaka's passing in 2004 and also the change of government in 2009. Yamanaka's departure was described as a kind of disjuncture by a senior business organisation official:

> There were cases where 'because Mr Yamanaka was there it could be done' or 'it was done in such a way'. I don't say it's right, but things smoothly working hitherto became unworkable [because of his death]. As often said, Mr Yamanaka's departure created a larger impact than the change of government from the LDP to the DPJ. (interview with a *Keidanren* official)

A retired senior civil servant offered a different view. He argued that the LDP's approach did not change with Yamanaka's death, suggesting that the influence of the 2009 change of government may have created more of an impact on the JFTC: 'Under the LDP government, a good relationship has been established [between the JFTC and the LDP] and the ruling parties treated the JFTC properly. But I am concerned how the DPJ actually treats the JFTC' (interview with a retired senior civil servant). The impact of the change of government in 2009 was described in a rather different way by a current JFTC civil servant, describing the influence of government change as a common experience among government organisations:

> After the DPJ government came, all government ministries had challenges to formulate policies. It probably resulted from issues related to something like governance, but the challenges have been shared by other government ministries. This isn't like 'AMA policies were good or bad', or 'the amendment was good or bad'; rather it resulted from things like the complexity or ambiguity of the power balance between political parties. (interview with a JFTC civil servant)

What then was the impact of the change of government? 'After the DPJ government started ... the relationship with the *Seimu sanyaku* intensified under the umbrella of the Policy Coordination Meeting. And we have policy issues and implementation issues, and policy issues have frequently been reported, I heard' (interview with a JFTC civil servant). The increased involvement of DPJ politicians on policy issues was also witnessed by other interviewees, including the following senior civil servant:

> The current AMA amendment bill was drafted under the leadership of the parliamentary secretary. It was written in the heated period just after the change of government ... 2009 saw a change of government, so from that autumn; on 9 December 2009, the direction was issued in the form of the *Seimu sanyaku* paper, and between these points the direction was contemplated under the leadership of the parliamentary secretary. This was distinctively led by the parliamentary secretary. (interview with a JFTC senior civil servant)

This changing relationship between party politicians and civil servants was also explained by a DPJ politician who was in the *Seimu sanyaku* in charge of the JFTC:

> The LDP government didn't assign the responsible senior vice-ministers and parliamentary secretaries. They assigned only the chief Cabinet secre-

> taries as the responsible Cabinet ministers. The DPJ government decided to create the responsible *Seimu sanyaku* and appointed those responsible for the JFTC. But it naturally has independent authority, so basically the job was the law by the Diet: the *Seimu sanyaku* is involved in what should be done about the law, but each member of the *Seimu sanyaku* had their respective idea on to what extent he should be involved in the daily business, and my approach was a restrained one. (interview with a member of the House of Representatives)

Together with the previous account by a senior JFTC civil servant, this account implies that the elected officials (*Seimu sanyaku*) of the DPJ played a significant role in anti-monopoly policy-making. This reveals a difference from the previous LDP-led Coalition government, where the chief Cabinet secretaries, who were the formally responsible Cabinet ministers, played only a ceremonial role. The DPJ's different approach was explained by Yukio Edano, the first DPJ Cabinet minister assigned to the JFTC:

> After the recent change of government, the *Seimu sanyaku* of the Cabinet Office to which the JFTC is administratively attached ... has been assigned to the JFTC ... I'll do my best to realise fair markets by strengthening the function and organisation of the JFTC. In particular, I'll make efforts to have Japanese industries develop under fair market competition in a significant change of global environment and markets. (The House of Representatives 2010a)

He also referred to the limits of his remit: 'Because the JFTC is an independent administrative commission as the law enforcement organisation, I can't directly command and control it' (The House of Representatives 2010b).

The above account indicates that DPJ politicians' approaches were not unified; some of them argued for a more proactive approach to anti-monopoly policies, while others preferred a more reserved one. A politician offered an explanation:

> There is a debate whether senior vice-ministers and parliamentary secretaries are really necessary. A JFTC chairman endorsed by the administration will solve the problem. And a chairman sufficiently communicates with the administration. But the chairman is from bureaucracy, from the finance ministry ... basically Mr Takeshima wasn't appointed because of the DPJ's wish. So as an interim approach, it is acceptable the *Seimu sanyaku* get involved so that the JFTC work in line with the DPJ's policy. (interview with a member of the House of Representatives)

Piecemeal transformation: anti-monopoly regulation 113

His account reveals that the DPJ's approach was a set of efforts based on each politician's method rather than a coordinated approach. Also, the politician highlighted the problem of accountability; because the current JFTC chairman was selected by the LDP, the DPJ government was distrustful of the chairman as its agent. At the same time, the DPJ was unable to sack the chairman because the AMA protects the chairman's tenure to safeguard the JFTC's independence. This suggests that the independence of authority created a new governance problem which the LDP never had during its long tenure.

The approach by the DPJ encountered criticism from observers outside the core executive. For example, a senior business organisation official stated: 'Surprisingly, I think nothing has emerged after the change of government. Nothing has changed in competition policies and anti-monopoly' (interview with a *Keidanren* official). This critical view was shared by an academic specialising in AMA:

> In most cases, they stopped listening to specialists' opinions. And all consulting committees, including those related law amendments and policy or law drafting, were stopped ... but debates have taken place nowhere. In such a way, anti-monopoly policies have stopped. (interview with an AMA academic)

A consumer group leader made a similar comment as the same events emerged throughout government organisations:

> Since the DPJ took power the executive branch hasn't worked. In short the *Seimu sanyaku* decides things, and councils and committees in each government ministry almost stopped and became their own committees and examination meetings, and they have been working instead ... civil servants had difficulty with moving and working and they have been waiting, I heard. I suggested such a situation undermined their morale. (interview with a consumer group leader)

These accounts from outside observers indicate that the DPJ dismantled the LDP's governing system and failed to establish its own. This suggests an unstable situation where no established rules controlled the governing machine.

Changing power relations and the core executive's continued dominance

In drawing the above together, what emerges is the sustained dominance of the core executive. Party politicians have retained their decision-making role. During the LDP government, this role was played by key party politicians including Yamanaka. The change of government in 2009 dismantled the LDP's traditional governing machine. What emerged instead was an uncoordinated intervention from party politicians in the Cabinet. There is a possibility that the change of government and the emergence of Cabinet ministers specifically responsible for the JFTC have created a challenge to the independence of the JFTC. The independent authority of the JFTC fends off the intervention of politics regarding policy implementation, the major elements of which are law-enforcement issues, for example AMA breach investigations and subsequent administrative proceedings. The JFTC chairman selected by the Cabinet can be regarded as an agent assigned tasks by the Cabinet as a principal. Under the LDP government, this caused few problems because the chairmen were selected by the LDP's Cabinet. The change of government in 2009 dismantled this precondition; it transformed the JFTC's independence of authority to a challenge over accountability. Elsewhere, unlike ICT regulation, anti-monopoly regulation has not seen the emergence of a new actor but the gradual enhancement of the traditional regulator, whose approach is different from that of other government ministries such as the MITI and the MPT/MIC. The JFTC's policy-making activities were not particularly strategic; however, its skilful management enabled it to control anti-monopoly regulation. The overall change of relative strength among the actors in the sector is revealed in Table 5.7.

What can be observed in Japan's anti-monopoly regulation is a version of the fluid change of power within the core executive. The dominance of party politicians is distinctive. Under the LDP, the government's key decision makers such as Yamanaka demonstrated their dominant power in the policy-making process. This framework was retained after

Table 5.7 Relative strength of the actors in anti-monopoly regulation

	1980s–1989 LDP government, Yamanaka period	1990s–2004 LDP government, Yamanaka period	2004–09 LDP government	2009– DPJ government
The Cabinet and the *Seimu sanyaku*	negligible	negligible	negligible	enhanced
Party politicians outside the Cabinet	dominant	dominant	dominant (became unstable)	significantly declined
JFTC	weak, stagnated	enhanced	enhanced	enhanced

Note: Party politicians outside the Cabinet include the LDP's AMA Examination Committee.

Yamanaka's death in 2004. After the 2009 change of government, the DPJ established a new framework of governing by designating responsible Cabinet ministers and their teams (*Seimu sanyaku*). The change of dominant actor occurred within the group of party politicians. The continuous characteristic of this set of frameworks is the dominant nature of party politicians as the key decision makers. The power and role of the JFTC in policy-making processes is subject to the dominance of party politicians and the nature of its power has been policy implementation and a limited range of policy steering within the LDP's decisions. In contrast to the change that had taken place within the group of party politicians, no significant change can be observed in the relative strength of the JFTC vis-à-vis party politicians. Its bureaucratic management and independent implementation of the AMA have shaped the detail of anti-monopoly regulation under the supervision and dominance of party politicians.

Party politicians have had access to not only the JFTC but also its opponents such as the MITI and *Keidanren*. For actors such as the MITI and *Keidanren*, one of the major ways of opposing the JFTC was by lobbying party politicians. Key party politicians such as Yamanaka have been in a position to make decisions, taking account of the views of related actors such as the JFTC, the MITI and *Keidanren*. This system reveals a similarity to the British core executive analysed by Smith (1999: 251). Party politicians' role as the key decision makers places them at the centre of the policy community on anti-monopoly regulation. It is party politicians such as Yamanaka who decide which direction and views the government will employ. The *Seimu sanyaku* in the DPJ government played a similar role to Yamanaka because it made key decisions on anti-monopoly regulation such as formulating bills. The group of party politicians including Liberal Democrats and Democrats has decided key policy issues such as the final content of bills. Other actors including the JFTC have lobbied party politicians to realise their goals. This implies that the relationship between the group of party politicians and other actors has been asymmetric; the former has had the discretion to make final decisions.

A key characteristic of the core executive in Japan's anti-monopoly regulation can also be understood as its asymmetric dominance mobilised by ruling party politicians. Strategic management in anti-monopoly regulation by officials has been limited; the major decisions shaping the regulatory framework have been made by the key party politicians. The power of the JFTC stemmed from its institutional authority as an independent anti-monopoly regulator. Its power in legislation was not dominant and its scope was within the decisions made by the LDP; it had no capacity to counter the LDP's decisions. What it did was to manoeuvre the legislative process as well as monopolising implementation through its independence of authority.

116 Evolving regulation and governance

Here the nature of the JFTC's independence becomes a topic of scrutiny; how the JFTC has retained its independent status as a rare independent administrative commission in Japan is key to exploring the transformation of the commission and the sector. The next chapter examines the independent status of the JFTC and its impact on anti-monopoly policies.

Notes

1 The SII was a bilateral process between the governments of Japan and the US from 1989 to 1990, which was launched as a joint initiative by President George H. W. Bush and Prime Minister Uno in June 1989, and whose final agreement was signed in June 1990, following a year of concentrated formal negotiations and informal meetings (Matsushita 1991: 436; Mastanduno 1992: 235). Its major focus was a trade imbalance between Japan and the US resulting from the non-tariff barrier, mainly on the Japanese side (Matsushita 1991: 436). Its follow-up talks continued throughout 1991 (Morita 1991: 778).
2 Yamamura (1967: 9) explains that the first version of Japan's AMA was based on the draft presented by the Anti-Trust Division of the US Justice Department.
3 Eleanor Hadley was a member of the SCAP Cartel Division in Tokyo (Schaede 2000: 72).
4 Yamamura (1967: 196–216) has the full text of the AMA as enacted in 1947 and amended in 1953.
5 The JFTC proceeded against sixty-six cartels in 1973, and forty-four cartels, four unfair trades and thirteen other cases in 1974. The JFTC formally recognised these cases as AMA breaches, and placed them into its administrative processes pursuant to the provisions of the AMA, the results of which include issuing a recommendation (*Kankoku*).
6 After the enactment of the AMA in 1947, there were only four precedent criminal cases before the oil cartel cases; three of them were in 1949 under the administration of the SCAP, and one an unfair promotion by an estate agency prosecuted in 1970 (Miwa and Ramseyer 2004).
7 Japan's segmented industrial groups aligned with distributors and financial institutions (Calder 1993: 142). Hadley (1970: 205–90) presents detailed typology and analysis about *Keiretsu*.
8 The Japanese asset bubble was an economic bubble from 1986 to 1991, in which real estate and stock prices were greatly inflated.
9 Privately owned industrial empires (Johnson 1982: 23). According to Hadley (1970: 20) *Zaibatsu* were family-oriented 'combines', i.e. complexes 'of corporations displaying unified business strategies arising primarily out of an ownership base'.
10 From January 2006 Japan introduced a leniency programme, under which the JFTC can treat cartel participants leniently when imposing surcharges, despite the clear fact that the informant has also obtained profits from the cartel (Uesugi 2005: 362; JFTC 2012a). The JFTC affords full immunity for the

first informant, a 50 per cent reduction in penalties to the second informant, and a 30 per cent reduction for the third informant, so long as they provide necessary information before the start of the JFTC investigation (Uesugi 2005: 362; JFTC 2012a). A certain number of informants can also enjoy the benefit of this programme after the start of the JFTC investigation (JFTC 2012a).

11 Article 27 (2) of the AMA stipulates: 'The Fair Trade Commission shall be administratively attached to the office of the Prime Minister.'
12 Article 8 empowers the chief Cabinet secretary to organise the Cabinet Office's official duties in cooperation with the Prime Minister and supervise them under the instruction of the Prime Minister, except for those assigned to other Ministers of State.

6
Breaking the egg shell

The JFTC's independence is an unusual feature within Japan's political tradition. As demonstrated by the 1977 AMA amendment, the commission's independence emerged as a notable element that characterised policy-making in anti-monopoly regulation (Beeman 2002). Elsewhere, the prioritisation of the sector after the 1990s gradually changed the conditions surrounding and shaping anti-monopoly regulation. This change had the potential to reframe the JFTC and the sector, including the commission's independence and state capacity within the sector.

Prompted by the above observations, this chapter examines the JFTC's independence and state capacity within the sector. To elaborate, it first pinpoints the independent characteristic of the JFTC. What follows is an assessment of the impact of transformation through analysing the capacity of the state in anti-monopoly regulation. The third section pulls together the points raised in both the previous chapter and this chapter and considers the nature of state transformation in anti-monopoly regulation after the 1980s.

The nature and limitations of the JFTC's independence

When the focus of the interviews moved to the JFTC's independence, the majority of the interviewees offered cautious and reserved, if not critical, views. With respect to the reason why the JFTC has retained its independent status, a retired JFTC civil servant offered an explanation based on its historical background; the JFTC has retained its independent administrative commission status because it had no predecessor before the Second World War:

> The meaning of independence and independent organisations wasn't understood at that time [in the 1940s–50s]. The JFTC happened to survive

in this period, for no government ministry accepted its tasks. The MITI said it wanted that in the 1950s and 1960s, but it took time [after the JFTC's establishment] and transferring the JFTC to the MITI would probably have provoked significant resistance in society, so it didn't materialise. (interview with a retired JFTC senior civil servant)

Another retired senior civil servant offered a similar view:

The reason why only the JFTC remained [as an independent administrative commission in the 1950s] is that competition and anti-monopoly policies undertaken by the JFTC emerged after the Second World War and didn't exist before that. Therefore, nobody did the job before the war. The JFTC administered anti-monopoly policies, so nobody would accept the JFTC's tasks if it were abolished. Such a background may have led to the conclusion that some kind of organisation was necessary, and the JFTC may have survived. (interview with a retired JFTC senior civil servant)

He argued that the benefit of independence was to counter pressure from opponents, including other government ministries and party politicians acting for vested interests: 'Because the AMA covers all sectors and corporations, each investigative raid involves some members of the Diet; accepting such politicians' claims every time would significantly undermine the JFTC's job' (interview with a retired JFTC senior civil servant). Independence of authority could fend off such external interventions. Referring to the fact that the JFTC was politically weak compared with its opponents in the past, he argued: 'The JFTC has become very large and powerful. In the past, it was the government office that could be crushed or transferred at any time. Now, nobody will agree if someone argues for abolishing the JFTC. Such a guy could be kicked out' (interview with a retired JFTC senior civil servant). In his view, the new challenge for the enhanced JFTC is policy-making as well as implementing the AMA. Transforming to a policy-making organisation would require a re-evaluation of the JFTC's status as an independent administrative commission, because 'Law enforcement is based on independent authority, but policy [making] can't be independent. Independent policy-making is a kind of dictatorship' (interview with a retired JFTC senior civil servant).

Another retired JFTC official offered a view that the JFTC's independent status made it apolitical and saved it as a government organisation, taking past pressure on the JFTC seriously: 'The 1950s was the JFTC's most severe "winter". So it [independent status] protected the JFTC from being crushed. If the JFTC were noisier, like a noisy puppy, or if it had a more substantial presence to the extent that it couldn't be left, it could have been crushed' (interview with a retired JFTC senior civil servant).

A similar view was offered by a major business organisation official who argued that distance from party politicians and the basis to confront other government ministries are the major benefits of the JFTC's independence: 'The most important thing is that the JFTC's status as an Article 3 organisation independent of the Cabinet prevents the JFTC from being influenced by an idiot when he becomes the premier ... and it enables the JFTC to confront the METI' (interview with a *Keidanren* official). This perspective was seconded by an AMA lawyer: 'I suggest independence enabled the JFTC to resist pressures from various interest groups and other government organisations' (interview with an AMA lawyer). The relationship between the Cabinet and the JFTC was elaborated on by a DPJ politician previously responsible for the JFTC:

> A commission can have the merit of having a more transparent process of selecting a chairman than an agency; the nature of the difference is an appointment issue. But in my view a commission will have fewer inadequate political interventions. In an agency a crap Cabinet minister can make a crap instruction, and everyone has to obey that; such a thing can happen ... but if a respectable private-sector person is appointed as the head of an agency things should be the same [as a commission-style organisation]. I think so, but we haven't yet done it to that extent in Japan; even employing external resources in government offices hasn't been done yet. (interview with a member of the House of Representatives)

To pull these accounts together, a significant benefit of the JFTC's independence was the distance it created from the Cabinet. This distance has contributed to enhancing the JFTC's power in its confrontations with opponents such as other government ministries.

A group of interviewees including a law professor, an AMA lawyer and a former civil servant argued that another benefit of an independent commission was that it suits a complaints system (*Shinpan seido*) – the JFTC's quasi-judicial system. Until 2005 most cases in which the JFTC found substantial violations were referred to as complaints, where identified private firms could submit their arguments in writing. If the private firms alleged by the JFTC to be AMA violators accepted the allegation, the subsequent complaint process would be short; it would be terminated by recommendation decisions typically utilising the JFTC's cease-and-desist orders (Schaede 2000: 116). If the firms did not accept the allegation, the complaint process would be substantial, with hearings from the firms and final consent decisions (*Dōi shinketsu*, if the JFTC and the firm agreed the terms) or complaint decisions (*Shinpan shinketsu*, if no agreement was reached)

(Schaede 2000: 114, 116). The nature of this complaints system was 'a quasi-judicial system under which cases of AMA violation were judged by the authority with expertise' (interview with an AMA lawyer). This ex ante based complaints system was transformed into an ex post based complaints system by the 2005 AMA amendment, under which suspected firms receive the JFTC's cease-and-desist orders first and then file complaints if they disagree with the orders (see Table 5.4 and Appendix 2).

The quasi-judicial nature of the complaints system has been regarded as a reason why the JFTC has to be independent. For instance, the above AMA lawyer commented that 'The JFTC has to be independent to have a quasi-judicial function, for the judicial function can be compromised if it were in the executive branch; it's like a kind of separation of powers' (interview with an AMA lawyer). A law professor specialising in the AMA concurred: 'The complaints system is a framework in which things like the court system are done within the administrative system. It's done because the JFTC is an independent administrative commission' (interview with a law professor). These accounts regard the quasi-judicial function of the JFTC as a significant reason for its independence.

Along similar lines, a current JFTC senior civil servant revealed a view highlighting the nature of the AMA and the JFTC's independence:

> The independence of the JFTC is not only because of the provision of Article 28 that it shall perform its authority independently; this provision emphasises the framer's intention, but it is rather explained that independence stems from the nature of the assignment, and is ensured in a number of ways ... discussed by five commissioners, who are specialists in their respective fields. And the discussion reaches adequate settlements. This is how things work. I think there is an understanding that AMA violation cases should be sorted out in such a way. Analyses from various angles and the resulting debates should be the basis of a conclusion. (interview with a senior civil servant)

Her viewpoint focusing on the nature of the AMA was shared by another JFTC official: 'The AMA, which is called the constitution of economy, is a basic legal document for maintaining the liberalist or capitalist economy. Such a characteristic requires neutral law enforcement based on economic theories ... I suggest there is a consensus on this in Japan' (interview with a JFTC civil servant). He also differentiated the AMA from other regulatory laws: 'The JFTC has received much criticism such as "it doesn't know the industry", but because what a law violation is is evident, it can apply the law to whatever the product and whatever the boundaries [between the product's market]' (interview with a JFTC civil servant). In a similar vein, a senior JFTC civil servant highlighted a characteristic of the JFTC as concentrating on regulation:

> If the JFTC were such a government organisation as overseeing and developing responsible industries it would have two kinds of responsibilities and have conflicts [of interest], but it doesn't have responsible industries and just implements so-called regulation; in that way, the JFTC just regulates and can decide and implement according to the provisions of the AMA. (interview with a senior JFTC civil servant)

According to these accounts, the AMA was a basic law which could be applied in a generalised manner and, concentrating on the AMA, the JFTC was free from a conflict of interest between a developmental orientation described by Johnson (1982) and a regulatory orientation.

The above accounts reveal the issues related to the JFTC's independence: the JFTC's unique responsibilities, which cannot be assumed by others; an institutional necessity as a quasi-judicial organisation; and a shield whereby the distance from the Cabinet offered by the JFTC's independent status contributed to enhancing its power in confrontations with opponents such as other government ministries.

When Japan's independent administrative commissions were reorganised in the 1950s, no government ministry emerged as a suitable successor to the JFTC with appropriate expertise, because the AMA regime was newly established in 1947. This historical background can be understood as one reason why no other government organisation absorbed the JFTC and the AMA. A second reason is that the JFTC has a quasi-judicial complaints system, equipping it with quasi-judicial characteristics. There has been an understanding that a quasi-judicial task such as the complaints system is better handled by an independent commission rather than an ordinary government ministry supervised by elected officials.

The abolition of the complaints system by the 2013 AMA amendment undermines the second reason. This abolition stemmed from the growth of the JFTC's power and conflicts of interest, as Okiharu Yasuoka (2008: 120), who was the chairman of the LDP's AMA Examination Committee in 2006 and led the debate about the abolition of the complaints system, comments:

> The JFTC has the investigative and complaint functions which resemble 'a merger between the public prosecutor and the judge' but no other similar example exists in the world or other institutions in Japan ... As corporate activities are globalised and trade becomes complicated, the JFTC, which has obtained great power including the surcharge system, needs a comprehensive review of its institutional framework and adequate enhancement

and division of power. Therefore, abolishing the complaint system and leaving its function to the revocatory lawsuits in court is an idea.

A view presented in the interviews was that the abolition of the complaints system would undermine the status of the JFTC as an independent commission, because other government organisations such as the National Tax Agency, the Financial Services Agency and the Public Prosecutor's Office also have investigative functions based on the principle of neutral and independent law enforcement. For example, a law professor who specialised in the AMA and had a long relationship with the JFTC commented: 'If the complaints system is abolished, the JFTC's independence will disappear in the future; in my view it has independence because its task contains something similar to a court' (interview with a law professor). A similar comment was offered by an AMA lawyer: 'When the current AMA amendment bill abolishes the complaints system and private firms directly complain to the courts, then the argument that the quasi-judicial function should be independent will disappear.' Another view highlighted mainly by JFTC officials offers a defence of independence by referring to the nature of the AMA, which enables a general application to various cases and requires a neutral approach to implementation. The JFTC has had no conflict of interest between regulation and industry promotion up to now. Taking account of the fact that other government organisations also require neutral law enforcement, this does not seem a robust argument to defend the independence of the JFTC.

Instead, this book highlights as a third reason emerging from the interviews that independence has offered a kind of shield with which the JFTC can face its opponents such as the METI. This was commented on by several interviewees. This benefit seemed important when the JFTC was a low-profile government organisation. At the same time, the more powerful the JFTC becomes in bureaucracy, the less important the benefit will be.

Interviews also revealed a problem caused by the JFTC's independent status. The JFTC lacks democratic control in its policy-making process, for its senior officials are democratically unaccountable. This problem is evident when new policies are introduced. Many of them are introduced in the form of legal amendments. Because the commission members are unelected, there is a possibility that an AMA amendment bill could be drafted without substantial supervision by democratically elected officials. The JFTC's official paper justifies this system by arguing that a close relationship between planning/formulating and law enforcement is important:

> In the administration of competition policy ... planning and formulating can effectively achieve the goal of competition policy, retaining and

> promoting fair and free competition, only when it is based on and closely related to the practical usage of law. Therefore, in competition policy, the most effective and efficient approach is assigning the JFTC planning and formulating and law enforcement together. (JFTC 1997)

It further refers to the relationship between the JFTC's independence of authority and the Cabinet's administrative responsibility:

> Despite the JFTC's independence of authority, policy formulation such as AMA amendments by such an organisation does not create a problem vis-à-vis the Cabinet's administrative responsibility and the unity of the government's economic policy ... the JFTC formulates the draft and sufficiently coordinates with related parties such as other government organisations and the ruling parties; the bill then is put before the Diet pursuant to the formal procedures. (JFTC 1997)

This argument does not fully address the challenge of accountability: the lack of substantial supervision of elected officials in policy-making processes. This caused few problems up to the 1980s when AMA amendments were infrequent. As anti-monopoly regulation attracted more public attention after the SII, more demands for AMA amendments emerged.

If the case of the JFTC is compared with the guidelines of the OECD (2002: 95–6: see Table 6.1), which are widely disseminated as a consensus formulated by an international organisation, one can recognise that 'To shield interventions from captured politicians and bureaucrats' was

Table 6.1 The merits and demerits of an independent regulator

Merits:
- guards against interventions from politicians and bureaucrats subject to regulatory capture
- improved transparency
- more stable regulation
- better conditions for having expertise
- possibility of improved accountability if an independent regulator has explicit objectives and a specific report system to the government or parliament

Demerits:
- possibility of slowing structural changes, losing potential gains to consumers
- remaining risk of capture if the regulator faces structural weaknesses
- possibility of inadequate democratic accountability
- possibility of fragmenting governmental policies and actions

Source: OECD 2002: 95–6. See also Table 4.1.

highlighted by the interviewees, while accountability emerged as a major shortcoming. The fact that the DPJ appointed Cabinet ministers with responsibility for the JFTC can be understood as an effort to cope with this challenge. Its real impact is a topic for future research.

The independence of the JFTC was shaped by an exogenous factor: the SCAP's policy. The subsequent path to retaining this organisational characteristic was shaped by the JFTC's preference for maintaining the status quo and other core executive actors' indifference. This sequence can be regarded as an example of self-reinforcing path-dependency formed by the consensus among the core executive. The JFTC has been in favour of retaining anti-monopoly regulation by an independent administrative commission, because independence gives it a shield from its opponents and suits the JFTC's quasi-judicial function: the complaints system. Since the 1980s, core executive actors such as party politicians have been indifferent to the JFTC's independence of authority. No government organisation was interested in absorbing the JFTC's functions. This set of factors has influenced the retention of the JFTC's independent status. The response of the core executive on this issue is to maintain the status quo, through the key actor's strong will and others' indifference.

In analysing the independence of the JFTC, there emerges the possibility that the expansion of the role of anti-monopoly regulation has significantly changed the traditional framework. A significant cause of such transformation pointed out by interviewees and the literature is the growth of the enhanced JFTC after the SII. The capacity of the state in anti-monopoly regulation, including the JFTC, is therefore key to exploring how the field has been transformed. The next section examines this issue.

Growing bureaucracy and the regulatory capacity of the state

Similar to the case of ICT regulation, interviewees focused on the JFTC in their description of the capacity of the Japanese state in anti-monopoly regulation. Most interviewees regard the organisational growth of the commission after the 1980s revealed in Table 5.6 as a significant enhancement of the state in anti-monopoly regulation.

Enhancing the JFTC has been viewed as having limited salience for party politicians in general, because enhancing a government organisation does not have a significant impact on their respective constituencies. A former LDP Cabinet minister made this point, referring to the case of another government organisation (the Ministry of Justice): 'We tried hard to increase the staff of the Ministry of Justice, judges, and the sum of the justice related budget. Not many politicians do such a thing, because it doesn't attract votes' (interview with a former

Cabinet minister). Rather, some of them opposed strengthening the JFTC, as a retired JFTC senior civil servant commented: 'Around the 1980s and before some politicians opposed enhancing the JFTC ... when we explained the draft of the next financial year's budget, they said that's too much; some politicians opposed that' (interview with a retired senior JFTC civil servant). Given such circumstances, one can highlight the election of the Koizumi government (2001–06) as the most significant event after the 1980s:

> He [Koizumi] increased by 30 officials a year, 150 in 5 years, and he, or his staff, or the Koizumi government had a significant impact [on the AMA]. Enforcement by a very small number of staff has limitations. In addition, it said 'unacceptable is unacceptable' to something about the regulatory methods, like the case of the post office. These two were of significant assistance [to the JFTC]. (interview with a retired JFTC senior civil servant)

Another party politician argued that appointing an appropriate JFTC chairman was vital for establishing capacity:

> We need to properly embrace competent officials in government organisations including the JFTC. Concerning the JFTC, we change the chairman to somebody interested in such a recruitment policy, possibly one from the private sector, and let him do it his way. This could be an indirect political intervention but I don't think it is a proper political intervention. If we have such a chairman, the commission can recruit competent candidates regardless of their previous sectors more easily than other government organisations. Well, to tell the truth, other government organisations can also do that if the ministers want, but the administration is stopping all staff changes now. (interview with a member of the House of Representatives (DPJ))

These accounts reveal that party politicians' influence in enhancing the JFTC has been insignificant in general and that the impact of party politicians was significant when they expressed a clear will to strengthen the JFTC, as the case of the Koizumi government demonstrates.

Elsewhere, a group of interviewees recognised the intention of the state as a whole to enhance the JFTC: 'The fact that we have got significant manpower under the severe budget condition of the state means we have got sufficient attention. When I entered the commission we had 506; now we have 799 officials; the 60 per cent increase is significant' (interview with a JFTC civil servant). This observation was shared by an outside observer: 'Manpower has increased as the statistical data indicates, even under tax revenue shortages resulting from the recession. This means the JFTC's capacity is needed so much and politicians have understood that, I guess' (interview with an AMA lawyer). This set of responses indicates that the JFTC's organisational expansion has been interpreted as the government's intention to strengthen its anti-monopoly regulation capacity.

The impact of staff increases was witnessed by a retired JFTC senior civil servant:

> Although we needed more people to fully function for anti-monopoly regulation we had about 400 or 450; therefore, we couldn't actively undertake various things ... enhancing authority is important, but for instance, we significantly enhanced authority in 1977, but with the staff increase of several officials a year, we couldn't do so many things ... regarding authority and manpower, we've enhanced authority through a series of debates, but without manpower we couldn't do so much, in my opinion. (interview with a retired JFTC senior civil servant)

He also compared the current situation with that in the early 1990s: 'Probably they don't stop proceeding with cases because of manpower or money shortages today. I did such things in the early 1990s. At that time the situation was like that, and it was the largest obstacle to actual enforcement' (interview with a retired JFTC senior civil servant). This demonstrates the impact of staff increases on the JFTC's capacity and supports the view that the JFTC's organisational expansion can be understood as effective for enhancing Japan's anti-monopoly regulation capacity.

The steady staff and budget increases for the JFTC offer a contrast to the professional expertise of the staff. A number of interviewees gave negative views regarding the professional expertise of the JFTC's staff from a couple of viewpoints. The above retired JFTC senior civil servant, for instance, highlighted the lack of employees with professional training:

> The JFTC officials are kind of generalists, and their posts frequently change. So it is hard to develop people like those specialised in and very good at mergers and acquisitions. But other countries have already employed such professionals, including those with a ten-year history or so, with which it's difficult for Japan to cope. We need to offer better treatment and invite competent, qualified and able people; they may go to somewhere like universities, but we need to increase such people; within Japan the JFTC staff is not so inferior; because other government offices employ the same approach. We do business in international conferences, or investigate and cope with the same cases together; in such cases, counterparts are those with PhDs. Our people are university graduates, some of whom don't have even Masters; is this really all right? (interview with a retired JFTC senior civil servant)

He also highlighted the difference between the JFTC and its American counterpart:

> Anti-monopoly policies include mergers and acquisition regulation; the US counterpart employs more than 100 PhD holders engaging in such tasks. In Japan, commissioners may have a PhD but they don't directly engage in mergers and acquisitions regulation cases, so one PhD holder, a post-doc or PhD holder; the reality is something like that. (interview with a retired JFTC senior civil servant)

This lack of trained specialists was pointed out by a current JFTC official:

> Focusing the staff's professional expertise is very important when compared with the US and the EU. Because for instance public prosecutors implement anti-monopoly law and economists analyse the economy; the EU is also an international organisation, so holding a PhD or a Masters in law is common among its staff. Such people are examining … I fear if our [officials'] professional expertise is inferior to the US's and the EU's. (interview with a JFTC civil servant)

This observation was shared by an AMA lawyer:

> The JFTC should be a specialist organisation, but it doesn't employ sufficient professionals. For example, I don't think 16 lawyers are enough, and regarding economists, one piece of evidence that the JFTC doesn't take economic analysis seriously is it employs only a few economists. It doesn't think about identifying AMA breaches by economic analysis. In other countries, half of the US FTC's staff are economists. This is a problem. (interview with an AMA lawyer)

Indeed, his concern is shared by the US authorities, who claim that Japan's enforcement remains lax by international standards, with the JFTC's economic analysis capacity regarding anti-competitive behaviour falling behind that of the US and the EU (Vogel 2018: 102). Such a situation can be summarised in the following comment: 'The organisational size can quickly be strengthened but professional expertise can't' (interview with a *Keidanren* official). All these views highlight the insufficient professional expertise of the JFTC's staff, in contrast to the enhanced staff numbers and budget.

In pulling the above interview comments together, what emerges is a lack of party politicians' explicit interest except for the Koizumi administration, organisational expansion in terms of the size of the budget and staff numbers, and the insufficient professional expertise of the staff. At the beginning of the 1980s, party politicians were not actively involved in anti-monopoly regulation and their support for strengthening the JFTC was small. State capacity in anti-monopoly regulation was limited because of staff shortages. The change of state power emerged in the form of the organisational expansion of the JFTC in terms of its staff numbers and budget, as Table 5.6 indicates. This trend continued throughout the period after the 1980s. Although the influence of the majority has been small, some party politicians such as Koizumi made a significant impact. The state in anti-monopoly regulation has therefore grown in the form of the JFTC's bureaucratic expansion. Similar to the case of ICT regulation, the transformation of state capacity can be understood as the expansion or the adaptation of responsible civil servants since the 1980s; resistance to strengthening anti-monopoly regulation has gradually waned and the JFTC has retained significant discretion in the details of its regulatory function.

Within the community of the core executive, the JFTC's power has gradually grown in relation to other actors. With supervision by party politicians of the JFTC, the expansion of the commission's power can be understood as a policy endorsed by politicians, although few, with exceptions such as Koizumi, have shown explicit interest. This process of change can be viewed as the gradual growth of state power initiated by the core executive in anti-monopoly regulation. With the rise of the JFTC's capacity, state capacity in anti-monopoly regulation has also become stronger.

Elsewhere, the nature of state capacity in anti-monopoly regulation has not changed. It is not easy to identify who has steered state power in anti-monopoly regulation. Although after the 2009 change of government the *Seimu sanyaku* responsible for the JFTC played a more active role in policy-making processes than nominally responsible chief Cabinet secretaries before 2009, its impact does not hitherto seem significant on state capacity: the approach of the *Seimu sanyaku* has been indirect control through the JFTC chairman.

A different path, the same nature

Anti-monopoly regulation in Japan has not experienced a significant disjuncture that transformed the structure of the sector such as the 1985 regulatory reform in ICT. Instead, the relative strength of the state grew after the 1980s through the enhancement of the JFTC and the AMA. This has led to a gradual change in the framework of anti-monopoly regulation. Indeed, the whole process can be evaluated as the expansion of the state, characterised as a process in which the government machine and demands for accountability have grown. The development of state capacity has forced the institutional framework of anti-monopoly regulation to face the challenge of democratic control. The change has been gradual rather than rapid after the SII.

A major characteristic of the sector is the significance of party politicians and their power. A limited number of LDP politicians surrounding Yamanaka dominated the decision-making process. Their influence was aimed at key decision-making such as endorsing AMA amendment bills, and left the detail untouched. Another characteristic of Japan's anti-monopoly regulation until the late 1980s was the opposition to change, as the compromised impact of the 1977 AMA amendment demonstrated. This can be interpreted as the significant power of opponents – a significant group of the core executive (e.g. some LDP politicians, the MITI) – deterring the development of the sector in the form of more stringent regulatory enforcement.

Important turning points were brought by the SII and the election of the Koizumi government. These events contributed to the development of state capacity in anti-monopoly regulation. Indeed, throughout the period after the SII, anti-monopoly regulation emerged as a changing sector, with the bureaucratic machine of the JFTC significantly enhanced in terms of its budget and staff. The 2009 change of government from the LDP to the DPJ transformed party politicians' approach to anti-monopoly regulation, although its impact on the relationship between party politicians and civil servants was not distinctive.

The exploration of the internal relationship within the core executive in anti-monopoly regulation reveals the change of key actors and power relations and the exchange of resources between them. Party politicians outside Cabinet had dominant power until 2004, when Yamanaka died, with the chief Cabinet secretaries (as the formally responsible Cabinet ministers for the anti-monopoly field and the JFTC) engaging in ceremonial tasks rather than substantial supervision. This policy-making framework was retained after the death of Yamanaka. It was the emergence of the DPJ government that changed the framework under the LDP by dismantling the LDP's internal examination system and assigning responsibility for the JFTC to the competent *Seimu sanyaku*. The fact that the *Seimu sanyaku* became actively involved in drafting AMA amendment bills suggests the enhanced dominance of party politicians in anti-monopoly regulation. This set of events came with a consensus among the core executive; it was the core executive that steered and implemented enhanced anti-monopoly regulation. The case of anti-monopoly regulation in Japan after the 1980s can be understood as an example of the asymmetric dominance of the core executive as it collectively held a dominant position in steering regulation throughout the period.

Elsewhere, the relationship between party politicians and civil servants has been significantly influenced by the JFTC's status as an independent regulator pursuant to Article 28 of the AMA, which requires the commission to perform its role independently, unlike other government ministries. This has traditionally fended off party politicians' intervention in AMA enforcement by the JFTC. The analyses revealed that the initial decision that the JFTC be left independent has shaped its path as an independent administrative commission. This can be understood as an example of self-reinforcing path-dependence. Indeed, the political circumstances surrounding the JFTC up to the 1980s suited it as an independent administrative commission. Independent status offered the JFTC a shield in its confrontations with opponents such as the MITI and its concentration on enforcing the AMA, fending off interventions from party politicians. With few legal amendments, the JFTC did not need frequent access to ruling party politicians in the 1980s; this meant that party politicians did not exercise significant power over the JFTC and had limited exchange of resources, for example opportunities to consult with party politicians on AMA amendment bills, as power emerges from the exchange of resources within the core executive (Smith 1999: 31). This offers a contrast with the case of ICT regulation, where the initial decision that the regulatory function inside the MPT be retained after the 1985 NTT privatisation shaped the regulator's organisational framework. Additionally, the quasi-judicial nature of the complaints system through which AMA breaches were processed was regarded as requiring the JFTC to be at arm's length from the executive branch.

After the SII, these circumstances significantly changed. As the JFTC gained more power, the benefits of independent status as a tool to confront opponents waned. More active policy-making inspired by the SII has developed a potential problem with accountability, because policy-making activities including drafting bills have no supervision from elected officers such as Cabinet ministers. A more robust system of accountability could better contribute to the governance of anti-monopoly policy-making in response to the transformation of the sector and state power. State power within the sector has grown in the form of the strengthened bureaucratic machine, that is, new legal authority and staff and budgetary resources have increased, in response to circumstantial changes. In other words, the transformation of state power can be described as the enhancement of law-enforcement capacity through the enlarging of the JFTC's organisation and responsibilities. Since relying on law enforcement is a characteristic of the regulatory state, the nature of the transformation of anti-monopoly regulation can be viewed as an example of the emergent Japanese regulatory state.

What emerges here is the transformation of the state through changes of circumstances surrounding the regulator. Independent status has fended off party politicians' interventions in the JFTC, whose primary focus was implementing the AMA. The JFTC's increasing involvement in the policy-making process as an independent administrative commission has provoked a potential challenge: establishing clear accountability for policy-making. The growing power of the JFTC has also gradually undermined the need for independent status as a shield from its adversaries. These changes could lead to a review of the nature of the JFTC's independence. By enhancing its power and obtaining opportunities for more frequent policy-making activities, the commission has gained the potential to develop its activities beyond its traditional institutional framework. Elsewhere, in spite of the fact that independence of authority has fended off the interventions of party politicians, key decisions required the endorsement of party politicians including Yamanaka. The change of the institutional framework was steered by party politicians such as those in the LDP's AMA Examination Committee. The change of government in 2009 enhanced party politicians' involvement in anti-monopoly policies through assigning responsibility for the JFTC to the *Seimu sanyaku*.

What emerges here is a different version of the dominance of the core executive. Party politicians have dominated policy decisions, leaving investigative cases to civil servants in the JFTC; overall, the core executive has successfully dominated policy-making and implementation. The decision-making process has involved discretionary negotiations within the core executive: party (typically LDP) politicians and JFTC civil servants. Increasingly prioritised anti-monopoly regulation needs intensified policy-making with resulting politicisation; this leads to the increasing involvement of party politicians. The negotiations demonstrated the exchange of resources within the core executive. Indeed, the governing of the core executive in Japan's anti-monopoly regulation in which party politicians and civil servants exchange their resources reveals a variation of the model proposed by Smith (1999). The transformation of the sector – prioritisation, growing state power, increasing policy-making and resulting politicisation – has been undertaken by the core executive's collective decisions, concomitant with the change of power relations within itself. This example shows that the core executive as a collective political group has demonstrated its asymmetric dominance within the sector through its discretionary approach to regulation.

By focusing on the core executive in anti-monopoly regulation, this chapter has revealed the asymmetric dominance of the core executive based on the state's unique set of resources (e.g. legitimacy, state bureaucracy, legislation) at a macro level (Marsh et al. 2001: 248). The state at a macro level has retained its control over society through the change of power relations within the core executive; this adaptation process is an example of a state reconstituting itself by establishing a variation of the regulatory state with the growing power of the state (regulator) and politicisation in response to the sector's prioritisation and increasing demand for regulation. Indeed, this set of events characterises a form of anti-monopoly regulatory state in Japan constructed through transformative processes in response to the challenge of governance after the 1980s.

Together with Chapter 4, this chapter has shown how dominant the core executive has been in another key regulatory sector, heeding the broader context of the state at a macro level. What one can observe in this chapter through an elitist approach is how the Japanese state has been reconstituted in a sector where a crucial and salient issue of state transformation (regulation) has been administered by illuminating the dominance of the core executive. The final part draws together and analyses the implications of the findings in relation to both the literature on and current approaches to understanding the nature of the Japanese state and the impact of transformation over the last thirty years.

Part III

The nature of Japanese governance with the transformation of the state

7

Regulatory transformation and the core executive

Japan and its politics has long been a significant topic of research. With the emergence of observers highlighting the transformation of the state after the 1980s, the nature and transformation of the Japanese state of the period offers a timely contribution to understanding governance and public policy scholarship. The case studies in Part II explicitly disclose the significance of the core executive as key to explaining governance and regulation, with its unusual approach based on the conventional process – the path-dependent process – to shaping regulators and growing state capacity in regulation. Indeed, the emergence of the regulatory state in Japan, dominated by the core executive within the two chosen sectors, corroborates the proposition by revealing the reconstitution of the Japanese state, rather than the hollowed-out state, in response to the changing nature of governance.

This chapter undertakes a systematic analysis of the results drawn from the case studies of Part II. The analysis shapes the foundation on which this book sets out its core argument. The chapter first considers the nature of regulatory development in the two chosen sectors. In both, the regulatory framework has evolved in response to changes of circumstances such as the 1985 telecommunications liberalisation and NTT privatisation, the SII, and concomitant changes of power relations within the core executive. The impact of the disjuncture reshaped both the structures and actors with the change of power relations. What comes next is an analysis of changing power and the core executive. It is the heart of this study; indeed, the state at a macro level has had an asymmetric dominant position in relation to societal actors, drawing on fluid changes of power within the core executive. The evolution of Japan's regulatory framework in ICT regulation and anti-monopoly regulation exemplifies state transformation dominated by a loose network of the core executive. The next two sections analyse specific examples that demonstrate the dominance of the core executive in the case studies: the sequence of shaping regulators and the capacity of the Japanese regulatory state. While the former demonstrates how a political tradition has shaped a particular policy outcome – enlarging the existing regulatory organisations – the latter offers a view that the sector elites collectively enhanced state capacity in regulation. What is common in these two examples is the core executive's consensus to set particular policy goals. This set of analyses is followed by an examination of the extent to which the core theme of this book has been corroborated.

The nature of regulatory development

In the period around the 1985 telecommunications reform, the major protector of the previous system, NTT, did not have or exercise strong veto power over the decisions of the dominant actor, the LDP. NTT also did not have the discretion to flexibly interpret or enforce existing rules; most of them were under the supervision of the Diet, namely party politicians. In the post-1985 regulatory reform period, the emergent MPT/MIC gained significant discretion in interpreting and enforcing the rules as the responsible executive ministry (see Table 3.1). However, the unchanged dominance of party politicians made the veto power of the possible defenders of the sector weak. Under this mode, ICT regulation has retained its approach of employing a government ministry as the regulator. Anti-monopoly regulation has seen a gradual expansion of its independent regulator and the AMA. The process of institutional expansion has been piecemeal rather than striking. This sequence of changes in both case studies reflects fluid changes of power within the core executive. Both studies have revealed the development and concomitant transformation in regulation, which has changed power relations. What is remarkable in the transformative process is the extent to which the role of the core executive actors has formed and reshaped the governance of the sector through fluid changes of relative strength within the core executive in response to challenges. They have defended the status quo, overseen rules within the sector, and determined the mode of change.

The core executive as key in regulation

In both ICT regulation and anti-monopoly regulation, the position of key decision maker has been retained by party politicians, either those outside the Cabinet or Cabinet ministers. This has resulted in their dominance over civil servants as well as the core executive's dominance in the context of state–society relations.

The decision-making process under the LDP/LDP-led Coalition governments was dominated by party politicians outside the Cabinet in the 1980s and 1990s. Their dominant position lasted until the end of the LDP-led Coalition government, although this traditional system was gradually undermined by a set of administrative reforms including the introduction of the *Seimu sanyaku* system. The change of government in 2009 ended the dominance of party politicians outside the Cabinet and intensified the influence of Cabinet ministers. This can be understood in terms of a fluid change of power within the group of party politicians. Regulatory approaches have also changed. ICT regulation has shifted its approach from direct service provision to ex ante regulation to ex post regulation. Anti-monopoly regulation has significantly expanded after the SII with a similar shift of its regulatory approach. The change of approaches identified above is a response to challenges in the fields as well as the cause of changes of power. ICT regulation saw the rapidly growing power of the new regulatory ministry, the MPT/MIC, whose emergence took place under the supervision and steering of party politicians. Similarly, the JFTC's gradual expansion in terms of its staff and budget has been implemented under the control of party politicians. Indeed, the rise of the bureaucratic machine has happened under the supervision of party politicians. This can be understood in terms of the core executive expanding its capacity and power in the two sectors.

Change within the core executive indicates not only the dominance of party politicians but also the fact that regulatory bureaucracy has been transformed under the steering of party politicians. In ICT regulation, key actors emerged (e.g. the MPT, Cabinet ministers) and declined (party politicians outside the Cabinet) within the core executive based on the fluid and relational nature of power; this set of events demonstrates the transformation of the state at a macro level in the sector. Similarly, what anti-monopoly regulation has seen is a change of power relations between party politicians and the rise of the regulator. A limited number of LDP politicians around LDP Member of the House of Representatives Yamanaka dominated the decision-making process of anti-monopoly regulation in the 1980s and 1990s. Under this regime, significant turning points came about with the SII and the Koizumi government. These events contributed to the development of state capacity in anti-monopoly regulation; the bureaucratic machine of the JFTC has been significantly enhanced in terms of its budget and staff numbers.

The change of government from the LDP to the DPJ in 2009 transformed the party politicians' approach and highlighted the power of the Cabinet minister. It exacerbated the internal change within the group of party politicians by sidelining those outside the Cabinet but within the ruling party in Japanese politics. Yet the resulting gap was not filled by any actor. Although the Cabinet and its elected officials have been enhanced since the 2000s under both the LDP and DPJ administrations, the evidence of this study reveals their failure to establish stable steering capacity in policy-making that is sufficiently competent to take over their predecessors' role. What emerged was a power vacuum; the gap created by the exit of formerly powerful ruling party politicians outside the Cabinet was not filled by other key actors, including Cabinet ministers, officials and private-sector actors. Elsewhere, although the changes within the LDP in the 2000s and the 2009 change of government from the LDP to the DPJ had a significant impact on the decision-making mechanism, party politicians retained a significantly stronger position than their bureaucratic and private-sector counterparts. Indeed, party politicians' relative strength in relation to officials and private-sector actors has remained. Therefore, one can conclude that the core executive has been dominant in policy-making since the 1990s.

In drawing the analyses together, in both ICT regulation and anti-monopoly regulation since the 1980s fluid and relational changes of power have taken place between the core executive actors. With these changes, the core executive retained control over the two regulatory sectors. This control was asymmetrical because the core executive actors have held power and dominated the sectors, while other actors have not had power to counter the core executive's dominance. This set of findings – the flexible responses of the core executive through fluid changes of power within itself and its asymmetric dominance of society – can be regarded as core in transforming the Japanese state at a macro level in regulation.

Path-dependent sequences dominated by the core executive

Exploring the issue of an independent regulator illuminates the striking difference between ICT regulation and anti-monopoly regulation, in that the former is regulated by a ministry and the latter is overseen by an independent administrative commission. In ICT regulation, the abolition of a US-style independent administrative commission in radio regulation in 1952 significantly impacted on the core executive's perspective about having an independent ICT regulator, shaping a self-reinforcing path-dependent sequence of retaining the status quo through ministerial regulation. Institutional characteristics such as the constitutional framework and the inflexible nature of Japanese law could also have contributed to this process; the Constitution requires all executive organisations to be under the supervision of the Cabinet; the inflexible interpretation of existing laws limits the possibility of the executive branch making policy within its own jurisdiction and requires frequent consultations with the Diet through legal amendments. The analysis in this book identified no clear benefit to the core executive in establishing an independent ICT regulator. A number of interviewees disclosed their concern that independent regulation could compromise the regulator's capacity by jeopardising the close interaction between regulation and industry promotion, including sharing information on technological development. What emerges from the views of the opponents of creating an independent ICT regulator is an established political context, which started from an initial decision that the regulatory functions be retained within the MPT.

In spite of its strikingly different outcome – regulation supervised by an independent administrative commission rather than a government ministry – there is a similar pattern in anti-monopoly regulation. The contingent factor that anti-monopoly regulation was newly introduced in 1947 ensured that the JFTC remained independent; no government organisation had experience of anti-monopoly regulation or was willing to take over the JFTC's responsibilities. What the experiences of the two regulatory sectors demonstrate is a set of self-reinforcing path-dependent dynamics. The sequence of events was determined by the initial contingent events. The chosen paths have been persistent; in both sectors, no substantial institutional change occurred after the initial contingent events (ICT regulation: the 1985 regulatory reform; anti-monopoly regulation: the establishment of the JFTC in 1947). The prioritising of anti-monopoly regulation since the 1990s may result in future change, as public policy-making requires extensive involvement in political processes; for example, frequent legal amendments pose a challenge to the institutional framework of an independent administrative commission, because being independent of politics can be an obstacle to participating in public policy-making activities such as legislation, which requires a significant degree of political coordination. Therefore, strengthening the AMA and the JFTC could undermine the previous system by increasing contact with politics.

What has contributed to shaping this path are the initial events and the political tradition rather than power relations within the core executive. In both cases, the initial decisions (retaining regulatory function within the MPT; establishing and retaining the JFTC as an independent administrative commission) had a significant impact on the subsequent sequence. The political tradition, such as the narrow interpretation of the law and the frequency of legal amendments, formed self-reinforcing path-dependent sequences. The core executive's decision to retain its regulatory functions within the government ministry in ICT regulation reveals that no endogenous incentive to change has emerged within the core executive. The disjuncture of the 1985 telecommunications reform did not offer an opportunity to debate the independent implementation of regulation or the establishment of an independent ICT regulator, in contrast to the case in Europe. The lack of endogenous incentives and exogenous pressures contributed to maintaining the regulatory approach.

The emergence of the new Japanese regulatory state

The capacity of the state in both ICT regulation and anti-monopoly regulation was regarded as that of the bureaucratic machine: the manpower, financial resources and statutory authority of the MPT/MIC and the JFTC. In the case of ICT regulation, the decline of the capacity of civil servants can be directly regarded as a decline of regulatory capacity. The rise of Cabinet ministers as party politicians in bureaucracy has not filled the vacuum created by the retreat of civil servants, but brought about an unstable situation, since Cabinet ministers have failed to consolidate their resources and take over the role of civil servants because of their short tenure in office and their lack of experience. These obstacles have prevented Cabinet ministers from managing regulatory policy-making. It is within this complex environment that significant contention emerges in evaluating how the capacity of the state has been developed in ICT regulation. Whereas a group of interviewees argued that a significant regulatory capacity has been developed, mainly in the government ministry and based on a newly established bureaucratic power base, another group highlighted different aspects of regulatory capacity including the inconsistent approach of civil servants stemming from their short tenure, the lessening of the government ministry's legal authority, and the lack of political will to impose strict measures.

In anti-monopoly regulation, the Japanese state has expanded its power to respond to circumstantial changes by strengthening the bureaucratic machine, with new legal provisions, staff increases and budget increases. This has involved the enhancement of law-enforcement capacity through the enlargement of the JFTC's organisation and responsibilities. Since relying on law enforcement is a characteristic of the regulatory state, the nature of the transformation of Japan's anti-monopoly regulation can be viewed as the emergent form of the Japanese regulatory state. The bureaucratic machine has been transformed under the supervision of party politicians; that is, the policy has been endorsed by them. Given the fact that it has been considered and determined within the core executive, one can also say that the core executive has retained a significant degree of discretion over state capacity in regulation. The transformation of state capacity in ICT regulation and anti-monopoly regulation can be viewed as an adaption of the core executive to the regulatory challenges of the period, reflecting a fluid change of power within the core executive.

Regulatory transformation and the core executive   143

What emerges in the above analysis is the enhanced regulatory capacity of the organisations in both sectors, which can be described as the emergence of a variation of the regulatory state under the initiative of the core executive in response to the challenges of governance. This new regulatory state lacks some of the characteristics observed in other examples; the lack of a new independent regulator in liberalised markets is an example. As this study has shown, a number of reasons contributed to this unusual outcome. What is clear is that a strikingly different consensus has formed within the core executive, if specifically compared to the cases of the UK and New Zealand. What is common among these three significantly different cases is the status of the core executive as key. The question of regulators and state capacity unfolds specific examples regarding to what extent political elites in the sector have been influential over policy-making and implementation.

State reconstitution drawing on fluid changes of power in response to the challenges of governance

The above sections disclosed the core characteristics of the two regulatory sectors after the 1980s: the core executive asymmetrically dominant over society flexibly addresses challenges through the change of power relations, which have been fluid in response to internal and external challenges and salient in the process of state transformation. Indeed, fluid changes of power relations within the core executive enabled it to retain its dominant position in policy-making and implementation. This is the mechanism that mobilises the core executive to respond to the challenge of governance regarding the specific issues examined in this book.

ICT regulation and anti-monopoly regulation have continually been subject to steering by party politicians. Under their supervision, regulatory capacity in the two sectors has been strengthened through the adaptation process of the bureaucratic machine. In anti-monopoly regulation, the bureaucratic machine has continuously expanded; that in ICT regulation has been transformed to cope with the changing regulatory environment. Within the group of party politicians, power has shifted from those outside the Cabinet to the *Seimu sanyaku*, including Cabinet ministers. This change of power relations and the rise of the Cabinet have characterised the core executive since the 2000s. Indeed, explicit political efforts to augment the Cabinet begun by the LDP/LDP-led Coalition governments include the introduction of the *Seimu sanyaku* system under the Obuchi government (1998–2000) (Neary 2002: 127). Prime Minister Koizumi's success in elections and resulting strength in the political arena further enhanced the power and authority of the Cabinet and its members in relation to other state actors. This move was intensified by the change of government in 2009 together with the sidelining of the previously powerful LDP politicians outside the Cabinet. Throughout this transformative process, power fluidly changed between the core executive actors in response to the challenges of governance in the sectors and beyond; these changes have shaped the present power relations in the two sectors. Upon this foundation, the core executive has collectively retained its dominance within policy-making and implementation. This set of reconstitution processes in the case studies explicitly reveals the transformation of the Japanese state at a macro level in regulation.

Discretionary regulation within the inner regulatory policy community

The above analysis reveals a number of factors underpinning the dominance of the core executive. An important factor is party politicians' dominant position as the key decision makers in both ICT regulation and anti-monopoly regulation. The relationships between party politicians and other actors are asymmetric; party politicians determine and other actors have no other option than to follow their decision. Party politicians have had an interdependent relationship with civil servants and have been lobbied by societal groups such as NTT and *Keidanren*. In both case studies actions are taken within the limits of decisions by party politicians, who need civil servants to mobilise bureaucratic machines. The significance of party politicians in Japanese public policy-making and implementation has been evident.

Elsewhere, this book has also revealed the impact of a structural factor: the informal rules in Japanese politics. The two Japanese examples since the 1980s are different from British executive politics analysed by Smith (1999: 115–30), as the impact of the ruling parties' internal rules resulting from the long dominance of the LDP within the administration has been significant. Shaped by political parties outside the formal institution of the state, the ruling parties' internal rules are informal; the impact of informal rules is a key factor explaining the nature of the power of party politicians outside the Cabinet. This example demonstrates the impact of informal rules at the core of the political arena, where the key decisions of the sector are shaped. The gradual decline of their power together with the emergence of the *Seimu sanyaku* was intensified by the change of government in 2009. This change of power within the group of party politicians exemplifies the fluid changes of power within the core executive in Japan. However, the nature of power exercised by party politicians does not seem to have been affected by internal changes of power; their political power has been discretionary, given the fact that no explicit rule binding them exists.

The nature of civil servants is different. Representing state power in relation to societal actors such as private firms, the impact of civil servants has been significant (e.g. Johnson 1982; Vogel 1996). However, the nature of their power in both case studies is in line with the analysis of Smith (1999): their power has been under the supervision of party politicians. Party politicians' authorisation was vital in order for civil servants to exercise their power.

Societal groups have the potential to mobilise the core executive, as demonstrated in the cases of the 1977 AMA amendment and the 1997 NTT break-up. The power of societal groups can be understood as analogous to the British case introduced by Smith (1999: 226–7), which reveals the impact of pressure groups on the core executive and policy-making. Societal actors such as NTT, *Keidanren* and consumer groups can be understood as members of policy networks. Business actors such as NTT and *Keidanren* directly lobby party politicians. Others such as consumer groups and academics tend to access bureaucracy rather than party politicians; their approach includes joining the government's policy deliberation councils such as the Information and Communications Council. The fact that key decisions such as the content of government bills are finalised by party politicians indicates that bureaucracy works as a mediator. In line with Smith's (1999) model drawing from the British core executive, party politicians and civil servants in Japan need each other within the community of the core executive. Elsewhere, other actors do not have the resources indispensable to core executive actors. The relationship between the core executive actors and other societal actors is asymmetric. The core executive has the discretion to control other actors' access to policy-making and implementation.

Drawing on the above, this book sets out as its argument that the core executive under the LDP government sustained its asymmetric dominance in ICT regulation and anti-monopoly regulation through its decision-making process, in which key decisions were shaped within a closed community composed of key party politicians. Operating in an interdependent relationship with civil servants in line with Smith's analysis, party politicians under the LDP government exercised discretionary policy-making in the political parties' internal organisations such as the LDP's PARC. Ruling parties' internal organisations functioned as a key governing tool for the core executive within the two sectors in the early part of the period between the 1980s and 2000s. As time passed, actors with a formal institutional basis such as the Prime Minister and the *Seimu sanyaku* became more significant and previous key governing tools such as the PARC lost their influence (Krauss and Pekkanen 2011: 242). This change was highlighted by longitudinal data obtained by Muramatsu and his associates, revealing that civil servants recognised the decline of *Zoku gi'in* and the PARC between 1987 and 2002 (Krauss and Pekkanen 2011: 242). Despite its internal change, the group of ruling party politicians as a whole has sustained its position of asymmetric dominance in ICT regulation and anti-monopoly regulation, in conjunction with their civil servant counterparts. This can be understood as a version of the asymmetric dominance of Japan's core executive between the 1980s and 2000s. The 2009 change of government did not produce a significant impact on this set of approaches by the core executive according to the evidence of the interviews.

Given this development, this study concludes that the nature of the Japanese regulatory state is asymmetric dominance on the part of the core executive. The empirical evidence drawn from the case studies supports this claim. Although the limited scope of the research in concentrating on two specific regulatory cases implies that further research, including examining other regulatory cases and other policy areas such as distributory and stabilising examples (Majone 1996), is needed to firmly establish the case, the two case studies are representative of the core part of Japan's policy-making arenas; as discussed in Chapter 1, the significance of ICT regulation and anti-monopoly regulation in Japan's policy-making and implementation and regulation as core functions of the state suggests that the development of these two cases is not isolated but exemplary. Indeed, the outcome of the two case studies is strongly indicative of the transformation of the Japanese state beyond the two sectors. In particular, I would like to illuminate the fact that the core of Japan's governing network has flexibly changed over this period. Within the network, the significance of ruling party politicians outside the Cabinet is a strikingly different feature compared with Westminster-style parliamentary systems such as the UK's, where their equivalents are usually outside policy networks. It could rather offer a parallel to presidential systems such as the US, where key parliamentarians mobilise policies. The decline of Japan's party politicians outside the Cabinet not only exemplifies the fluid changes of power within respective inner policy circles in the Japanese system but also the country's transformation from a governing system influenced by the US-style division of powers to a Westminster model. This set of analyses comprehensively covering governing systems demonstrates the benefit of highlighting the core as crucial.

Referring to the argument above, the final chapter reviews the political development of the two sectors after the 2012 change of government from the DPJ to the LDP. The chapter then sets out the implications of this research, drawing on the argument of this chapter and recent political developments.

8

Governance in Japan: the implications of the research

The downfall of the DPJ in December 2012 was unsurprising, given its growing unpopularity (Reed et al. 2013: 34–46). Defeating the Yoshihiko Noda government in the general election of 16 December 2012, the LDP's Shinzō Abe won his second term as Prime Minister. After his first brief tenure between 2006 and 2007 was widely seen as a failure, not many expected a revival. Therefore, his return as the premier in December 2012 was received with surprise.

The power of Abe's LDP-led Coalition administration has generally been regarded as strong, given a set of landslide victories in consecutive national elections: the 2012 general election of the House of Representatives, the 2013 House of Councillors election, the 2014 snap general election of the House of Representatives, the 2016 House of Councillors election, and the 2017 snap general election of the House of Representatives. The impact of the MMM system[1] in the Lower House election also contributed to shaping Abe's power within the LDP through selecting the registered LDP candidates in constituencies. The power of the administration is concomitant with the weak opposition parties that allowed the LDP to win the elections. In particular, the power of the DPJ, which was transformed into the DP (Democratic Party: *Min'shin'tō*) in March 2016, has significantly declined, with its share of seats diminishing from 308 in 2009 to 73 in 2014 in the Lower House alone; the party's split into three groups in 2017 seems to have exacerbated the situation. This can be interpreted as significant popular distaste for the DPJ. This set of factors leads to an understanding that the LDP's Abe administration has significant power in Japan's policy-making arenas (Tazaki 2014: 229–34).

The foundations of the Abe administration's power include the two-party system based on the MMM system and his record as electoral leader in the past, and the enhanced *Kantei* (Prime Minister's Office) from the 2001 administrative reform. The fact that Abe's own faction, *Seiwa-ken* (*Seiwa seisaku kenkyūkai*: Seiwa Policy Research Association) is the largest in the LDP may also strengthen his internal authority. In addition, the enhanced capacity of the Cabinet and Prime Minister resulting from the 2001 administrative reform would have significantly contributed to the power of the administration. Most of these factors constituting the structural foundations of the Abe administration are shared with the previous LDP-led Coalition government before 2009.

The continuity between the LDP-led Coalition administration before 2009 and the Abe administration can also be found in Abe's approach to policy-making and implementation. Indeed, the impact of the Abe administration regarding policy-making processes does not seem as salient as its rhetoric. As a major accomplishment, the administration restored the LDP's preliminary examination system – the PARC's preliminary examination of government bills – within policy-making processes after the 2012 change of government (Takenaka 2013). This could have enabled Liberal Democrats outside the Cabinet to regain power over government organisations such as the MIC and the JFTC; however, what has actually been observed is their lack of explicit influence in policy-making arenas (Yomiuri online 2014).

In ICT regulation, Abe's abrupt call for mobile phone charge reductions and the subsequent sequence in 2015 reveals the characteristics of policy-making processes and power relations within this sector under the administration. Abe publicly disclosed his explicit concern over the financial burden incurred by mobile phone charges in a meeting of the Council on Economic and Fiscal Policy (CEFP) in September 2015 and instructed MIC Minister Sanae Taka'ichi to consider ways to cut such fees (*The Japan Times* 2015). As the council formulates the government's core economic strategy, Abe's remark had a significant impact. Taka'ichi responded by explicitly stating her intention to formulate a plan to reduce rates by the end of the year (*The Japan Times* 2015). The MIC launched an internal taskforce regarding mobile phone tariffs and other service conditions the following month; on 16 December, the taskforce unveiled a policy statement requesting new fee plans for small data users, tariff reductions, an end to call charge income subsidising mobile handset costs, and the setting up of an interconnection system for mobile virtual network operators, emerging as new competitors to the existing mobile network operators (MNOs) (MIC 2015a). Two days later the ministry itself issued its plan for mobile services and set out an official request to MNOs to reduce call charges (MIC 2015b). In April 2016 the MIC issued an official request to MNOs to stop reducing mobile handset prices by subsidising; this was followed by the ministry's review in the meeting of its internal policy taskforce (MIC 2016).

What appear in this sequence of events are explicit actions by Cabinet members, including Prime Minister Abe's remark in a September CEFP meeting, MIC Minister Taka'ichi's prompt response in the same meeting and the following media conferences, and her explicit efforts to formulate a policy package aimed at mobile phone services reform. Elsewhere, no one has reported the active involvement of LDP politicians outside the Cabinet in the process. Given the fact that some media articles suggest the possibility that Taka'ichi had had preliminary briefings (Ishikawa 2015), and that she reacted swiftly to Abe's remark in the official meeting and set up the taskforce, some suggest that MIC officials could have been informed before Abe's abrupt remark and become involved with the process. What this set of processes reveals is the striking difference from the traditional approach of Japanese officials, in which ministries' policy deliberation councils set out proposals based on their examination of key issues, which continues typically for several months, and officials then draft government bills drawing on the proposals. A possible explanation is that this set of events was originally planned by the *Kantei* including Abe and it mobilised the MIC to realise the whole process.

The events regarding mobile call rate reductions in 2015 reveal the explicit impact of Cabinet ministers such as Abe and Taka'ichi. Chief Cabinet Secretary Yoshihide Suga's abrupt call for mobile phone charge reductions in August 2018 not only recalls the similar event in 2015 but also reiterates the significance of this approach mobilised by the *Kantei* in the sector (*The Japan Times* 2018). Their strong power on this policy issue as indicated in the media coverage contrasts sharply with the absence of previously powerful party politicians outside the Cabinet specialising in communications policy, including LDP *Yūsei-zoku*. The role and power of MIC officials have not been explicitly reported by observers; what appears is their smooth reaction to Abe's abrupt request and skilful approach to the issue.

Turning to anti-monopoly regulation, the Abe administration retained the post of the Cabinet minister responsible for the JFTC created by the DPJ government. The observable impact of this post is not significant and no explicit assignment regarding the JFTC appears on the official government website as of September 2016 (*Kantei* 2016a). The previously influential AMA Examination Committee was renamed the Competition Policy Examination Committee in 2013 with the appointment of a new chairman, Yoshiaki Harada. A significant event that emerged in anti-monopoly regulation under the Abe administration was the 2013 AMA amendment; effectuated in 2014, the amendment replaced the JFTC's quasi-judicial complaints system (*Shinpan seido*) with the courts. This policy was first proposed under the LDP-led Coalition administration before 2009 (Yasuoka 2008) and the resulting bill was first formulated in 2010 under the DPJ administration. The 2010 bill was abandoned for technical reasons in the Diet in 2012, and was transformed into the 2013 AMA amendment bill with practically the same contents (JFTC 2014: 19). This sequence indicates that it was not started by the Abe administration but was a broader consensus shared by both the LDP and the DPJ. After the effectuation of the 2013 amendment, few political events with significant impacts on the sector seem to have emerged; for example, the fact that Chairman Harada posted only one brief article regarding anti-monopoly issues on his Facebook page between 2015 and September 2016 indicates that the sector was involved in few political issues.

Pulling the above together, developments within ICT regulation have confirmed the change of power relations within the sector. The power of elected officials has explicitly been demonstrated, whereas few report the observable impact of party politicians outside the Cabinet. With respect to the MIC, what one can observe in ICT regulation after 2012 is its skilful process management rather than its significant impact as an influential strategic actor. Turning to anti-monopoly regulation, developments after 2012 can be characterised by the continuous governing framework and a low profile. Although the *Seimu sanyaku* has had the capacity to engage in anti-monopoly regulation, no evidence indicates that it has explicitly exercised this power; a key policy-making event, the 2013 AMA amendment, was drawn from the consensus shared by both the LDP and DPJ governments. Indeed, no clue reveals explicit political change in anti-monopoly regulation after 2012. In conclusion, developments since 2012 seem to reveal a similar set of structures and actors to the DPJ administration's.

Although examining the political developments of the period in the two sectors and beyond requires further rigorous research with strong evidence, what explicitly appears in the two sectors drawn from the secondary sources seems to confirm the findings of this study; it also concurs with the assessment of other examples (Takenaka 2017). In addition, the impact of Abe's prioritised economic project, with the mantras of 'Abenomics' and 'three arrows' (*Sanbon no ya*), has had little impact on the two sectors or on Japan's regulatory system as a whole, although Abenomics' third arrow was meant to address structural reforms by pursuing a growth strategy including imperative regulatory reforms (*The Economist* 2016a; *Kantei* 2016b).

The reconstituted Japanese state since the 1980s

The exploration of the two case studies on regulation has revealed the reconstitution of the Japanese state in responding to challenges after the 1980s: the period after the emergence of Johnson's (1982) developmental state thesis. Drawing on this finding regarding the regulatory sectors, this book sets out a perspective that the reconstituted state is a key characteristic of the Japanese state since the 1980s.

Regulation is a key issue for the transformed modern state: the increasing employment of principal–agent regulation by the modern state is one of the major characteristics since the 1980s (Sorensen 2004; Smith 2009). Exploring the case of regulation therefore has the potential to address how the state has been transformed in response to challenges by focusing on a salient characteristic of the transformed state. In particular, regulatory sectors experiencing a significant disjuncture concomitant with challenges to the state such as privatisation can offer a distinctive example of the transformation of the state to cope with challenges. By exploring ICT regulation and anti-monopoly regulation, this book has the potential to expose the key nature of the transformation of the Japanese state.

Johnson's (1982) developmental state concentrates on developmentally oriented goals. The Japanese state's developmentally oriented approach was also identified by Vogel's (1996) study of Japan's ICT regulation and financial regulation. In line with this previous literature, the evidence of this book identifies this traditional tendency through the accounts of current and former civil servants, revealing an orientation to industrial development in the ICT sector in the 1980s and 1990s.

The reconstitution of the Japanese state has been accompanied by changes of power within the core executive, which has also resulted in the transformation of a developmental state led by civil servants as described by Johnson. Powerful party politicians outside the Cabinet acting as decision makers and civil servants acting as strategists administered key sectors such as ICT and anti-monopoly regulation in the 1980s and 1990s (Muramatsu and Krauss 1987). In the 2000s the Cabinet emerged as a dominant actor but failed to take over the strategic role of civil servants. Mobilised by changes of power among the core executive actors – Cabinet ministers, party politicians outside the Cabinet and civil servants – the reconstitution of the state has transformed the developmentally oriented characteristic of the Japanese state. The detail of change in Japan at a micro level was partially reported by researchers including Vogel (2006) and Schaede (2008), although their major concerns were elsewhere. The retreat of civil servants from their role as economic strategists was a piece of the puzzle forming the transformation of the Japanese state. In line with Vogel and Schaede, the evidence in this book reveals that the mode of the Japanese state led by developmentally oriented civil servants has ended.

The transformation of the Japanese state has not, however, changed its core nature: the asymmetric dominance of the core executive. Rather, it is the core executive that has mobilised the reconstitution of the Japanese state. By identifying the significance of the core executive in the Japanese state, this study reveals a different perspective from Vogel's. Vogel (1996) set out the strategic nature of Japan's telecommunications regulation and financial regulation in the 1980s and 1990s, focusing on state actors: party politicians and civil servants. His analysis highlighted Japan's political tradition in telecommunications and financial regulation, which he called 'strategic'. Vogel argued that the strategic nature of Japan's telecommunications and financial regulation offers a striking contrast to that of the UK, where competition promotion was the focus. By focusing on the state at a macro level and power relations within the core executive, this book has highlighted the asymmetric dominance of the core executive within the Japanese state in ICT regulation and anti-monopoly regulation.

Although Vogel highlighted an important characteristic of the Japanese state – strategically oriented approaches – analogous to Johnson's model of the developmental state, he failed to illuminate the core nature of the Japanese state. What the literature such as Johnson and Vogel illuminates is not the nature of the Japanese state but the approach employed by Japan's core executive during the period. The Japanese state employed a developmentally oriented approach because the core executive of the time chose that option. If the core executive had chosen an alternative, the Japanese state would have employed a different method. Therefore, the nature of the Japanese state can be explained not through concrete approaches such as a developmental orientation, but via what the Japanese state was made to employ, a developmentally oriented approach: the dominance of the core executive in Japanese politics.

The Japanese state gradually changed its approach and sought alternatives when the traditional approach of developmentally oriented policy encountered challenges in the 1990s (Yamamura 1997; Vogel 2006; Schaede 2008). This book delineates what happened in the middle of the transformation. The situation in 2011, when many of the interviews in this book were collected, was unstable rather than under equilibrium; political development since then seems to have disclosed the same trend; some of the findings of this study suggest that further change will take place in the future. The core characteristic observed in the Japanese state after the 1980s is the asymmetric dominance of the core executive. It is the core executive that has chosen the path of a developmental state. The Japanese state has been reconstituted as a response of the core executive to cope with challenges since the 1980s; some measures in the reconstitution could be market oriented, and others could be reserved or protectionist. However, the nature of what has happened in Japan is a dynamic process of state reconstitution led by the core executive. This is the perspective that addresses the nature of what has happened in Japan's political arena since the 1980s.

The nature of the Japanese regulatory state

If our functional definition in Chapter 2 is revisited, the Japanese regulatory state is a concept that describes an aspect of the Japanese state that administers regulation which existed in Japan even before the 1980s, when Johnson illuminated the impact of the Japanese developmental state. After the 1980s, because of key events such as the 1985 telecommunications regulatory reform and the SII, the regulatory function of the Japanese state attracted the interest of researchers (e.g. I'io 1993; Vogel 1996). What emerged in ICT regulation after 1985 and in anti-monopoly regulation after the SII was a new form of regulatory state replacing the previous one.

The case studies in this book reveal the transformation of the Japanese regulatory state. The previous form of regulatory state was service provision based on state corporation monopoly (e.g. NTT in the ICT sector) and cooperation between private firms (e.g. AMA exemptions in specific sectors) with ex ante approaches by the state (e.g. entry prohibition in domestic telecommunications markets, holding company prohibition in anti-monopoly regulation) rather than competition in markets. The new form of regulatory state emerged after key events such as the telecommunications regulatory reform in 1985 and the SII, employing principal–agent regulation and competition in markets as key tools. In ICT regulation, the intensified use of principal–agent regulation has emerged with the rise of the MPT/MIC as a key regulatory ministry. In anti-monopoly regulation, it has come to light with the enhancement of the JFTC.

Elsewhere, the analysis of the case studies has revealed the core executive's path-dependent view of regulatory independence, in which a significant reluctance to establish flexible independent regulators within the traditional political tradition was evident in ICT regulation. The self-reinforcing path-dependency starting from the JFTC's establishment in 1947 contributed to defending the commission's independence of authority. This path-dependent history gives the Japanese regulatory state an unusual outlook; many of its regulators (e.g. ICT, transport, utilities) are still located within government ministries.

Another characteristic is the tendency that prioritising a regulatory sector leads to politicisation. Because of this, party politicians in Japan have had the opportunity for a significant role in the Japanese regulatory state. The regulatory process and the decision-making process within the regulatory state tend to be politicised because of the significant role of party politicians within the core executive.

The process of shaping the Japanese regulatory state after the 1980s has been mobilised by the core executive. Indeed, a key characteristic of the Japanese regulatory state is the dominance of the core executive. The core executive has been in a discretionary position to administer regulation and its tools: rule-making, monitoring and enforcement. The significance of the core executive in shaping a new regulatory state is highlighted by Moran (2003) in his analysis of the British regulatory state.

154   The nature of Japanese governance

Commentators such as Kelsey (1995) also illuminate the role of elites in the core executive as key for New Zealand's regulatory reform. The Japanese regulatory state has also been dominated by the core executive in shaping its framework since the 1980s. The transformation of the Japanese regulatory state, which Vogel (1996) highlights as the emergence of re-regulation as an explicit response of the state actors, can be understood as a response of the core executive reconstituting the new form of the regulatory state with its asymmetric dominance.

If the dominance of the core executive is a key feature of the Japanese regulatory state, what makes the Japanese regulatory state shape its specific approach to regulation? This book proposes that the Japanese regulatory state can be explained as an equilibrium between the following elements:

- *Accountability*
  A key factor in controlling the relationship within the core executive is accountability. This typically means oversight by elected officials such as Cabinet ministers and the legislature. Accountability is an important instrument for party politicians to control the government. It offers the basis of political legitimacy on which both party politicians outside the Cabinet and the *Seimu sanyaku* exercise their control over civil servants. If a regulator is independent of politics, it is not under the direct control of the elected government. In the case of the JFCT, it is democratically controlled through the appointment of its commission members, including the chairman, and the endorsement of key policy issues including AMA amendment bills. The change of government in 2009 from the LDP to the DPJ created a problem with this chain of democratic control. The fact that JFTC Chairman Takeshima (2002–12) was appointed by the LDP Koizumi government could have been a problem for the DPJ government regarding democratic control of the JFTC; it had to embrace a chairman selected by somebody else. Accountability also has the potential of restricting flexible rule changes; it may require rules to be adopted within the democratic process. Democratically adopted rules such as laws need a long process involving a significant number of interested parties. Because the political cost of rule-change processes, such as coordination among interested parties, is significant, frequently changing democratically adopted rules costs more than changing less formal rules such as decrees and government orders. When the former are needed, regulators will face difficulty without politicians' assistance
- *Independent implementation*
  The neutral implementation of regulation in fending off interested parties such as private firms is vital for effective competition in

markets. The JFTC's independence of authority ensures independent implementation of regulation; it was not a prioritised idea in ICT regulation, where elected officials directly supervise regulation.

Independent implementation of regulation has the potential to conflict with accountability, because with independence a regulator distances itself from direct supervision by elected officials. It also has the potential to conflict with rule changes. A political element is inherent in regulatory rule changes as they involve various interested parties. Increasingly frequent rule changes require regulators to more heavily engage in political processes.

- *Frequent rule changes in response to circumstantial changes*
  Flexible rule changes in regulation are key to coping with changing circumstances through updated regulatory rules. In rapidly developing sectors such as ICT, technological and social development can make established rules quickly obsolete. Timely and flexible rule-making and rule changes are imperative for such sectors to keep themselves updated and competitive in response to their challenges. Rule changes involving formal processes such as legal amendments may politicise not only the change processes but also the issues examined and those involved. This is a challenge emerging in anti-monopoly regulation, since its prioritisation has required more frequent legal amendments.

The present situation in ICT regulation and anti-monopoly regulation can be explained as the equilibrium of these factors.

The case study chapters regarding ICT regulation have shown that political accountability and frequent rule changes have been prioritised. Regulation has been under the influence of dominant party politicians, for example key Liberal Democrats outside the Cabinet and Cabinet ministers. Elsewhere, the rise and transformation of civil servants in the ICT sector reflects the sector's rapidly changing circumstances. The MPT as an emergent regulator filled the gap created by the NTT privatisation. The government ministry has changed regulatory approaches in response to the development of the ICT sector. The dominance of party politicians and the nature of the quickly changing ICT sector have prioritised accountability and frequent rule changes. The state tradition that requires detailed provisions in regulatory laws also could have contributed to involving party politicians. This set of factors has resulted in a regulatory approach in which a government ministry regulates in close consultation with party politicians.

In anti-monopoly regulation, the regulator's independent status and the lack of interest from party politicians resulted in a lesser influence of party politicians and fewer demands for accountability than in ICT regulation. Only a limited number of party politicians surrounding

Yamanaka steered key issues such as AMA amendments. As Japan prioritised anti-monopoly regulation and the AMA after the 1990s, this set of circumstances gradually changed. The prioritisation of the sector resulted in more frequent AMA amendments and increased the involvement of party politicians; anti-monopoly regulation and the AMA have attracted more attention than before from party politicians. The abolition of the complaints system under the 2013 AMA amendment has the potential to undermine the JFTC's quasi-judicial nature, which has been regarded as a significant reason why the commission needs a status as an independent administrative commission, and to reshape the sector.

In pulling the above considerations together, this study shows Japan's ICT regulation and anti-monopoly regulation vis-à-vis the three elements. In Figure 8.1, Japan's ICT regulation is placed on one side of the triangle; it is located in the most distant place from 'independent implementation', meaning that Japan's ICT regulation by no means prioritises independent implementation. Elsewhere, it is just in the middle between 'accountability' and 'frequent rule changes', meaning that Japan's ICT regulation prioritises them to the same extent. Japan's anti-monopoly regulation is located in a place remote from 'frequent rule changes', meaning that the sector has not had either frequent rule changes or the preparation to cope with them, but has managed its challenges so far. It is located between 'accountability' and 'independent implementation', but closer to the latter than the former. This means that Japan's anti-monopoly regulation has prioritised its independence of authority, and concern for accountability has been less than that for independent implementation. This reflects the fact that the JFTC does not have a robust tie with politics, unlike other government ministries.

If Figure 8.1 is compared to the case of other countries, the characteristics of the Japanese case can be illuminated. The following seeks

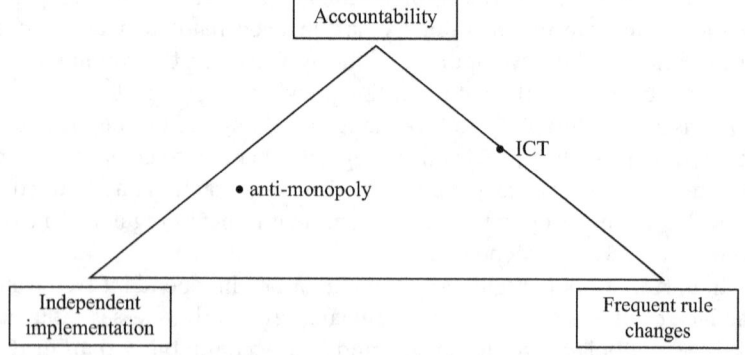

Figure 8.1 The mode of regulation in the Japanese regulatory state

to examine the Japanese regulatory state in generalisable terms by referring to the cases of the UK and New Zealand. In the British case, a new form of institution – regulators neither in the executive branch nor the private sector – has emerged under the informal dominance of ministers. British regulators are required to be less accountable to party politicians and have more authority to implement policy programmes without legislation. Some literature calls this characteristic 'depoliticisation', meaning that the activities remove certain subjects from the scope of everyday politics (Roberts 2010: 5). A key characteristic of depoliticisation is its foundational legal instruments (e.g. laws, treaties, contracts) that purport to transfer authority to technocrats specialised in the sector or thoroughly proscribe certain policy choices (Roberts 2010: 5). New Zealand promoted economic reforms based on pure deregulation without re-regulation. The effort to reverse this reform through reprioritising policy goals from efficiency-oriented to those that take account of welfare in the 2000s has been successful in part, but has faced the opposition of the established structure, for example the reluctant response of Commerce Commission officials in the 2000s (Carter 2008).

Analysing the cases of the UK and New Zealand in terms of accountability, independent implementation and frequent rule changes can reveal different characteristics to the Japanese ones. The UK offers examples in which independent implementation and frequent rule changes are prioritised more than the Japanese cases. As a result of depoliticisation, British regulators have significant authority to set rules without consulting the legislature. In New Zealand's light-handed regulation, the lack of regulatory procedures enables the formation of a wide range of rules without consulting the government and regulators. The independent nature of the regulator (the Commerce Commission) and the limited scope for administrative intervention prevent party politicians from intervening. In short, the impact of accountability in New Zealand's regulation has been small with its framework of light-handed regulation. The equilibrium of these cases is shown in Figure 8.2.

Figures 8.1 and 8.2 illuminate the key characteristics of the Japanese regulatory state – the more extensive response to the external requirements of accountability – compared with those of the UK and New Zealand. Based on the analytical framework focusing on the Japanese state at a macro level with the concept of the core executive, the analysis of the Japanese regulatory state explains the state in generalisable terms, that is, accountability, independent implementation and frequent rule changes, not in contrasting and particularistic terms such as 'strategic', 'regulatory' and 'developmental'. This account offers a framework to illuminate the key characteristics of the regulatory state in Japan and beyond through further development.

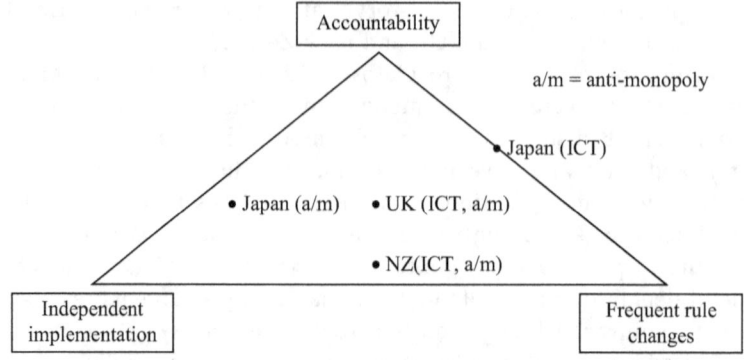

Figure 8.2 The mode of regulation in the Japanese regulatory state compared with the UK and New Zealand

Japanese governance and beyond

The above is drawn from theoretical and conceptual challenges to established methods in earlier literature: an approach focusing on the Japanese state at a macro level with the concept of the core executive as a key analytical tool. It offers a broad perspective explaining the core of Japanese politics after the 1980s by focusing on how the state has been reconstituted in response to changes in governance. The transformation of Japan's governing in the 1980s was characterised by the growing power of *Zoku gi'in* – LDP politicians outside the Cabinet – together with the gradually declining power of government officials: the change of power relations within the core executive under the established political framework (Muramatsu and Krauss 1987). This framework encountered explicit political transformation after the late 2000s, including the 2009 and 2012 changes of government, which attracted scholars (e.g. Kushida and Lipscy 2013; Pekkanen et al. 2013, 2016; Shinoda 2013) who illuminated individual issues but lacked what is needed to address the extent to which political factors reshaped the mechanism of policy-making and implementation, leaving the changing governance of Japan's political arena as a whole untouched. A body of literature (e.g. Amyx and Drysdale 2003; JPSA 2008, 2015; Pekkanen et al. 2013, 2016) has debated issues related to 'governance' with specific focus on individual policy issues, but few have heeded the state's adaptation in response to the challenges of governance after the 1980s. Indeed, the transformation after the 1990s through key reform projects including the 1994 political reform and the 1997 administrative reform has reshaped the country's key political structures, including the Cabinet system, the significance of the *Kantei*, the nature of the House of Representatives and its constituencies, and the political parties' electoral machine. The explicit impact of political changes culminated in the emergence of the Koizumi government, which enjoyed a significantly long tenure through exploiting the outcome of these changes. The resulting assessment regarding Koizumi as a strong Prime Minister strikingly contrasts with the administrations of his successors in both the DPJ and the LDP, including the first Shinzō Abe administration. The unexpected revival of the Abe administration in 2012 and its long tenure afterwards implies that the sequence of events after the 2000s exhibits a type of governance different from earlier.

This study argues that political developments after the 2009 change of government created an unstable situation rather than a new equilibrium in both ICT regulation and anti-monopoly regulation – i.e. a lack of strategic actors – considering the nature of governance in Japan with specific attention to the state rather than individual issues, when recent political events including the 2009 and 2012 changes of government drew public attention to the extent to which the Japanese state has demonstrated its governing capability. The documents regarding the 2012 change of government from the DPJ to the LDP and the resulting LDP-led Coalition administration suggest continuity rather than disjuncture with the previous DPJ government regarding power relations between key state actors (e.g. Takenaka 2017). Despite its political rhetoric criticising the opposition DP and its robust measures in monetary policy and fiscal policy, the historical sequence of the Abe administration has engaged in insignificant structural reforms (*The Economist* 2016b). If summarised, the outcome of the administration hitherto is the politicisation of independent monetary policy overseen by the central bank, a willingness to restore the traditional fiscal expansionist policy – the track record of the administration implies that it has failed to demonstrate significant strategic capacity to reshape the course of the country's traditional fiscal expansionist policy – and the lack of a robust approach to substantial structural reforms, an issue of political difficulty with significant opponents with vested interests in politics and business, despite Abe's explicit resolution to accomplish his 'Abenomics' project. Commentators argue that in significantly depending upon the weak opposition parties including the DPJ/DP (Noble 2016: 166; Scheiner et al. 2016), the strength of the Abe administration is not as solid as it looks (Endo and Pekkanen 2016: 53). If one turns to the Cabinet ministers, the administration's approach to mobile phone charge reductions suggests that the nature of the Cabinet ministers under the Abe administration regarding decision-making and strategic management is ostensibly strong but, in reality, insubstantial and unstable.

This prompts an exploration of the nature and power of the core executive, heeding the unusual relationships between Cabinet ministers, ruling party politicians outside the Cabinet, and civil servants in Japanese politics, which responds to the 'Who is the strategist?' question. This has the potential to offer an insight into the nature of the reconstituted Japanese state, in particular when the traditional interdependence between these two key actors in Britain has been transformed into a more universal command and control relationship that is seen as necessary to meet the demands of accountability and transparency (Richards and Smith 2016). Elsewhere, exploring the nature and power of the core executive will uncover another significant issue in Japanese politics: the separation of powers and governance.

The key characteristics of political development since the 1980s include the enhanced power of the Prime Minister and his office. The change of power relations within the core executive of the period has come with the increasing influence of the Prime Minister and the Cabinet on ministry officials. The resulting transformation has undermined the power of party politicians outside the Cabinet, whose power is drawn from their status as specialist parliamentarians. This implies that the policy-making process in Japan has seen close interconnection between the government and the legislature, with the Prime Minister leading the general election campaign of the ruling party, and parliamentarians, who are supposedly under the supervision of the head of the ruling party, namely the Prime Minister, controlling the ruling party's preliminary examination of key policy issues including government bills. The relationship between the two actors can be sufficiently explained through the framework of the core executive; at the same time, one can doubt to what extent Japan's central governing system, including the Prime Minister and the legislature, can be separated. The 1994 political reform accelerated this analytical challenge in enabling the Prime Minister to exercise stronger leverage to control the party through the selection of party candidates under the MMM electoral system.

This set of issues prompts one to consider whether or not the concept of a constitutional government with three separate branches (*Sanken bun'ritsu*), which has been regarded as the key constitutional framework that has characterised Japan's democracy since 1945 by a large group of researchers including constitutional scholars, is applicable to the Japanese case. Given the current policy-making process in which party politicians outside the Cabinet exercise power in planning and implementing key policy issues, the Cabinet minister selection system in which many of those politicians, namely *Zoku gi'in*, have been appointed as key specialists and would-be powerful Cabinet ministers, and the Prime Minister's natural role as the chief of the ruling party's general election campaign and the appointer of all the key positions within the party, the possible and practical extent of separation between the executive branch under the Prime Minister and the legislative branch dominated by the ruling party, whose head is the Prime Minister as the chief of the ruling party, seems to be limited. The author doubts whether the executive branch under the parliamentary system can be separated from the legislative branch dominated by the ruling party, which is headed by and selects the Prime Minister in most cases. The contradictory relationship between the executive branch and the legislative branch under the mainstream interpretation of Japan's executive politics, in which the Prime Minister is independent of the Diet in which her/his party dominates, offers no cogent explanation; this explanatory approach strikingly differs from other parliamentary systems, including that of the UK. Although the challenge of reconceptualising the polity and governance of Japanese politics needs further and careful examination, analysis of the change of governance since the 1980s offers an opportunity to reconsider and reframe the previous awkward approach by setting out an alternative that collectively analyses the complicated relationships between the key actors, heeding the relevant structures, and mobilised by the pursuit of the nature and exercise of power in actual political arenas rather than one's ideological view on democracy. The resulting approach will be compatible with those aimed at other examples of parliamentary systems and is therefore generalisable, unlike Japan's mainstream framework of a constitutional government with three separate branches of government under a parliamentary system, probably a rare example in political analysis across the globe.

In pulling the above together, governance as a political issue presents a set of significant challenges to Japan's politics and public policy. It relates to the traditional scholarly question: 'Who governs Japan?' (Wright 1999); it also relates to another long-ignored but emerging question in response to growing challenges in the governing machine and society: 'How is Japan governed?' In this sense, exploring state transformation, a key issue in the change of governance, not only unfolds the significant impact of the challenge of governance since the 1980s but also questions the nature of governance in Japan after 1945, requiring theories and approaches that set the issue of governance as their core concern. Therefore, the challenge of governance in Japan raises two questions: the change of governing including its approaches, structures and actors, and the reappraisal of the traditional perspective of governing and democracy in the country: the governance of Japan's democracy and politics after 1945. The core theme of this book – the transformation of the state – is located within the pivot of the new and old challenges of governance: the state is the core of the challenge of governance in political arenas throughout the world and also a central and indispensable issue in the consideration of the separation of powers; these are addressed by this book's explicit approach of focusing on the state at a macro level. As an example of the new body of governance literature addressing questions of governance in a Japanese context, this book sets out a new strategy.

The implications for policy-making is another issue for reflection. This study has revealed that the transformation of politics and the state in Japan has resulted in unstable policy-making processes in two regulatory sectors, whose characteristics include the highly politicised nature of decision-making. Unlike other examples such as Europe's, where the emergence of independent regulators has prompted debates about depoliticisation among political science commentators, the development of a key sector administered by a regulatory ministry and one administered by an independent regulator exhibits the explicit and continuous politicisation of regulatory policy-making in Japan. This suggests that Japan's regulation is free from the challenges prompted by depoliticised regulation but affected by those of politicised public administration, including compromised professional discernment and incoherent regulatory policy-making and implementation; some may recognise elements of such problems in the mobile phone charge reductions initiated by Shinzō Abe. Addressing these challenges probably requires not the examination of technical details such as regulatory organisations but more essential factors mobilising regulatory policy-making and implementation; particularly vital are policy decisions based on evidence, the general understanding of the importance of apolitical regulation in society, and established approaches to regulatory appraisal including identifying best practice. These measures aim at the structures of regulatory policy-making and implementation.

Evidence-based policies and a preference for apolitical regulation in society contribute to forming more effective regulation and competition by preventing discretionary approaches that prompt politicians to interfere and result in ineffective regulation and competition. Regulatory appraisals identify what regulatory efforts are effective in a country. We have seen Japan's unusual characteristics in regulation in this study: its regulation is an unusual version of hyper-politicisation in regulation (Moran 2003), with a lack of independent regulators. Therefore, the response to Japan's regulatory challenges will differ from that of many others. To shape a more concrete idea of how it will respond, we probably need to establish Japan's successful best practice templates in regulation, applicable to other examples in the country and beyond. Following a set of reform programmes in Japan's regulatory sectors mobilised by ideologies such as neoliberalism, what is required now are measures that suit Japan's political tradition. Whatever emerges, Japan's new form of regulation will probably divulge significant lessons for regulation and governance study in a broader context through its adaptation to the country's unusual preference for politicisation.

Note

1 The MMM system counts single-member district seats and PR seats independently: 'There is a fixed number of seats assigned to each tier, and each party "earns" its proportional share of the PR seats, plus as many SMD as its candidates win' (Rosenbluth and Thies 2010: 105).

Appendix 1

List of Ministers of Post and Telecommunications (before January 2001) and Ministers of Internal Affairs and Communications (after January 2001)

Minister of Post and Telecommunications[1]

1. LDP government

Name	Prime Minister	From	To	Notes
Masao Ō'nishi	Masayoshi Ō'hira	11/1979	07/1980	
Ichirō Yamanouchi	Zenkō Suzuki	07/1980	11/1981	
Noboru Minowa		11/1981	11/1982	
Tokutarō Higaki	Yasuhiro Nakasone	11/1982	12/1983	
Keiwa Okuda		12/1983	11/1984	
Megumu Satō		11/1984	12/1985	
Bunsei Satō		12/1985	07/1986	
Shunjirō Karasawa		07/1986	11/1987	
Masateru Nakayama	Noboru Takeshita	11/1987	12/1988	
Sei'ichi Kata'oka		12/1988	06/1989	
Kenzō Muraoka	Sōsuke Uno	06/1989	08/1989	
Senpachi Ō'ishi	Toshiki Kaifu	08/1989	02/1990	
Takashi Fukaya		02/1990	12/1990	
Masatsugu Sekiya		12/1990	11/1991	
Hideo Watanabe	Ki'ichi Miyazawa	11/1991	12/1992	
Jun'ichirō Koizumi		12/1992	07/1993	
Ki'ichi Miyazawa		07/1993	08/1993	Prime Minister

2. Non-LDP Coalition government

Noritake Kanzaki[2]	Morihiro Hosokawa	08/1993	04/1994	
Tsutomu Hata[3]	Tsutomu Hata	04/1994		Prime Minister[4]
Katsuyuki Higasa[5]		04/1994	06/1994	

3. LDP/LDP-led Coalition governments

Shun Ō'ide[6]	Tomi'ichi Murayama	06/1994	08/1995	
Issei Inoue[7]		08/1995	01/1996	
Ichirō Hino[8]		01/1996	11/1996	
Hisao Horinouchi	Ryūtarō Hashimoto	11/1996	09/1997	
Shōzaburō Jimi		09/1997	07/1998	
Seiko Noda	Keizō Obuchi	07/1998	10/1999	
Eizaburō Maejima		10/1999	04/2000	
		04/2000	07/2000	
Kōzō Hirabayashi	Yoshirō Mori	07/2000	12/2000	
Toranosuke Katayama		12/2000	01/2001	Held other offices[9]

Minister of Internal Affairs and Communications

1. LDP-led Coalition government

	Prime Minister	From	To	Notes
Toranosuke Katayama	Yoshirō Mori	01/2001	04/2001	
	Jun'ichirō Koizumi	04/2001	09/2003	
Tarō Asō		09/2003	10/2005	Held other office[10]
Heizō Takenaka		10/2005	09/2006	Held other office[11]
Yoshihide Suga	Shinzō Abe	09/2006	08/2007	Held other offices[12]
Hiroya Masuda		08/2007	09/2007	Held other offices[13]
	Yasuo Fukuda	09/2007	09/2008	
Kunio Hatoyama	Tarō Asō	09/2008	06/2009	Held other office[14]
Tsutomu Satō		06/2009	09/2009	Held other offices[15]

2. DPJ government

Kazuhiro Haraguchi	Yukio Hatoyama	09/2009	06/2010	Held other office[16]
	Naoto Kan	06/2010	09/2010	
Yoshihiro Katayama		09/2010	09/2011	Held other office[17]
Tatsuo Kawabata	Yoshihiko Noda	09/2011	09/2012	Held other offices[18]
Shinji Tarutoko		10/2012	12/2012	Held other offices[19]

3. LDP-led Coalition government

Yoshitaka Shindō		12/2011	09/2014	Held other offices[20]
Sanae Taka'ichi	Shinzō Abe	09/2014	08/2017	Held other offices[21]
Seiko Noda		08/2017	10/2018	Held other offices[22]
Masatoshi Ishida		10/2018		Held other offices[23]

Notes

1. Unless otherwise stated, ministers were members of the LDP.
2. Japan Renewal Party member (originally from the Komeito Party).
3. Japan Renewal Party member (originally from the LDP).
4. Interim ministership by Prime Minister (one day: 28 April 1994).
5. Japan Renewal Party member (originally from the Komeito Party).
6. Member of the SDPJ.
7. Member of the SDPJ.
8. Member of the SDPJ.
9. Katayama was concurrently assigned to the posts of the Minister of Home Affairs and the director general of the Management and Coordination Agency. The Ministry of Post and Telecommunications, the Ministry of Home Affairs and the Management and Coordination Agency were merged into the Ministry of Internal Affairs and Communications on 6 January 2001. He became the first Minister of Internal Affairs and Communications.
10. Also concurrently served as the Minister for National Sports (09/2004–10/2005).
11. Also concurrently served as the Minister for Postal Services Privatisation (10/2005–09/2006).
12. Also concurrently served as the Minister for Postal Services Privatisation (09/2006–08/2007) and the Minister for Devolution (12/2006–08/2007).
13. Also concurrently served as the Minister for Postal Services Privatisation, the County System and Regional Gap and the Minister for Devolution.
14. Also concurrently served as the Minister for Devolution.
15. Also concurrently served as the Minister for Devolution and the chairman of the National Public Safety Commission (06–07/2009).
16. Also concurrently served as the Minister for Promotion of Local Sovereignty.
17. Also concurrently served as the Minister for Promotion of Local Sovereignty.
18. Also concurrently served as the Minister for Promotion of Local Sovereignty, Okinawa and Northern Territories Affairs.
19. Also concurrently served as the Minister for Promotion of Local Sovereignty, Okinawa and Northern Territories Affairs, and Regional Revitalisation.
20. Also concurrently served as the Minister for National Strategic Special Zones and Devolutionary Reform.
21. Also concurrently served as the Minister for the My-Number System.
22. Also concurrently served as the Minister for the My-Number System.
23. Also concurrently serves as the Minister for the My-Number System.

Appendix 2
The anti-monopoly case process

1. Before January 2006 (based on Schaede 2000: 114)

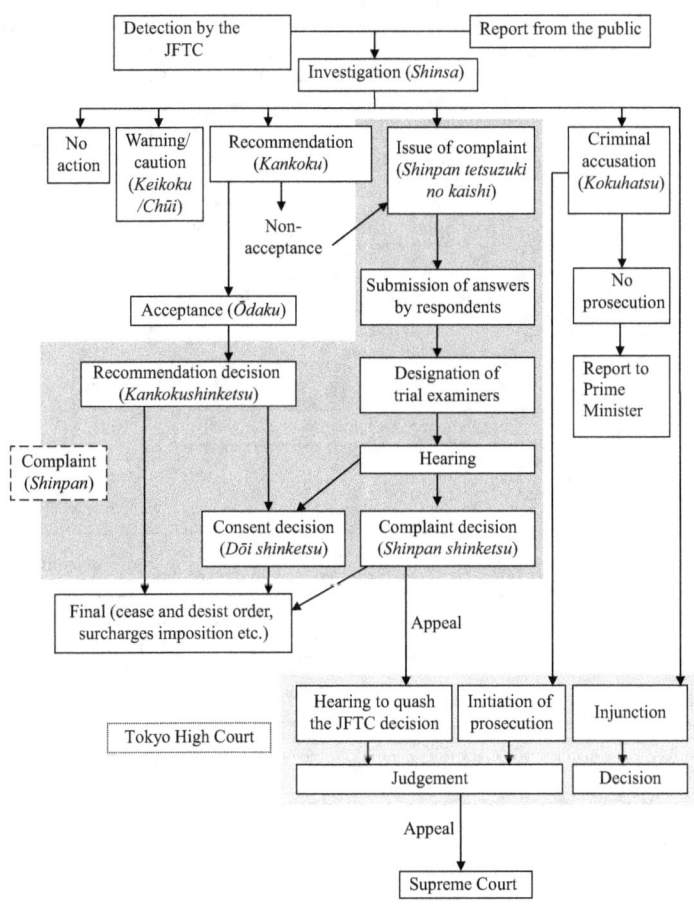

168 Appendix 2

2. After January 2006: the 2005 AMA amendment effectuated (based on JFTC 2012b)

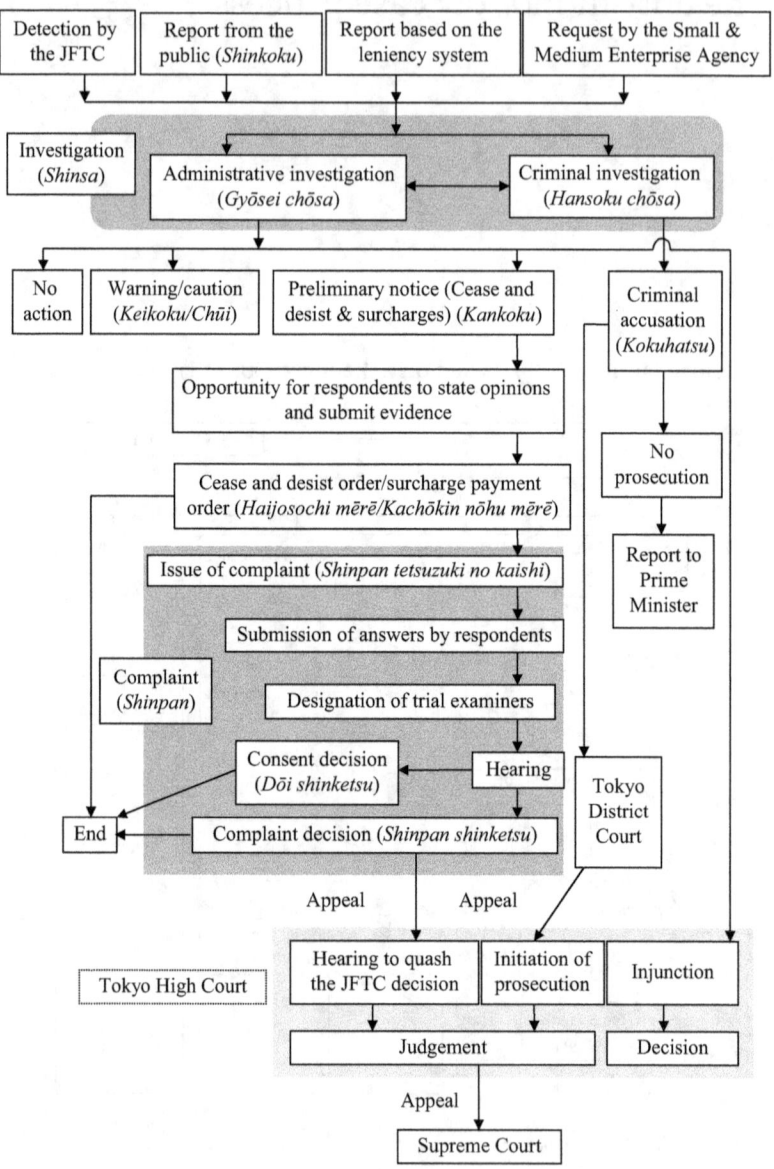

Appendix 2   169

3. After April 2015: the 2013 AMA amendment effectuated (based on JFTC 2016a, 2016b)

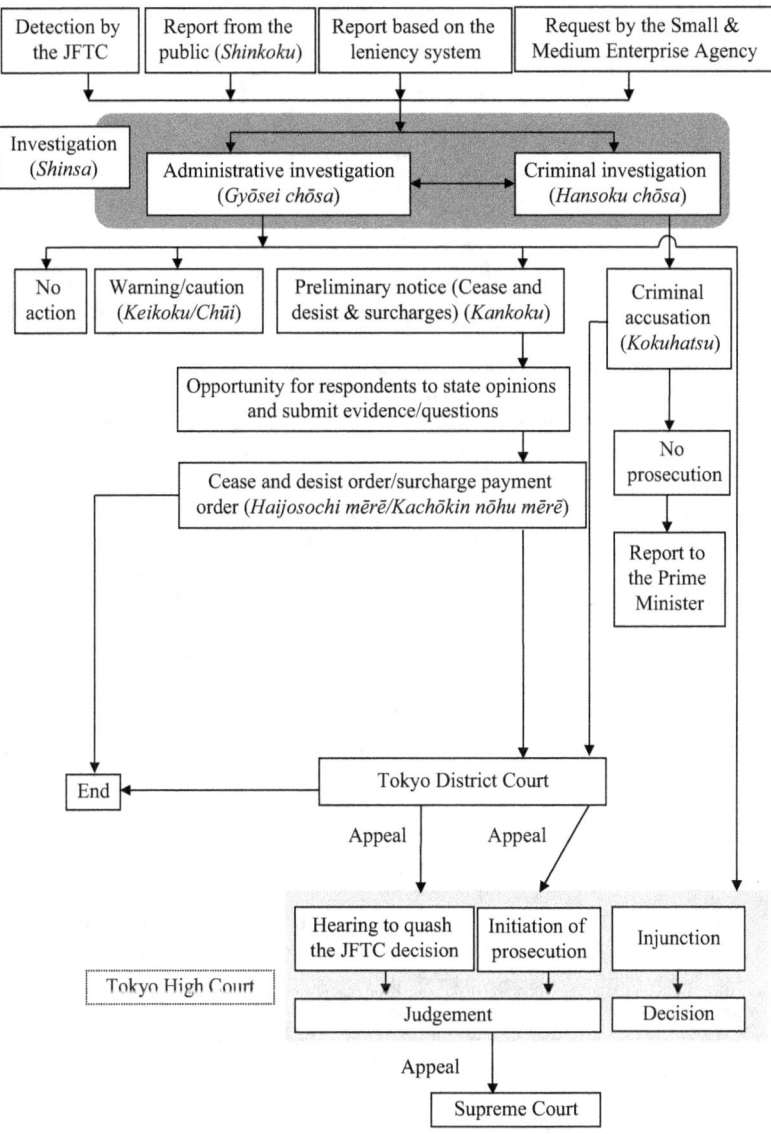

References

Amyx, J., and Drysdale, P. (2003), 'Background', in J. Amyx and P. Drysdale (eds), *Japanese Governance: Beyond Japan Inc.*, New York: Routledge Curzon, 1–14.

Beeman, M. L. (2002), *Public Policy and Economic Competition in Japan: Change and Continuity in Antimonopoly Policy, 1973–1995*, London: Routledge.

Braithwaite, J. (2000), 'The New Regulatory State and the Transformation of Criminology', *British Journal of Criminology*, 40, 222–38.

Cabinet Office of Japan (2012), '*Gaiyō*', in *Keizaizaisei Shimon Kaigi* [online] ['Abstract', in the Council on Economic and Fiscal Policy], Cabinet Office of Japan, http://www5.cao.go.jp/keizai-shimon/about/about.html [accessed 5 January 2012].

Calder, K. E. (1993), *Strategic Capitalism: Private Business and Public Purpose in Japanese Industrial Finance*, Princeton, NJ: Princeton University Press.

Carter, D. B. (2008), 'Crossing the Wires: The Interface between Law and Accounting and the Discourse Theory Potential of Telecommunications Regulation', PhD thesis, Victoria University of Wellington, http://researcharchive.vuw.ac.nz/bitstream/handle/10063/1048/thesis.pdf?sequence=1 [accessed 30 June 2012].

Collins, R., and Murroni, C. (1996), *New Media, New Policies: Media and Communications Strategies for the Future*, London: Polity.

Department for Business, Innovation & Skills (2013), *Focus on Enforcement: List of National Regulators and their Remits*, Department for Business, Innovation & Skills, http://discuss.bis.gov.uk/focusonenforcement/list-of-regulators-and-their-remit/ [accessed 18 January 2013].

DPJ (Democratic Party of Japan) (2009), *Policy Index 2009*, http://www.dpj.or.jp/policy/manifesto/seisaku2009/img/INDEX2009.pdf [accessed 22 April 2010].

Dunleavy, P., and Rhodes, R. A. W. (1990), 'Core Executive Studies in Britain', *Public Administration*, 68(1), 3–28.

Easton, B. (1989), 'The Commercialisation of the New Zealand Economy', in B. Easton (ed.), *The Making of Rogernomics*, Auckland: Auckland University Press. [AQ]

The Economist (2016a), 'Abenomics: Overhyped, Underappreciated', *The Economist*, 30 July 2016, http://www.economist.com/news/leaders/217027

51-what-japans-economic-experiment-can-teach-rest-world-overhyped-und erappreciated [accessed 21 September 2016].
The Economist (2016b), 'Three-piece Dream Suit', *The Economist*, 30 July 2016, http://www.economist.com/news/finance-and-economics/21702756-abeno mics-may-have-failed-live-up-hype-it-has-not-failed-and [accessed 21 September 2016].
Elgie, R. (2011), 'Core Executive Studies Two Decades On', *Public Administration*, 89(1), 64–77.
Elster, J. (1989), *Nuts and Bolts for the Social Sciences*, Cambridge: Cambridge University Press.
Endo, M., and Pekkanen, R. J. (2016), 'The LDP: Return to Dominance? Or a Golden Age Built on Sand?', in R. J. Pekkanen, S. R. Reed and E. Scheiner (eds), *Japan Decides 2014: The Japanese General Election*, Basingstoke: Palgrave MacMillan, 41–54.
Evans, L., Grimes, A., Wilkinson, B., and Teece, D. (1996), 'Economic Reform in New Zealand 1984–95: The Pursuit of Efficiency', *Journal of Economic Literature*, 34, 1856–902.
Evans, P. B. (1995), *Embedded Autonomy: States and Industrial Transformation*, Princeton, NJ: Princeton University Press.
Freyer, Tony A. (2006), *Antitrust and Global Capitalism, 1930–2004*, New York: Cambridge University Press.
Fukuyama, F. (2016), 'American Political Decay or Renewal? The Meaning of the 2016 Election', *Foreign Affairs*, July/August 2016, https://www.foreignaf fairs.com/articles/united-states/2016-06-13/american-political-decay-or-renewal [accessed 20 June 2016].
Fukuyama, F. (2017), 'Francis Fukuyama: Democracy Needs Elites', *TheHuffingtonPost.com*, 2 March 2017, http://www.huffingtonpost.com/ entry/francis-fukuyama-democracy-elites_us_58b5a2cfe4b0780bac2d8ea3?n cid=engmodushpmg00000004 [accessed 29 April 2017].
George Mulgan, A. (2005), *Japan's Interventionist State: The Role of the MAFF*, Abingdon: Routledge Curzon.
George Mulgan, A. (2006), *Japan's Agricultural Policy Regime*, Abingdon: Routledge.
Graham, J. (1991), *Dictionary of Telecommunications*, rev. Sue J. Lowe, London: Penguin Books.
Hadley, E. M. (1970), *Antitrust in Japan*, Princeton, NJ: Princeton University Press.
Harada, Y. (2011), '*Denpakanri I'inkai no Igi Kyōkun*' [The Meaning and Lessons of the Radio Regulation Commission], *Jōhōtsūshin seisaku review* [ICT Policy Review] (2), 31 January 2011, http://www.soumu.go.jp/iicp/chousakenkyu/ data/research/icp_review/02/harada2011.pdf [accessed 24 January 2011].
Hayashi, S. (2008), '*Showa 52-nen Dokusenkinshihō Kaisei no Jitsuzō*' [The Reality of the 1977 Anti-monopoly Act Amendment], *Housei ronshū*, 226, 311–65.
The House of Councillors (2003), *Kaigiroku* [Record of the Session], 22 May 2003, 156th Session, Internal Affairs and Communications Standing Committee, Vol. 13 (26/226), http://kokkai.ndl.go.jp [accessed 7 November 2012].

References

House of Lords (2007), *UK Economic Regulators*, House of Lords Select Committee on Regulators, 1st Report of Session 2006–07, Vol. I, London: The Stationery Office, http://www.publications.parliament.uk/pa/ld200607/ldselect/ldrgltrs/189/189i.pdf [accessed 18 January 2013].

The House of Representatives (1984a), *Kaigiroku* [Record of the Session], 20 June 1984, 101st Session, Communications Standing Committee, Vol. 10 (269, 273/286), http://kokkai.ndl.go.jp [accessed 8 November 2012].

The House of Representatives (1984b), *Kaigiroku* [Record of the Session], 17 July 1984, 101st Session, Communications Standing Committee/Cabinet Standing Committee/Local Government Standing Committee/Commerce Standing Committee/Standing Committee for Price Issues [Joint Standing Committee], Vol. 1 (201/299), http://kokkai.ndl.go.jp [accessed 8 November 2012].

The House of Representatives (2004), *Kaigiroku* [Record of the Session], 23 March 2004, 159th Session, Plenary Session, Vol. 17, http://www.shugiin.go.jp/itdb_kaigiroku.nsf/html/kaigiroku/000115920040323017.htm [accessed 17 April 2012].

The House of Representatives (2010a), *Kaigiroku* [Record of the Session], 10 March 2010, 174th Session, Economy and Industry Standing Committee, Vol. 1, http://www.shugiin.go.jp/index.nsf/html/index_kaigiroku.htm [accessed 10 November 2012].

The House of Representatives (2010b), *Kaigiroku* [Record of the Session], 21 May 2010, 174th Session, Economy and Industry Standing Committee, Vol. 13, http://www.shugiin.go.jp/index.nsf/html/index_kaigiroku.htm [accessed 10 November 2012].

Howell, B. (2008) 'From Competition to Regulation: New Zealand Telecommunications Sector Performance 1987–2007', working paper presented at the International Telecommunications Society European Region Conference, LUISS Guido Carli University, Rome, 17–20 September 2008, New Zealand Institute for the Study of Competition and Regulation, http://www.iscr.org.nz/n49.html [accessed 15 March 2010].

Howell, B. (2010), 'Politics and the Pursuit of Telecommunications Sector Efficiency in New Zealand', *Journal of Competition Law & Economics*, 6(2), 253–76.

ICT Policy Taskforce for a Global Era [*Gröbarujidai niokeru ICT Seisaku ni kansuru Tasukufōsu*] (2010), *Hikari no michi Kōsō Jitsugen ni mukete – Torimatome (Gaiyō)* [To Realise the Path of Light: Summary (Abstract)], MIC, http://www.soumu.go.jp/main_content/000094715.pdf [accessed 6 January 2011].

Ida, T. (2011), *Jisedai Intānetto no Keizaigaku* [The Economics of the Next Generation Internet], Tokyo: Iwanamishoten.

I'io J. (1993), *Min'eika no Seijikatei* [The Political Process of Privatisation], Tokyo: University of Tokyo Press.

I'io, J. (2007), *Nihon no Tōchikōzō* [Japan's Governing Structure], Tokyo: Chūōkōron shinsha.

Inoguchi, T., and Iwai, T. (1987), *Zoku gi'in no Kenkyu – Jimintōseiken o Gyūjiru Shuyaku tachi* [The Study of the Tribe Members of the Diet: The Major Player Dominating the LDP Administration], Tokyo: Nikkei.

Ishikawa, T. (2015), 'Sōmushō no "Kētairyōkin Nesageseyo" ga Ukeirerarenai Riyū' [The Reason Why the MIC's Mobile Call Charge Drop Request has been Rejected], Mag2 News, 17 November 2015, http://www.mag2.com/p/news/123750 [accessed 16 September 2015].

Itō, M. (2006), *Kanteishudōgata Seisakukettei to Jimintō – Core Executive no Shūkenka* [Policy Decision Making Led by the *Kantei* and the LDP: The Centralising Core Executive], *Leviathan*, 7–40.

The Japan Times (2015), 'Government Leans on Mobile Carriers to Simplify Pricing', *The Japan Times*, 20 October 2015, http://www.japantimes.co.jp/news/2015/10/20/business/government-leans-on-mobile-carriers-to-simplify-pricing/#.V9p_UxCKS00 [accessed 15 September 2016].

The Japan Times (2018), 'Mobile Phone Operators Take ¥1 Trillion Blow after Suga Says Bills Could be Cut by 40%', *The Japan Times*, 21 August 2018, https://www.japantimes.co.jp/news/2018/08/21/business/mobile-phone-operators-take-1-trillion-blow-suga-says-bills-cut-40/#.W8szwrt1PIU [accessed 20 October 2018].

JFTC (Fair Trade Commission, Japan) (1997), *Kōseitorihiki i'inkai setsumei shiryō (6-gatsu 25-nichi)* [The JFTC's Position Paper (25 June)], http://www.kantei.go.jp/jp/gyokaku/980428kotori.html [accessed 11 November 2012].

JFTC (Fair Trade Commission, Japan) (2011a), *Heisei 22-nendo ni okeru Dokusenkin'shihōi'hanjiken no Shorijōkyō (Pointo)* [Breaches of the Antimonopoly Act in Financial Year 2010: Key Point], http://www.jftc.go.jp/pressrelease/11.june/110601point.pdfs [accessed 29 March 2012].

JFTC (Fair Trade Commission, Japan) (2011b), *Heisei 24-nendo Yosan'an ni okeru Kōsētorihiki'i'inkai no Yosan oyobi Kikō-tē'in ni tsuite* [The JFTC's Budget and Organisation/Number of Personnel in Financial Year 2012], 24 December 2011, http://www.jftc.go.jp/houdou/pressrelease/h23/dec/111224.html [accessed 6 October 2016].

JFTC (Fair Trade Commission, Japan) (2012a), *About the Leniency Program*, http://www.jftc.go.jp/en/policy_enforcement/leniency_program/about_leniency.pdf [accessed 27 March 2012].

JFTC (Fair Trade Commission, Japan) (2012b), '*Shinsashinpantetsuzuki*' [Investigation and Complaint Procedures], http://www.jftc.go.jp/dk/sinsa.html [accessed 22 October 2012].

JFTC (Fair Trade Commission, Japan) (2013a), *Heisei 25-nendo Yosan'an ni okeru Kōsētorihiki'i'inkai no Yosan oyobi Kikō-tē'in ni tsuite* [The JFTC's Budget and Organisation/Number of Personnel in Financial Year 2013], 29 January 2013, http://www.jftc.go.jp/houdou/pressrelease/h25/jan/130129_1.html [accessed 6 October 2016].

JFTC (Fair Trade Commission, Japan) (2013b), *Heisei 26-nendo Yosan'an ni okeru Kōsētorihiki'i'inkai no Yosan oyobi Kikō-tē'in ni tsuite* [The JFTC's Budget and Organisation/Number of Personnel in Financial Year 2014], 24 December 2013, http://www.jftc.go.jp/houdou/pressrelease/h25/dec/131224.html [accessed 6 October 2016].

JFTC (Fair Trade Commission, Japan) (2014), *Heisei 25-nendo Nenjihōkoku* [The 2013 Annual Report], http://www.jftc.go.jp/houdou/pressrelease/h26/oct/141007.files/h25nennpou.pdf [accessed 18 September 2014].

JFTC (Fair Trade Commission, Japan) (2015a), *Heisei 26-nendo ni okeru Dokusenkinshihōi'hanjiken no Shorijōkyō nitsuite* [Breaches of the Antimonopoly Act in Financial Year 2014], 27 May 2015, http://www.jftc.go.jp/houdou/pressrelease/h27/may/150527_1.html [accessed 5 October 2016].

JFTC (Fair Trade Commission, Japan) (2015b), *Heisei 27-nendo Yosan'an ni okeru Kōsētorihiki'i'inkai no Yosan oyobi Kikō-tē'in ni tsuite* [The JFTC's Budget and Organisation/Number of Personnel in Financial Year 2015], 14 January 2015, http://www.jftc.go.jp/houdou/pressrelease/h27/jan/150114_1.html [accessed 5 October 2016].

JFTC (Fair Trade Commission, Japan) (2015c), *Heisei 28-nendo Yosan'an ni okeru Kōsētorihiki'i'inkai no Yosan oyobi Kikō-tē'in ni tsuite* [The JFTC's Budget and Organisation/Number of Personnel in Financial Year 2016], 24 December 2015, http://www.jftc.go.jp/houdou/pressrelease/h27/dec/151224_2.html [accessed 5 October 2016].

JFTC (Fair Trade Commission, Japan) (2016a), *Revisions of the Procedures prior to Issuing Final Orders and the Appeal Procedures*, 9 December 2013, http://www.jftc.go.jp/en/pressreleases/yearly-2013/Dec/individual131209.files/Attachment2.pdf [accessed 8 October 2016].

JFTC (Fair Trade Commission, Japan) (2016b), *Outline of the Bill to Amend the Antimonopoly Act*, 9 December 2013, http://www.jftc.go.jp/en/pressreleases/yearly-2013/Dec/individual131209.files/Attachment01.pdf [accessed 8 October 2016].

Johnson, C. (1982), *MITI and the Japanese Miracle: The Growth of Industrial Policy, 1925–1975*, Stanford, CA: Stanford University Press.

Jordana, J., and Levi-Faur, D. (2004), 'The Politics of Regulation in the Age of Governance', in J. Jordana and D. Levi-Faur (eds), *The Politics of Regulation: Institutions and Regulatory Reforms for the Age of Governance*, Cheltenham: Edward Elgar, 1–30.

JPSA (Japanese Political Studies Association) (2008), *Nenpō Seijigaku 2008-II: Seihukan Gabanansu no Henyō* [The Political Science Annual 2008–II: The Transformation of Intergovernmental Governance], Tokyo: Bokutakusha.

JPSA (Japanese Political Studies Association) (2015), *Nenpō Seijigaku 2014-II: Seijigaku ni okeru Gabanansuron no Genzai* [The Political Science Annual 2014–II: Governance Studies Today in Political Science], Tokyo: Bokutakusha.

Kalba, K. (1988), 'Opening Japan's Telecommunications Market', *Journal of Communication*, 38(1), 96–106.

Kamikubo, M. (2010), '"*En no kokusaika*" *ka* "*Gen no kokusaika*" *ka*: "*Asia Tsūkakyōryoku*" *no kokunai Seisakuritsu'ankateihikaku*' ['Internationalising Yen' or 'Internationalising Yuan': Comparing Domestic Policymaking Processes under the Asian Monetary Cooperation], working paper, Waseda University Global COE Program, http://www.waseda-giari.jp/jpn/research/achievements_detail/1019.html [accessed 15 August 2012].

Kantei (2016a), *Daisanji Abe Dainijikaizōnaikaku Kakuryōtōmeibo* [The List of the Third Abe Second Reshuffled Cabinet and its Adjuncts], http://www.kantei.go.jp/jp/97_abe/meibo/index.html [accessed 3 October 2016].

Kantei (2016b), *Abenomikusu Seichōsenryaku de Akarui Nihon ni!* [Abenomics: Cheerful Japan by the Growth Strategy!], http://www.kantei.go.jp/jp/headline/seicho_senryaku2013.html [accessed 19 September 2016].

Kato, J. (1994), *The Problem of Bureaucratic Rationality*, Princeton, NJ: Princeton University Press.

Kawabata, E. (2006), *Contemporary Government Reform in Japan: The Dual State in Flux*, New York: Palgrave Macmillan.

Kelsey, J. (1995), *Economic Fundamentalism*, London: Pluto Press.

Kojima, M. (2004), *Ikari o Hassuru Mono wa Gu ka* [Are Those Angered Stupid?], Tokyo: Fusōsha.

Krauss, E. S., and Pekkanen, R. J. (2011), *The Rise and Fall of Japan's LDP*, Ithaca, NY: Cornell University Press.

Kushida, K. E. (2006), 'Japan's Telecommunications Regime Shift: Understanding Japan's Potential Resurgence', in A. Newman and J. Zysman (eds), *How Revolutionary Was the Revolution? National Responses, Market Transitions and Global Technology in the Digital Era*, Stanford, CA: Stanford University Press, 125–47.

Kushida, K. E. (2013), 'Information Technology Policy in a Post-LDP Japan: Caught between Distributive Politics and Strategic Policy Again?', in K. E. Kushida and P. Y. Lipscy (eds), *Japan Under the DPJ: The Politics of Transition and Governance*, Stanford, CA: Shorenstein Asia-Pacific Research Center, 253–79.

Kushida, K. E., and Lipscy, P. Y. (eds) (2013), *Japan Under the DPJ: The Politics of Transition and Governance*, Stanford, CA: Shorenstein Asia-Pacific Research Center.

Levi-Faur, D. (2012), 'Regulating Capitalism: A Constitutive Approach', conference paper presented at 8th Transatlantic Dialogue on Transitions in Governance, Radboud University, Nijmegen, 6–9 June 2012.

Majone, G. (1996), 'The Rise of Statutory Regulation in Europe', in G. Majone (ed.), *Regulating Europe*, London: Routledge, 47–60.

Maloney, W. A. (2001), 'Regulation in an Episodic Policymaking Environment: The Water Industry in England and Wales', *Public Administration*, 79(3), 625–42.

Mann, M. (1993), *The Sources of Social Power*, Vol. II, Cambridge: Cambridge University Press.

Marinetto, M. (2003), 'Governing beyond the Centre: A Critique of the Anglo-Governance School', *Political Studies*, 51, 592–608.

Marsh, D., Richards, D., and Smith, M. J. (2001), *Changing Patterns of Governance in the United Kingdom: Reinventing Whitehall?*, Basingstoke: Palgrave Macmillan.

Marsh, D., Richards, D., and Smith, M. J. (2003), 'Unequal Power: Towards an Asymmetric Power Model of the British Party', *Government and Opposition*, 38(3), 306–22.

Mastanduno, M. (1992), 'Framing the Japan Problem: The Bush Administration and the Structural Impediments Initiative', *International Journal*, 47(2), 235–64.

Matsushita, M. (1991), 'The Structural Impediments Initiative: An Example of Bilateral Trade Negotiation', *Michigan Journal of International Law*, 12, 436–49.

McCargo, D. (2013), *Contemporary Japan*, 3rd edn, Basingstoke: Palgrave Macmillan.

McCubbins, M. D., and Noble, G. W. (1995), 'The Appearance of Power: Legislators, Bureaucrats and the Budget Process in the US and Japan', in P. F. Cowhey and M. D. McCubbins (eds), *Structure and Policy in Japan and the United States*, Cambridge: Cambridge University Press, 56–80.

MIC (Ministry of Internal Affairs and Communications, Japan) (2007), *New Competition Promotion Program 2010*, Tokyo: MIC.

MIC (Ministry of Internal Affairs and Communications, Japan) (2012), '*Gaiyou*', in *Jōhōtsūshinshingikai* ['Abstract', in Information and Communications Council], http://www.soumu.go.jp/main_sosiki/joho_tsusin/policyreports/joho_tsusin/index.html [accessed 8 January 2012].

MIC (Ministry of Internal Affairs and Communications, Japan) (2013), '2.4.1.(1) *Kokunaidenkitsūshinryōkin no Teirenka*', in *Tsūshinhakusho: 24-nendo ban* ['2.4.1.(1) The Number of Carriers', in 1997 Communications White Paper], http://www.soumu.go.jp/main_sosiki/joho_tsusin/policyreports/japanese/papers/98wp2-4-1a.html [accessed 5 July 2013].

MIC (Ministry of Internal Affairs and Communications, Japan) (2015a), 'Keitaidenwa no Ryōkinsonota no Teikyōjōken ni kansuru Tasukufōsu: Torimatome' [The Taskforce on Mobile Phone Service Conditions including Call Rates: The Concluding Statement], http://www.soumu.go.jp/main_content/000390882.pdf [accessed 15 September 2016].

MIC (Ministry of Internal Affairs and Communications, Japan) (2015b), 'Sumātofon no Ryōkinhutan no Keigen oyobi Tanmatsuhanbai no Tekiseika ni kansuru Torikumihōshin' [The Approach to Smartphone Charge Reduction and Rectified Mobile Handset Sales], http://www.soumu.go.jp/main_content/000390880.pdf [accessed 15 September 2016].

MIC (Ministry of Internal Affairs and Communications, Japan) (2016), 'Dai-7-shō ICT bunya no Kihondēta [Chapter 7 The Fundamental Data of the ICT Field], in *Jōhōtsūshinhakusho: 27-nendo ban* [FY 2015 ICT White Paper], http://www.soumu.go.jp/johotsusintokei/whitepaper/ja/h27/pdf/n7100000.pdf [accessed 5 October 2016].

Mogaki, M. (2015), 'The Evolving Power of the Core Executive: A Case Study of Japan's ICT Regulation after the 1980s', *Pacific Affairs*, 88(1), 27–49.

Moran, M. (2003), *British Regulatory State: High Modernism and Hyper-Innovation*, Oxford: Oxford University Press.

Morita, M. K. (1991), 'Structural Impediments Initiatives: Is It an Effective Correction of Japan's Antimonopoly Policy?', *University of Pennsylvania Journal of International Business Law*, 12(4), 777–810.

MPT (Ministry of Post and Telecommunications, Japan) (1997), '*11/12-zuke: Gyōseikaikakukaigi Teishutushiryō – Jōhōtūshingyōsei no Arikata –*' [12 November: Paper Submitted to the Administrative Reform Council – How ICT Should be Governed], http://www.soumu.go.jp/main_sosiki/joho_tsusin/pressrelease/japanese/sonota/971112j902.html [accessed 1 November 2012].

MPT (Ministry of Post and Telecommunications, Japan) (1998), *Manual for Market Entry into Japanese Telecommunications Business*, Tokyo: MPT.

Muramatsu, M. (1991), 'The "Enhancement" of the Ministry of Post and Telecommunications to Meet the Challenge of Telecommunications Innovation', in S. Wilks and M. Wright (eds), *The Promotion and Regulation of Industry in Japan*, Basingstoke: Macmillan, 286–308.

Muramatsu, M., and Krauss, E. S. (1987), 'The Conservative Policy Line and the Development of Patterned Pluralism', in K. Yamamura and Y. Yasuba (eds), *The Political Economy of Japan, Vol. 1: The Domestic Transformation*, Stanford, CA: Stanford University Press, 516–54.

Neary, I. (2002), *The State and Politics in Japan*, Cambridge: Polity.

Noble, G. W. (2016), 'Abenomics in the 2014 Election: Showing the Money (Supply) and Little Else', in R. J. Pekkanen, S. R. Reed and E. Scheiner (eds), *Japan Decides 2014: The Japanese General Election*, Basingstoke: Palgrave Macmillan, 155–69.

Norton, P. (2004), 'Regulating the Regulatory State', *Parliamentary Affairs*, 57(4), 785–99.

NTT (2013) '*Denkitsūshinshingikai no Tōshin to NTT no Hanron*' [The Telecommunications Council's Report and NTT's Refutation], in *NTT Group Shashi* [NTT Group's Corporate History], http://www.ntt.co.jp/about/history/pdf/p374_375.pdf [accessed 30 June 2012].

NTT East (2016), '*Tsūwaryō, Tsūshinryō*', in *Flet's Hikari* ['Call and Data Communications rates', in Flet's Light], http://flets.com/hikaridenwa/charge/phonecall.html [accessed 5 October 2016].

OECD (2002), *OECD Review of Regulatory Reform: Regulatory Policies in OECD Countries – From Interventionism to Regulatory Governance*, Paris: OECD.

OECD (2004), *OECD Review of Regulatory Reform: Japan: Progress in Implementing Regulatory Reform*, Paris: OECD.

Oikawa, K. (1999), *Ji-Sha-Sa Renritsu no Kyōkun – Seishinkaichō 463-nichi* [The Lessons of the LDP-SDPJ-*Sakigake* Coalition: 463 Days as the Policy Examination Council Chairman], Tokyo: Jōhōtsūshinmondai Kenkyūkai.

Patterson, R. (1998), 'Light-Handed Regulation in New Zealand Ten Years On', *Competition & Consumer Law Journal*, 6, 134–48.

Pekkanen, R., Reed, S. R., and Scheiner. E. (eds) (2013), *Japan Decides 2012: The Japanese General Election*, Basingstoke: Palgrave Macmillan.

Pekkanen, R., Reed, S. R., and Scheiner. E. (eds) (2016), *Japan Decides 2014: The Japanese General Election*, Basingstoke: Palgrave Macmillan.

Pempel, T. J. (1998), *Regime Shift: Comparative Dynamics of the Japanese Political Economy*, Ithaca, NY: Cornell University Press.

Pempel, T. J. (2010), 'Between Pork and Productivity: The Collapse of the Liberal Democratic Party', *The Journal of Japanese Studies*, 36(2), 227–54.

Peters, B. G. (1996), *The Future of Governing: Four Emerging Models*, Lawrence, KS: University Press of Kansas.

Peters, B. G. (2000), 'Governance and Comparative Politics', in J. Pierre (ed.), *Debating Governance: Authority, Steering, and Democracy*, Oxford: Oxford University Press, 36–53.

Peters, B. G., Rhodes, R. A. W., and Wright, V. (eds) (2000), *Administering the Summit: Administration of the Core Executive in Developed Countries*, Basingstoke: Macmillan.

Pierre, J. (2000), 'Introduction: Understanding Governance', in J. Pierre (ed.), *Debating Governance: Authority, Steering, and Democracy*, Oxford: Oxford University Press, 1–10.

Pierre, J., and Peters, B. G. (2000), *Governance, Politics and the State*, Basingstoke: Macmillan.

Ramseyer, J. M., and Rosenbluth, F. M. (1993), *Japan's Political Marketplace*, Cambridge, MA: Harvard University Press.

Reed, S. R., Scheiner, E., Smith, D. M., and Thies, M. F. (2013), 'The 2012 Election Results: The LDP Wins Big by Default', in R. Pekkanen, S. R. Reed and E. Scheiner (eds), *Japan Decides 2012: The Japanese General Election*, Basingstoke: Palgrave Macmillan, 34–46.

Rhodes, R. A. W. (1995), 'From Prime Ministerial Power to Core Executive', in R. A. W. Rhodes and P. Dunleavy (eds), *Prime Minister, Cabinet and Core Executive*, London: Macmillan, 11–37.

Rhodes, R. A. W. (1997), *Understanding Governance: Policy Networks, Governance, Reflexivity and Accountability*, Maidenhead: Open University Press.

Richards, D. (2008), *New Labour and the Civil Service: Reconstituting the Westminster Model*, Basingstoke: Palgrave Macmillan.

Richards, D., and Smith, M. J. (2016), 'The Westminster Model and the "Indivisibility of the Political and Administrative Elite": A Convenient Myth Whose Time Is Up?', *Governance*, 29(4), 499–516

RJIF (Rebuild Japan Initiative Foundation) (2013), *Minshutōseiken Shippai no Kenshō: Nihonseiji wa Nani o Ikasuka* [The Appraisal of the Failure of the Democratic Party of Japan Administration: Lessons for Japanese Politics], Tokyo: Chūōkōronshinsha.

Roberts, A. (2010), *The Logic of Discipline: Global Capitalism and the Architecture of Government*, Oxford: Oxford University Press.

Rosenbluth, F. M., and Thies, M. F. (2010), *Japan Transformed: Political Change and Economic Restructuring*, Princeton, NJ: Princeton University Press.

Sanekata, K. (1986), 'Antitrust in Japan: Recent Trends and Their Socio-political Background', *University of British Columbia Law Review*, 20(2), 379–99.

Sartori, G. (1970), 'Concept Misformation in Comparative Politics', *American Political Science Review*, 64(4), 1033–53.

Schaede, U. (2000), *Cooperative Capitalism: Self-regulation, Trade Associations, and the Antimonopoly Law in Japan*, Oxford: Oxford University Press.

Schaede, U. (2008), *Choose and Focus: Japanese Business Strategies for the 21st Century*, Ithaca, NY: Cornell University Press.

Scheiner, E., Smith, D. M., and Thies, M. F. (2016), 'The 2014 Japanese Election Results: The Opposition Cooperates but Fails to Inspire', in R. J. Pekkanen, S. R. Reed and E. Scheiner (eds), *Japan Decides 2014: The Japanese General Election*, Basingstoke: Palgrave Macmillan, 22–38.

Scott, C. (2004), 'Regulation in the Age of Governance: The Rise of the Post-Regulatory State', in J. Jordana and D. Levi-Faur (eds), *The Politics of Regulation: Institutions and Regulatory Reforms for the Age of Governance*, Cheltenham: Edward Elgar, 145–74.

Sekiguchi, S. (2016), '"Tasukufōsu" de Jisshitsu 0-en wa Zeseisaretanoka, Sōmushō de Forōappukaigō' [Does the 'Taskforce' Rectify the Practically

0 Yen: The Follow-up Meeting at the Ministry of Internal Affairs and Communications], *Kētai Watch*, 26 May 2016, http://k-tai.watch.impress.co.jp/docs/news/759366.html [accessed 16 September 2016].

Shinoda, T. (2013), *Contemporary Japanese Politics: Institutional Changes and Power Shifts*, New York: Columbia University Press.

Shiozaki, Y. (2013a), *Yamanaka Sadanori Sensei no Kyūsei o Itamu* [Condolence on Mr Sadanori Yamanaka's Sudden Demise], https://www.y-shiozaki.or.jp/oneself/index.php?start=420&id=4 [accessed 26 June 2013].

Shiozaki, Y. (2013b), *Dokkinhōkaisei'an, Rinjikokkai Teishutsu e* [The AMA Amendment Bill Goes To the Diet Extraordinary Session], https://www.y-shiozaki.or.jp/oneself/index.php?start=395&id=377 [accessed 26 June 2013].

Skocpol, T. (1985), 'Bringing the State Back In: Strategies of Analysis in Current Research', in P. B. Evans, D. Rueschemeyer and T. Skocpol (eds), *Bringing the State Back In*, Cambridge: Cambridge University Press, 3–37.

Smith, M. J. (1999), *The Core Executive in Britain*, Basingstoke: Macmillan.

Smith, M. J. (2005), 'Pluralism', in C. Hay, M. Lister and D. Marsh (eds), *The State: Theories and Issues*, Basingstoke: Palgrave Macmillan, 21–38.

Smith, M. J. (2009), *Power and the State*, Basingstoke: Palgrave Macmillan.

Sorensen, G. (2004), *The Transformation of the State: Beyond the Myth of Retreat*, Basingstoke: Palgrave Macmillan.

Spiller, P. T., and Vogelsang, I. (1996), 'The United Kingdom: A Pacesetter in Regulatory Incentives', in B. Levy and P. T. Spiller (eds), *Regulations, Institutions and Commitment: Comparative Studies of Telecommunications*, Cambridge: Cambridge University Press, 79–120.

Takahashi, H. (2009), *Innovation to Sekjigaku – Jōhōtsūshinkakumei <Nihon no Okure> no Seijikatei* [Innovation and Political Science: The Political Processes of ICT Revolution <Japan's Stagnation>], Tokyo: Keisōshobō.

Takenaka, H. (2013), *Japan in Pursuit of Westminster Democracy*, Tokyo: Nippon Communications Foundation, http://www.nippon.com/en/in-depth/a02301/ [accessed 5 May 2014].

Takenaka, H. (2017), *Hutatsu no Seikenkōtai: Seisaku wa Kawattanoka* [Two Changes of Government: Policies Changed?], Tokyo: Keisōshobō.

Takeshima, K. (2007), 'Endeavour to Establish a Rigorous Enforcement of the Antimonopoly Act in Japan', paper for Session 1 'Recent Development of Competition Law and Policy in East Asian Economies', at the 4th East Asia Conference on Competition Law and Policy, Hanoi, Vietnam, 3 May 2007, http://www.jftc.go.jp/en/policy_enforcement/speeches/070503.html [accessed 11 April 2012].

Tazaki, S. (2014), *Abe Kantei no Shōtai* [The Reality of Abe's *Kantei*] (Kōdansha Gendaishinsho), Tokyo: Kōdansha.

TDSC (Telecommunications Dispute Settlement Commission) (2016a), *Organisation of the Commission and the Secretariat*, http://www.soumu.go.jp/main_sosiki/hunso/english/commission/organisation.html [accessed 17 October 2016].

TDSC (Telecommunications Dispute Settlement Commission) (2016b), *Dispute Settlement Statistics*, http://www.soumu.go.jp/main_sosiki/hunso/english/activities/dispute.html [accessed 17 October 2016].

Telecommunications Council (1996a), *Report on the Status of Nippon Telegraph and Telephone Corporation*, Tokyo: Telecommunications Council, http://www.soumu.go.jp/main_sosiki/joho_tsusin/policyreports/english/telecouncil/NTT/Council-NTT.html [accessed 29 June 2013].

Telecommunications Council (1996b), *Basic Rules for Interconnection*, Tokyo: Telecommunications Council, 19 December 1996.

Thatcher, M. (1997), 'Institutions, Regulation and Change: New Regulatory Agencies in the British Privatised Utilities', *West European Politics*, 21(1), 120–47.

Thelen, K. (2009), 'First Annual Lecture of the BJIR: Institutional Change in Advanced Political Economies', *British Journal of Industrial Relations*, 47(3), 471–98.

Trade Compliance Center (2012), *Japan Structural Impediments Initiative Joint Report*, http://tcc.export.gov/Trade_Agreements/All_Trade_Agreements/exp_005583.asp [accessed 25 March 2012].

Tsuchiya, M. (2003), '*1990-nendai no Jōhōtsūshinseisaku – NTT keieikeitaimondai ni Torawareta 10-nen*' [ICT Policy in the 1990s: Ten Years Trapped by the Question of NTT's Structure], *Leviathan*, 72–96.

Tsuji, K. (1969), *Shinban Nihonkanryōsei no Kenkyū* [The Study of Japan's Bureaucracy, New Edition], Tokyo: University of Tokyo Press.

Tsuruta, T. (1997), *Kiseikanwa – Shijō no Kasseika to Dokkinhō* [Relaxing Regulation: Stimulating Markets and the AMA], Tokyo: Chikumashobō.

Uesugi, A. (2005), 'How Japan is Tackling Enforcement Against Cartels', *George Mason Law Review*, 13(2), 349–65.

Uesugi, A. (2007), *Dokkinhō no Kishikataikusue – Shiryū kara Honryū eno Ayumi* [The Path and Future of the AMA: From a Tributary to the Mainstream], Tokyo: Dai'ichihōki.

Vogel, S. K. (1996), *Freer Markets, More Rules: Regulatory Reform in Advanced Industrial Countries*, Ithaca, NY: Cornell University Press.

Vogel, S. K. (2006), *Japan Remodeled: How Government and Industry are Reforming Japanese Capitalism*, Ithaca, NY: Cornell University Press.

Vogel, S. K. (2018), *Marketcraft: How Governments Make Markets Work*, New York: Oxford University Press.

Ward, H. (2002), 'Rational Choice', in D. Marsh and G. Stoker (eds), *Theory and Methods in Political Science*, 2nd edn, Basingstoke: Palgrave Macmillan, 65–89.

Weber, M. (1978 [1925]), *Economy and Society: An Outline of Interpretative Sociology*, Berkeley, CA: University of California Press.

Weiss, L. (1998), *The Myth of the Powerless State: Governing the Economy in a Global Era*, Cambridge: Polity.

Williams, C. (2009), 'Ofcom Top of Tory Deathlist: Quangogeddon', *The Register*, 6 July 2009, http://www.theregister.co.uk/2009/07/06/cameron_ofcom/ [accessed 24 September 2012].

Wright, M. (1999), 'Who Governs Japan? Politicians and Bureaucrats in the Policy-making Processes', *Political Studies*, 47(5), 939–54.

Wright, M. (2002), *Japan's Fiscal Crisis: The Ministry of Finance and the Politics of Public Spending, 1975–2000*, New York: Oxford University Press.

Yamamura, K. (1967), *Economic Policy in Postwar Japan*, Berkeley, CA: University of California Press.

Yamamura, K. (1997), 'The Japanese Political Economy after the "Bubble": Plus Ca Change?', *Journal of Japanese Studies*, 23(2), 291–331.

Yasuoka, O. (2008), *Seijishudō no Jidai: Tōchikōzōkaikaku ni Torikunda Sanjū-nen* [The Era of Political Leadership: The Thirty Years Dedicated to the Governing Structure Reform], Tokyo: Chūōkōronshinsha.

Yomiuri online (2014), '"Seikōtōtei" Naze: Jimintōgi'in Chin'moku no Riyū' [Why 'Strong Cabinet & Weak Party'? The Reason for Liberal Democrats' Silence], Tokyo: Yomiuri Newspaper Co., http://www.yomiuri.co.jp/feature/shinso/20140417-OYT8T50015.html [accessed 5 May 2014].

Yoshikawa, S. (1983), 'Fair Trade Commission vs. MITI: History of the Conflicts between the Antimonopoly Policy and the Industrial Policy in the Post War Period of Japan', *Case Western Reserve Journal of International Law*, 15, 489–504.

Zakowski, K. (2015), *Decision-Making Reform in Japan: The DPJ's Failed Attempt at a Politician-Led Government*, Abingdon: Routledge.

Index

Abe, Shinzō 147–50, 159, 162, 165
   Abe administration 9, 147–8, 159
   Abenomics 150, 159
Administrative Management Agency 37
AMA (Anti-monopoly Act) vii, xii, 87–100, 102–11, 113–24, 126–32, 138–9, 141, 145, 149, 150, 153, 154, 156, 168, 169
   AMA Examination Committee 92, 93, 100, 104–6, 108, 109, 110, 114, 122, 132
Anglo-Governance School 20, 32

Cabinet vii, 5–9, 15, 16, 21–4, 29, 30, 32, 35, 36, 43, 46, 47, 55–60, 63, 66–8, 70–4, 78–80, 82–4, 88, 102, 103, 108, 114, 120, 122, 124, 130, 138, 139, 140, 143, 144, 146, 148–51, 154, 155, 158–60
   Cabinet Legislation Bureau 69
   Cabinet minister 5, 7, 9, 16, 22–4, 29, 35, 36, 46, 47, 55–60, 62, 77–84, 87, 102, 103, 107, 108, 111, 112, 114, 115, 120, 125, 126, 130, 131, 138–40, 142, 143, 149, 151, 154, 155, 159, 160
   Cabinet Office (Japan) 46, 63, 107, 112, 117
   Cabinet Office (UK) 21, 23
   Cabinet Secretariat 46
   chief Cabinet secretary 9, 103, 107, 110, 111, 112, 117, 129, 130, 149
CEFP (Council on Economic and Fiscal Policy) xii, 55, 63, 148
Chicago School of Economics 29, 31
Commerce Act (New Zealand) 28, 29
Commerce Commission 28–30, 157
Competition Policy Examination Committee 149
complaints system (*Shinpan seido*) 99, 120–3, 125, 131, 149
Constitution of Japan (Constitution) 71, 74, 88, 102, 103, 140
core executive v, vii, ix, 10, 14–18, 20–4, 28, 30–2, 35–7, 39, 41, 43, 45–9, 51, 53, 55, 57, 59–61, 63, 64, 66, 68, 70–2, 74, 78–85, 87, 103, 104, 109, 113–15, 125, 129–33, 137–46, 151–4, 157–61

Department of Justice (US) 98, 116
Diet (National Diet of Japan) xi, 6–8, 12, 32, 37–40, 45, 49, 50, 52, 53, 55, 57, 59, 70, 74, 80, 83, 91, 92, 95, 98, 102, 106–8, 110, 112, 119, 124, 138, 140, 149, 161
Douglas, Roger 30, 32
DPJ (Democratic Party of Japan) xii, xiii, 7–9, 36, 38, 41, 43, 47, 56–9, 62, 63, 67, 76, 77, 82–4, 87, 97, 98, 101–3, 110–15, 120, 125, 126, 130, 139, 140, 146, 147, 149, 150, 154, 159, 165, 166

Edano, Yukio 112
EU (European Union) 3, 128
Europe 3, 4, 14, 19, 25, 74, 142, 162
European Commission 25

FCC (Federal Communications Commission) xii, 64–8, 71

Index   183

governance
  the challenge of ix, 3, 88, 143, 144, 158, 161
Government Orders Amendment Consultation Committee (*Seirei kaisei shimon i'inkai*) 66, 80

Haraguchi, Kazuhiro 47, 58, 59, 62, 165
Hadley, Eleanor 88, 116
Hashimoto, Ryūtarō 6, 40, 165
Hata, Tsutomu 43, 164

Japan v, vii, ix, x, xii, xiii, 1, 3–20, 22–5, 28, 31, 32, 35–8, 40, 42, 43, 45, 47, 48, 53, 61, 62, 64–74, 76–83, 85–8, 90–4, 96–9, 102, 103, 106, 114–16, 118, 120, 121, 122, 127, 128–30, 132, 133, 137, 142, 144–7, 150, 151, 152, 153, 156–62
  Japanese state v, vii, ix, x, 1, 9, 10, 13, 14, 15–20, 23, 36, 75, 78, 80, 85, 88, 125, 133, 137, 140, 142, 144, 146, 150–3, 158–60
JFTC (Fair Trade Commission, Japan) vii, viii, xii, 17, 24, 61, 65, 67, 68, 70, 86–132, 139, 141, 142, 148, 149, 153–6, 167–9
  JFTC chairman 24, 99, 103, 107, 112–14, 120, 126, 129, 154
  JFTC commissioner 24, 95, 103, 121, 128

Katayama, Yoshihiro 58, 165, 166
Keidanren xii, 41, 70, 97, 98, 102, 106, 108, 110, 113, 115, 120, 128, 144, 145
Keiretsu 96, 97, 116
Koizumi, Jun'ichirō vii, 6–8, 46, 47, 55–7, 62, 77, 83, 87, 98, 104, 126, 128–30, 139, 143, 154, 159, 164, 165
Koyama, Moriya 52

LDP (Liberal Democratic Party, Japan) xii, 4–13, 16, 18, 22–4, 35–40, 43, 46, 47, 54–60, 62, 64, 65, 75, 78, 82–4, 87, 88, 90–3, 97, 98, 100–4, 106–15, 122, 125, 130, 132, 138–40, 143–50, 154, 158, 159, 164–6

light-handed regulation 28–30, 32, 157
Littlechild, Stephen C. 26, 27

METI (Ministry of Economy, Trade, and Industry) xii, 77, 85, 120, 123
MIC (Ministry of Internal Affairs and Communications) xii, 24, 35, 44–60, 62, 63, 65, 70, 71, 75–7, 79, 80, 83, 84, 114, 138, 139, 142, 148, 149, 150, 153
Ministry of Justice 125
MITI (Ministry of International Trade and Industry) xii, 10–12, 51, 77, 84, 85, 88, 91, 93, 97, 98, 102, 109, 114, 115, 119, 130, 131
MMC (Monopolies and Mergers Commission) xii, 27
MMM (mixed-member majoritarian) system xii, 6, 147, 160, 163
MNO (mobile network operators) xii, 148
MOF (Ministry of Finance) xii, 10, 11, 23, 37, 38, 40, 41, 106
MPT (Ministry of Post and Telecommunications) xii, 17, 24, 35, 38–45, 48–53, 55, 59–62, 66, 72, 75–7, 79, 80, 83, 84, 109, 114, 131, 138, 139, 141, 142, 153, 155

Nakasone, Yasuhiro 5, 36, 95, 164
NCC (New Common Carrier) xii, 35, 42, 44, 45, 49, 53, 65, 81
New Party *Sakigake* (New Harbinger Party) 43, 62, 97
New Zealand vii, 20, 25, 26, 28–32, 143, 154, 157, 158
Nonaka, Hiromu 43, 55
Non-Profit Organisation Law, 1998 6
NTT (Nippon Telegraph and Telephone Public Co. / Nippon Telegraph and Telephone Co.) vii, xii, 35–53, 57, 59–62, 65, 66, 68, 75, 77, 83, 95, 131, 137, 138, 144, 145, 153, 155

OECD (Organisation for Economic Co-operation and Development) 28, 72, 73, 124
Office of Rail Regulator 27
OFT (Office of Fair Trading) xii, 26, 27

184   Index

Oftel (Office of Telecommunications) xiii, 27, 70, 76

PARC (Policy Affairs Research Council) xiii, 5, 8, 23, 39, 40, 46, 56, 58, 83, 92, 93, 100, 101, 106, 110, 145, 148
parliamentary secretary 24, 32, 46, 47, 83, 111, 112
parliamentary vice-minister 24, 32, 46, 47, 57, 83
pluralist (ism) ix, x, 9–14, 17–19
price cap system 32
Prime Minister xii, 4–9, 12, 21–4, 36, 37, 46, 55, 57, 62, 63, 67, 84, 85, 90, 91, 98, 105, 107, 116, 117, 143, 145, 147, 148, 159–61, 164–9

rational choice ix, x, 9–14, 17–19
Reserve Bank 29
Rinchō (Second Provisional Commission on Administrative Reform) xiii, 36–8, 40, 51
RPI (Retail Price Index) xiii, 26, 32

SCAP (Supreme Commander for the Allied Powers) xiii, 65, 71, 86, 88, 90, 116, 125
SDPJ (Social Democratic Party of Japan) xiii, 38, 41, 43, 62, 97, 98, 101, 166
Second World War 65, 67, 71, 86, 118, 119
Seimu sanyaku 46, 47, 59, 60, 81, 83, 111–15, 129, 130, 132, 139, 143–5, 150, 154
senior vice-minister 24, 32, 46, 47, 83, 111, 112
SII (Structural Impediments Initiative) xiii, 86, 87, 95–8, 102, 103, 105, 108, 109, 116, 124, 125, 130, 131, 137, 139, 153
SNTV (single non-transferable voting) system 6
state
  developmental state 9, 10–12, 18, 150–3
  regulatory state v, vii, ix, x, 15, 17, 18, 20, 25, 26, 27, 30, 31, 46, 64, 75, 77, 85, 131, 132, 137, 142, 143, 146, 153, 154, 156, 157, 158
  state at a macro level ix, x, 10, 13, 14, 17, 24, 84, 85, 132, 133, 137, 139, 140, 144, 152, 157, 158, 161
Strategic Rail Authority 27
Suga, Yoshihide 149, 165

Taka'ichi, Sanae 148, 149, 165
Takeshima, Kazuhiko 99, 112, 154
Tanaka, Kakuei 5, 37, 40, 54, 62, 91
TDSC (Telecommunications Dispute Settlement Commission) xiii, 44, 45
Telecommunications Act, 1984 (UK) 70
Telecommunications Act, 2001 (New Zealand) 29
Telecommunications Commissioner 29
Telecommunications Inspectorate (*Denkitsūshin kanrikan*) 38, 75
Treasury (New Zealand) 29
Treasury (UK) 21, 23
Treaty of Peace with Japan (Treaty of San Francisco; the peace treaty with the Allies in 1951) 66, 85, 88

UK (United Kingdom of Great Britain and Northern Ireland) vii, xii, xiii, 3, 9, 17, 20, 22, 23, 25–7, 30, 31, 36, 62, 69, 70, 82, 143, 146, 152, 157, 158, 161
USA (United States of America) 3, 29, 36, 41, 68, 69, 72, 74, 86, 88, 98, 102, 116, 128, 140, 146

Yamanaka, Sadanori 92, 93, 100, 104–8, 110, 113–15, 130, 132, 139, 156
Yamazaki, Taku 43
Yoshida, Shigeru 66, 67, 80, 85
Yūsei-zoku 39, 40, 43, 46, 47, 49, 54, 55, 62, 149

Zaibatsu 98, 116
Zendentsū (Japan Telecommunication Workers Union) 38, 41
Zoku gi'in 5, 23, 24, 32, 36, 47, 54, 56, 58, 60, 62, 93, 106, 145, 158, 160

EU authorised representative for GPSR:
Easy Access System Europe, Mustamäe tee 50,
10621 Tallinn, Estonia
gpsr.requests@easproject.com

www.ingramcontent.com/pod-product-compliance
Lightning Source LLC
Chambersburg PA
CBHW071832230426
43672CB00013B/2821